Spiritual and Psychological Aspects of Illness

Dealing with Sickness, Loss, Dying, and Death

EDITED BY

Beverly A. Musgrave AND

Neil J. McGettigan, OSA

Paulist Press
New York/Mahwah, NJ

Cover and book design by Lynn Else

Library of Congress Cataloging-in-Publication Data

Spiritual and psychological aspects of illness : dealing with sickness, loss, dying, and death / edited by Beverly A. Musgrave and Neil J. McGettigan.
p. cm.
ISBN 978-0-8091-4661-1 (alk. paper)
1. Pastoral psychology. 2. Church work with the sick. 3. Diseases—Religious aspects—Christianity. 4. Death—Religious aspects—Christianity. 5. Loss (Psychology)—Religious aspects—Christianity. I. Musgrave, Beverly Anne. II. McGettigan, Neil J.
BV4460.S65 2010
253.5′2—dc22

2010000238

Published by Paulist Press
997 Macarthur Boulevard
Mahwah, New Jersey 07430

www.paulistpress.com

Printed and bound in the
United States of America

Contents

Introduction

In his famous book *The Varieties of Religious Experience*, the Harvard University didact William James demurred from attempting to define human saintliness, except to describe it as "the best things that human history has produced." However, he ventured to specify the source of saintliness in religious experience and to tell us how we can identify saints and know saintliness when we see it. To do so he fell back, finally, on a greater wisdom and a more powerful authority than his own by using the words of the wisdom found in the gospel: "By their fruits you shall know them." The "fruits," the results of the kind of life saints choose to live and especially the way saints choose to treat other human beings lovingly, name saints for who they are.

Of course, none of the authors of the chapters in this book began with an intention to explain human saintliness or to specify its source in religious experience. Nevertheless, in their writing you may find accounts of how dealing with sickness, loss, dying, and death can bring out "some of the best things" human beings are capable of in their personal relationships, that is, treating one another lovingly.

We can easily recognize these best things as the ordinary deeds that people do when family and friends are troubled and need help to live with sickness or face the reality of death. But the ordinary things that people do at those times—like being a friend and companion, listening and showing compassion, being patient and kind, or simply being present and willing to share as a partner in pain and suffering with another human being—these ordinary things often carry with them the power to heal and the grace to endure.

As the title of this book indicates, the "spiritual and psychological aspects of illness" serve as the inspirational matrix for all the chapters in the book and also give shape to the table of contents. Not surprisingly, the authors all find variations of spiritual and psychological dimensions in the experiences they relate and in whatever else they say about dealing with the intrusion of illness into our personal lives and relationships. Their explorations of the typical consequences of sickness in the lives of those suffering and the lives of their family members and friends reveal in different ways the benefit of a psychospiritual approach in the ministry of caregiving and healing.

Part I of the book presents six chapters that focus on theological dimensions. With the premise that the realities of loss, illness, and death are themselves only partially penetrable by our understanding, these theological dimensions are similarly open to an interpretation that is compatible with the kind of faith, or lack of it, through which they are perceived. Part II emphasizes how the impact of suffering sickness and caring for those who suffer sickness can impose psychological shifts on the way we approach life and attempt to find meaning and purpose in it.

From that perspective, the remaining articles relate personal responses to illness. Part III contains reflections that are useful for effective professional training or just the routine practice of being a caregiver, as it happens out of necessity for a family member or a friend. This part introduces the dimension of healing as a mysterious and consoling aftermath that can sometimes follow upon experiences of sickness, loss, and grieving. The authors note that ministry to the sick and partnership in the work of recovery are extraordinary aids in the process of healing, whether it follows upon physical suffering or personal trauma from loss of a loved one in death. Part IV contains examples of the common events that happen to ordinary people and that we also may expect to happen to us in family life or with friends. They are the familiar events of grief in all loving relationships because of the onsets of illness, or because of loss and eventually death.

The impetus for making such a collection of essays was an opportunity to give recognition to the benefits and healing results that are experienced through "partnership" with another caring human being when illness, loss, and death occur. That a caring partnership can bring about real benefit and sometimes healing is the collection's recurring theme. The book itself resulted from the inspiration and work of Beverly Anne Musgrave. Dr. Musgrave is principal editor of the book and founder of Partners in Healing, which is a model for its thematic construct. Partners in Healing is an interfaith and multiethnic group whose purpose is addressing the spiritual needs of ill and bereaved people. The dedication of its members working together selflessly as a group is a testament to the healing power present in all human partnerships that are rooted in love.

Being a partner to another human being through an experience of illness, loss, or death reminds us that God, too, is already a partner with us in all of those experiences of human life: the happy and the sad, the joyful and the painful. Suffering from illness and loss is a necessary and inevitable part of life, even though we struggle to explain why. Although spiritual and psychological perspectives of illness may help to provide an understanding of its necessity and inevitability, the final understanding comes only through acceptance of life itself as a gift. With all our uncertainties about illness, we can hold fast only to that truth—life itself is a gift and an act of love, an act of love from God. In the same way, to share generously with and to partner another human being, who needs help in the experience of illness or loss or death, is also a gift. But, by its nature, it can be given only as an act of love. Also by its nature, there is a ricochet that sends that gift back again as a gift to the partner. For those who take on the role of being a partner in healing, it somehow seems to work out that there is a kind of built-in reciprocity in the relationship between those who give care and those who receive it.

An ailing person whom we love dearly can weary us and may be physically and emotionally bereft and seem to have nothing to give in return. But the "return" may be what Mary Oliver calls "a box full of darkness" (in her short, enigmatic poem "The Uses of Sorrow"). It may take years for us to see through the weariness and the dark times of that experience of being a caregiver in order to really see what was hidden inside. In one way or another, each chapter touches on aspects of the darkness of illness and its aftermath. What each offers is not hope to avoid its onset but encouragement to seek blessedness within it.

Life is never totally without darkness, and it may appear to have nothing to offer in exchange for the love we give to one another in life. But life itself teaches us what we need to know about darkness. We are meant to grow in life, and only when we grow do we really know the value we receive in return for giving love. We live and we grow in spirit and in our loving. In their own unique ways, all the authors affirm that truth. Giving love and caring for one another are all we are able to do in the face of illness and loss. By that "all we are able to do," we lift the veil of darkness and see that what seemed to be only darkness—the darkness of sickness, dying, and death—is also a gift.

Neil J. McGettigan, OSA

Part I

Theological Dimensions of Loss, Illness, and Death

1

From Healing to Wholeness
A Psycho-Spiritual Approach

John J. Cecero

This is an exciting time in the fields of research and applied psychology, specifically in their openness to the importance of including a spiritual component in achieving a comprehensive assessment of psychological functioning and in designing treatment interventions. Keyes (2007) argues that, with the advent of the positive psychology movement and its emphasis on "flourishing" or optimal functioning as the goal of psychological intervention (Seligman and Peterson 2004), a new paradigm in approaches to mental health is emerging. He advocates a shift away from the previously exclusive focus on symptom reduction—a "pathogenic approach"—toward a more "complete model" that includes emphases on both symptom reduction and optimal functioning or wholeness. Within this complete model approach to health, spiritual values and practices may be considered as essential interventions to foster wholeness, over and above relief from symptoms.

Historical Psychological Approaches to Illness

Historically, the pathogenic approach in psychology (Keyes 2007), at least in the Western conceptualization of illness and its design of treatment interventions, mirrored the medical model by defining health as the absence of disability or disease and the prolongation of survival. As a result, the goal of psychological intervention was to restore the individual, as much as possible, to a premorbid state of functioning with as few symptoms of illness as possible. Against this pathogenic model, a second model—the "salutogenic approach" (Keyes 2007)—which defines health as the presence of positive states of human capacities and functioning in thinking, feeling, and behavior (Strumpfer 1995)—was proposed and popularized in the humanistic approaches of Carl Rogers and Abraham Maslow and in the existentialist approach of Irvin Yalom. These psychological approaches were less invested in designing cures for illness as they were in understanding the whole person and promoting optimal functioning, even in the midst of anxiety and suffering.

As noted above, Keyes (2007) argues that only the combination of the pathogenic and salutogenic approaches to mental health will lead to true population health. He notes that in the twentieth century the United States and other industrialized nations have undergone an "epidemiological transition" wherein the average life expectancy has increased by some thirty years; by the standards of the pathogenic model this may be considered an outstanding success. At the same time, however, Keyes notes a rise in a host of health-related problems during this same era, for example, a threefold increase in teen suicide, more adults with anxiety and depression, and more lifestyle and stress-related chronic physical health conditions. He concludes, "Increased life expectancy has increased the number of years spent living with chronic physical diseases and mental disorders rather than greater health, and continued attempts to improve population health solely by disease and illness prevention have proven extremely costly and largely ineffective" (96).

Positive Psychology: A New Paradigm

Against this backdrop of shortfalls in the pathogenic approach to mental health, a new emphasis on flourishing in the field of positive psychology appears especially warranted and welcome. In the face of limitation and illness, it is likely not enough to focus on symptom reduction; rather, one must focus on enhancing and maximizing human strengths and virtues (Seligman and Peterson 2004). For example, in the wake of a serious relationship failure, a person might recover from an episode of acute clinical depression with a reduction in sadness, an increase in energy, and a return to work and social relations but remain angry at the ex-partner and mistrustful about entering into future relationships. According to the pathogenic model, the person has been successfully treated but remains with a relational life that is impaired by unresolved anger, an inability to forgive, and a narrow range of relationships. In a real sense, this person may be said to be healed but certainly not whole.

In order for this person to attain wholeness, a more comprehensive approach to psychological assessment and treatment would include attention to the many facets of well-being that have been researched in recent years (Keyes, Shmotkin, and Ryff 2002; McGregor and Little 1998; Ryan and Deci 2001). They might be summarized under the headings of *hedonic* (e.g., emotional vitality and positive feelings toward one's life) or *eudaimonic* (e.g., self-acceptance, purpose in life, positive relations with others, sense of autonomy, sense of belonging, and interest in others). These facets have been factor analyzed and grouped under three broad domains of flourishing: (1) the presence of positive emotions; (2) positive psychological functioning; and (3) positive social functioning (Keyes 2005). Keyes (2007) proposes that, for a person to be diagnosed as flourishing in life, the individual must manifest high levels on at least one measure of hedonic well-being and high levels on at least six facets of positive functioning. By contrast, the individual with low levels on at least one measure of hedonic well-being and on at least six facets of positive functioning would be diagnosed as languishing.

Thus far, it appears that a focus on flourishing would indeed challenge the field of psychology to think beyond symptom reduction. But how about the case of a person who is not yet relieved of symptoms—can that individual at the same time flourish? Serious researchers and casual observers alike have speculated that some of the great saints who are lauded for their virtue and held up as models to emulate were indeed personally plagued by symptoms of anxiety, depression, and personality disorders, for example, Mother Teresa and Ignatius of Loyola (Meissner 1992). The answer to this question depends on the model of mental health endorsed by the respondent. If one ascribes to a single-factor model (for example, where illness and flourishing are conceptualized as polar opposites, such that the degree to which one is mentally ill is measured by the number of *Diagnostic and Statistical Manual of Mental Disorders* [DSM] Axis I or II symptoms and to that same degree the individual is removed from flourishing) then the answer is clearly and unequivocally no. It would be impossible to be symptomatic of illness and to flourish at the same time. If, on the other hand, one were to conceptualize a two-factor model of mental health, as proposed by Keyes and based on recent research (2007), where one factor is a continuous measure of mental illness and the other distinct but related factor is a measure of mental health or flourishing, then there would be the possibility for coexisting symptomatology and flourishing. As illustrated in figure 1 below, Keyes argues for a two-factor model of mental health, based on the results from a confirmatory factor analysis of the MacArthur Foundation Midlife in the United States (MIDUS) survey (Brim, Ryff, and Kessler 2004).

FIGURE 1. TWO-FACTOR MODEL OF MENTAL HEALTH

Pathogenic Model:
    Mental illness ________________ Absence of symptoms
Flourishing Model:
    Languishing ________________ Flourishing

Note. The correlation between Mental Illness and Flourishing is indicating that mental illness and flourising are inversely related in the data on the previous page.

As demonstrated by the direction and magnitude of the correlation between mental illness and flourishing, there is definitely a relationship between the two factors, such that as mental illness decreases, flourishing improves; however, the magnitude of the relationship is relatively modest, which indicates that flourishing is accounted for by much more than the absence of symptoms. Which factors may account for the additional variance in mental health and wholeness?

One promising direction for finding answers to this question may lie in the theory of positive psychology, which emphasizes the importance of fostering character strengths and virtues as the necessary components of mental health and wholeness (Seligman and Peterson 2004). Seligman and Peterson have identified twenty-four such strengths and virtues, classified them into broader constructs and generated an instrument to measure them, the Values in Action Inventory of Strengths (VIA-IS). At least four of these strengths appear especially complementary to, if not redundant with, spiritual values, and these are creativity, love, humility, and gratitude.

Creativity

The character strength of creativity may be conceptualized along a continuum, ranging on the one end from a complete absence of creativity manifested by those who never come up with an original idea to the other end of creative genius demonstrated by those great scientists, composers, poets, and so on, who may be Nobel laureates. In the middle of the continuum lies everyday creativity, or ingenuity, which may be characterized as the ability to generate creative solutions to the problems encountered at work and at home. A sample item to measure creativity on the VIA-IS is "When someone tells me how to do something, I automatically think of alternative ways to get the same thing done." The respondent is then instructed to endorse one of the following responses to this statement: "very much like me; like me; neutral; unlike me; and very much unlike me."

Seligman and Peterson (2004) point out that, while people who endorse everyday creativity may not necessarily demonstrate extraordinary intellectual brilliance, they generally have a wide range of interests, a greater openness to new experiences, and are risk takers. These traits position such creative people to flourish and not simply to maintain the status quo in coping with the demands of daily life.

In confronting distractions away from this creativity, a spiritual focus on staying in the present moment, which is the cornerstone of contemplative practice, appears especially useful. This spiritual focus will work against the enemy of creativity, an otherwise crippling obsession with achieving perfection. Recent empirical research has supported the efficacy of taking time away from the busyness of the workday simply to get lost in nature (Clay 2001). This "fascination time" is another term for contemplative spiritual experience, and it has been associated with significantly lower stress levels and greater creativity in the workplace. It is important to give ideas a chance to percolate in an environment of nonjudgmental acceptance in order to be able to evaluate successfully which ones are inspired and worthy of pursuit. By relieving performance anxiety and motivating openness to creativity, authentic contemplative practice fosters just this kind of environment.

Love

A second character strength that is at the same time a key spiritual value is love. There are at least three types of love. The first, in which the individual relies on another to make one's own welfare a priority, is akin to a child's love for a parent. A sample item on the VIA-IS to measure this kind of love is: "There are people in my life who care as much about my feelings and well-being as they do about their own." According to Maslow's hierarchy of needs and values (1954), the experience of love enables the realization of many of the other strengths and virtues that characterize self-actualization. For example, the experiential knowledge of love can motivate creativity and sometimes even serves as the very content of artistic endeavors. A second type of love, in which the individual comforts and protects another and makes sacrifices for the benefit of the other in order to make him or her feel safe, is more akin to a parent's love for a child. According to Erikson (1950), this generative love is the mark of psychosocial maturity, and it stands in stark contrast to stagnation, the opposite of flourishing. Finally, romantic love may be characterized by a passionate desire for sexual, physical, and emotional closeness with another person. Frankl (1984) notes that even in the midst of the most dehumanizing experience of the concentration camp, the thought of his wife, his love, would restore his sanity and give him hope. Frankl writes, "But my mind clung to my wife's image....A thought transfixed me—that love is the ultimate and the highest goal to which man can aspire" (56–57).

Empirical research has identified the physical and emotional correlates of love as including: fewer psychosomatic symptoms in response to stress, greater likelihood of seeking support when distressed, a greater likelihood of compromising in the face of conflict rather than turning to destructive strategies, and a higher sense of self-esteem.

From a spiritual perspective, the ultimate source of love is the experience of the Transcendent or the Divine. Father Pedro

Arrupe, SJ, former superior general of the Society of Jesus, wrote eloquently on the divine power of love: "Nothing is more practical than finding God. That is, than falling in love in a quite absolute, final way. What you are in love with, what seizes your imagination, will affect everything....It will decide what will get you out of bed in the morning, what you will do with your evenings, how you spend your weekend, what you read, what you know, what breaks your heart, and what amazes you with joy and gratitude. Fall in love, stay in love, and it will decide everything."

Humility

As contrasted with the narcissistic self-absorption that pervades Western culture and masquerades as self-esteem, humility is the mark of a person who neither overestimates nor underestimates a sense of his or her abilities and achievements. The item on the VIA-IS that measures humility is, "I am proud that I am an ordinary person." Not surprisingly, there are a host of benefits associated with humility. As elaborated on later in this chapter, one such benefit is the relative ease at exercising forgiveness. The humble person is less preoccupied with saving face in the wake of an interpersonal injury and more inclined to extend forgiveness. The sense of personal resilience associated with humility protects the individual against self-disintegration in the aftermath of some assault, threat, or criticism. Likewise, following such injuries, the humble person is less likely to soothe the self with desperate and impulsive behaviors, such as substance abuse, eating disorders, or even suicide attempts. This may explain why the cultivation of humility is an essential component of twelve-step programs designed to enable individuals to resist relapse to various addictions.

From a spiritual perspective, humility may be grounded in a secure knowledge of being unconditionally loved by God or some higher power. In a program of prayers designed to promote a radical embrace of the will of God in one's life, the *Spiritual Exercises of St. Ignatius Loyola* instructs the exercitant to consider that the love of God does not ignore his or her weaknesses, flaws, or deficiencies but instead embraces the individual, warts and all, as it were, as a finite being, who is nonetheless lovable.

Gratitude

Considered by some to be the cornerstone of all of the virtues, gratitude may be defined as an enduring thankfulness that is sustained across situations and over time. From a clinical perspective and by reason of raising a present awareness of the very giftedness of being alive, gratitude is restorative, that is, it has the capacity to relieve the sadness or fear of depressed and anxious clients. The grateful person perceives life itself more as a gift than as a burden. The item on the VIA-IS that assesses gratitude is straightforward, "I always express my thanks to people who care about me." As expected, gratitude has been empirically associated with a range of positive states, including an increase in positive emotions, life satisfaction, vitality, and optimism.

From a spiritual perspective, the enhancement of gratitude is a core practice. For example, germane to the practice of the *Spiritual Exercises* cited above, the cultivation of gratitude is recommended as a daily attitude and behavior. The Examen of Consciousness is proposed for this daily practice, and this involves setting aside ten to fifteen minutes each day simply to notice the many gifts bestowed by God in the ordinary persons and events of the day. Dennis Hamm, SJ (1994) details the specific steps of the gratitude exercise in his seminal article, "Rummaging for God: Praying Backward through Your Day."

Spirituality and Flourishing

While it seems clear thus far that the new focus emerging from within the paradigm of positive psychology on the cultivation of virtues and character strengths may hold much promise for the promotion of wholeness, the potential contribution of spirituality has been largely formulated and evaluated as a separate phenomenon. In their studies, the psychological researchers both in positive psychology and in spirituality or religiosity have not yet collaborated to evaluate their potential relationships. It was reported anecdotally at a recent meeting of the Division 36 (Psychology of Religion) of the American Psychological Association that Martin Seligman, a founder of positive psychology, was introduced recently to Kenneth Pargament, a prominent researcher in the psychology of religious coping, and that Seligman had not ever heard of the latter. This illustrates the lack of communication between these specialized disciplines, and it underscores the need for future collaborative research. Earlier in this chapter, the brief review of the character strengths and virtues and their potential enhancement through spiritual practice suggests that future empirical research may serve to substantiate further the role of spirituality to provide the context and motivation for fostering such virtues. In the meantime, one very promising direction in spirituality research is a focus on spiritual transformation, and especially on its implications for wholeness in the face of illness and suffering (Koss-Chiono and Hefner 2006). Following a review of this emerging area of concentration in spirituality, this chapter will conclude with proposed areas for the integration of positive psychological and spiritually transformative approaches that may tend to promote wholeness beyond healing in clinical and pastoral care.

Spiritual Transformation

Pargament (1997) describes two stages of spiritual development that precede spiritual transformation. In the "discovery stage," one's image of God develops as a mirror of the parental image. The psychoanalyst Anna Maria Rizzuto wrote in *The Birth of the Living God*, "The God representation changes along with us and our primary objects in the lifelong metamorphosis of becoming ourselves in a context of other relevant beings" (52). This stage does not require much, if any, conscious effort on our part, as the process of internalization of these representations is automatic. The second stage requires a more deliberate choice and effortful practice. In this "conservation" stage of spiritual development, the individual engages in prayer and other ordinary daily spiritual experiences to sustain a sense of God and the sacred. At this stage, spiritual development may be understood to be parallel to character and virtue development as described above. There is a probable overlap, but the rationale for integrating a spiritual focus in character and virtue development is not yet compelling, neither for the persons at this stage nor for the researchers who study them.

Instead, the context and motivation for appreciating the role of spirituality in personal development and optimal functioning often emerge in the wake of some personal trauma, illness, or serious life transition. These events occasion the stage of spiritual transformation, where the place and the character of the sacred are radically questioned and reoriented in one's life and among one's priorities. Pargament points out that the person at this stage will move from a self-centered to a more God-centered view of the universe. Likewise, the character of God is frequently called into question and redefined. For example, Pargament points out that Rabbi Harold Kushner, after the death of his small child, could no longer endorse an omnipotent God but rather a God who is limited in the face of suffering. For some at this stage of transformation, God is experienced as less distant and more near and loving.

According to the definition endorsed by the Metanexus Institute, which specializes in spirituality research, spiritual transformation involves dramatic changes in world and self views, purpose in life, religious beliefs, attitudes, and behavior. In other words, spiritual transformation involves a fundamental shift in identity. In the New Testament, this spiritual transformation is exemplified in the story of the woman with a hemorrhage (Matt 9:18–22), who is called out of her shame and anonymity to identify herself at the time of healing. Jesus reassures her, "Take heart, daughter, your faith has made you whole." The word *whole*—in Greek, *sōthēsomai*—denotes not just a physical healing, from the hemorrhage in this case, but perhaps more importantly an identity transformation. From this moment forward, this woman who had previously identified herself as accursed and shameful would now see herself as beloved and worthy of respect.

This shift in identity that precedes spiritual transformation and may prepare the way for it has been described by William May in *The Patient's Ordeal* (1991). May claims that illness often occasions certain negative shifts in identity. More specifically, the sick person may become more fearful and mistrustful of his or her own body. In addition, one's relationship with others may become burdened by a sense of heightened dependency and the resentment that often accompanies it. One's own relationship to God may also shift from one of trust to one of anger and resentment. How could a benevolent God permit this kind of suffering to visit me?

Spiritual transformation permits the individual to grow beyond symptom reduction and to adapt a new vision of self, others, and God, with a new way of relating to each. Its component spiritual strategies correspond to the exercise of the character strengths and virtues outlined above, with an emphasis on living in the present (cornerstone of creativity), shifting from negative to positive appraisals of oneself, others, and God (practicing love), extending forgiveness (the fruit of humility), and developing a heightened sense of grace at each moment (gratitude).

Toward Wholeness: Some Clinical and Pastoral Guidelines

This final section of the chapter will offer some guidelines for integrating elements of spiritual transformation with character strengths and virtues in the service of promoting wholeness.

In the first place, the pastoral agent will likely assist the person who is recovering from some trauma to reconstruct his or her personal story so as to enhance personal identity and dignity. In the aftermath of the devastating physical, emotional, and spiritual assaults on one's identity that are occasioned by such trauma, one primary goal of the clinical or pastoral intervention is to help the individual to aspire to personal growth. Positive psychology emphasizes the importance of creativity in flourishing, and this may be a vital time to exercise this creativity. For example, the person might be encouraged to write his or her personal story and to emphasize especially the heroic choices made in the face of the illness, abuse, or other trauma. A spiritual focus on the nature and power of grace, that is, the abiding presence and labor of God with the recovering person, may foster and sustain this creative endeavor, even in the face of disillusionment and despair. For some, this spiritual focus may be the only avenue to promote successfully an interest in creativity, and it may therefore serve as a uniquely powerful instrument to enhance wholeness.

Pargament has differentiated between positive and negative religious coping (1997). The former is characterized by a collaborative relationship with God in times of trial and stress—for example, God is collaborating with me to get through this. The latter is characterized by negative appraisals of self, God, or others—for example, God is punishing me.

Whereas positive religious coping has been associated with a host of physical and emotional benefits, negative religious coping has been even more strongly associated with toxic effects.

From a positive psychological perspective, the harmful appraisals associated with negative religious coping may be attenuated, if not completely eradicated, by a focus on the character strength and virtue of love. Rather than focus on the evil at work in one's life, one can be encouraged to focus on the loving and caring people who are reaching out in time of need. This cognitive shift will most likely reduce the despondency associated with stages of recovery from illness and trauma. At the same time, for at least some people, it may be difficult to perceive love in these caring people. Instead, their benevolence may be perceived more as motivated by duty or obligation. The recovering person may even fear that the kindness of others may wear thin and eventually be withdrawn, the result of compassion fatigue or the like. For such persons, the spiritual focus on the absolute love of the Transcendent One may greatly assist them to begin to perceive and eventually to accept the possibility of unconditional love. The acceptance and reciprocation of love will very likely assist the recovering person to advance from healing to wholeness.

The affront to one's sense of being an ordinary person is yet another challenge to wholeness for the recovering person. For some perhaps still unknown reason, an illness or calamity has interrupted the normal and expected flow of life, and the individual may be living with an extraordinary sense of vulnerability. Instead of the normal and expected flow, this person may be more prone to withdraw into interpersonal shelter and resentment, all for the sake of safety. For such people, the spiritual exercise of forgiveness may hold the power to enable the humility that is so germane to flourishing. Jack Kornfield, in *The Art of Forgiveness, Lovingkindness, and Peace* (2002, 19), writes: "Without forgiveness, life would be unbearable. Without forgiveness, our lives are chained, forced to carry the sufferings of the past and repeat them without release." But how does the clinical or pastoral agent help another person to exercise forgiveness at this point of perceived vulnerability?

First, it is important to educate the person about the meaning of forgiveness. Forgiveness is not forgetting the offense or assault on one's well-being. After all, it is wholly unrealistic to expect amnesia for such a hurtful event or circumstance. At the same time, however, forgiveness requires a decision to stop ruminating about the offense, because such elaborative rehearsal very likely serves to more deeply encode it in memory, which only strengthens its potency to cause distress.

Also, forgiveness does not necessarily mean reconciliation. Reconciliation implies a desire to repair the relationship, and in some cases it is important for the individual to establish a permanent distance with the offending person, for example, an abusive partner.

Finally, forgiveness is not always rooted in justice. While it may be easier to forgive someone who acknowledges wrongdoing and is willing to make reparation, forgiveness does not depend on this. Indeed, there are circumstances that preclude such an acknowledgment of fault, for example, acts of nature (God).

According to some of the leading researchers in this area, forgiveness may be better defined as "the decision to reduce negative thoughts, affect, and behavior—such as blame and anger—toward an offender or hurtful situation, and to begin to gain better understanding of the offense and the offender" (McCullough and Worthington 1994, 3).

Clinically and pastorally, one can assist another with making this decision to forgive in at least three ways. First, the injured person might be challenged to view the offense less personally, that is, as less intentional on the part of the offender purposely to inflict harm and more as a consequence of a thoughtless action. Second, the offended party might be challenged to take more responsibility for emotional experiences (hurt, sadness) rather than to blame the offender for these feelings—he or she *made* me feel this way. And finally, the clinical and pastoral agent might challenge the offended person to let go of the grievance story that underscores helplessness and victim status and instead to create a new narrative that emphasizes his or her own heroism in the wake of injury, as manifested in a commitment to personal growth and transformation.

Thus far in this section, the focus has been on psychological and spiritual interventions to foster individual flourishing. However, trauma and illness affect not only the injured person but also the community of one's family, friends, and colleagues as well. Warren Brown, in "Physicalism, Suffering, and Disability" (2005), argues that spiritual transformation and the enhancement of flourishing for those who are suffering or disabled must involve creative action on the part of the immediate community to intervene in ways that enhance personal relatedness. Brown dispels the dichotomy between the "disabled" and the "non-disabled." Instead, he contends that throughout our lives, all of us move back and forth along this continuum.

If one accepts this argument of the need and benefit of community participation in the spiritual transformation, then it is not simply a matter of applying certain psychological and spiritual approaches to the sick or traumatized person; rather, it is an embodied transformation of all involved in caring for that person. This transformation precipitates a shift in self-identity and sense of dependency on the part of *all* who are involved, including the clinical and pastoral agent. Character strengths and virtues and their spiritual correlates (creativity, love, humility, and gratitude) are evoked and deepened in all who care for the sick person, enriching the healing process with the promise of flourishing and spiritual transformation, the hallmarks of wholeness.

References

Brim, O., C. Ryff, and R. Kessler, eds. 2004. *How Healthy Are We? A National Study of Well-Being at Midlife*. Chicago: University of Chicago Press.

Brown, W. S. 2005. "Physicalism, Suffering, and Disability." *Journal of Psychology and Christianity* 24, no. 2: 149–55.

Clay, R. 2001. "Green Is Good for You." *APA Monitor* 32, no. 4: 1–7.

Erikson, E. 1950. *Childhood and Society*. New York: Norton.

Frankl, V. 1984. *Man's Search for Meaning*. New York: Simon & Schuster.

Hamm, D. 1994. "Rummaging for God: Praying Backward through Your Day." *America*, May 14, 1994.

Keyes, C. 2005. "Mental Illness and/or Mental Health? Investigating Axioms of the Complete State Model of Health." *Journal of Consulting and Clinical Psychology* 73:539–48.

———. 2007. "Promoting and Protecting Mental Health as Flourishing." *American Psychologist* 62:95–108.

Keyes, C., D. Shmotkin, and C. Ryff. 2002. "Optimizing Well-Being: The Empirical Encounter of Two Traditions." *Journal of Personality and Social Psychology* 82:1007–22.

Kornfield, J. 2002. *The Art of Forgiveness, Lovingkindness, and Peace*. New York: Bantam Books.

Koss-Chiono, J., and P. Hefner. 2006. *Spiritual Transformation and Healing*. New York: AltaMira Press.

Maslow, A. 1954. *Motivation and Personality*. 3rd ed. New York: Harper Collins.

May, W. 1991. *The Patient's Ordeal*. Bloomington: Indiana University Press.

McCullough, M., and E. Worthington, Jr. 1994. "Encouraging Clients to Forgive People Who Have Hurt Them: Review, Critique, and Research Prospectus." *Journal of Psychology and Theology* 22:3–20.

McGregor, I., and B. Little. 1998. "Personal Projects, Happiness, and Meaning: On Doing Well and Being Yourself." *Journal of Personality and Social Psychology* 74:494–512.

Meissner, W. W. 1992. *Ignatius of Loyola: The Psychology of a Saint*. New Haven, CT: Yale University Press.

Pargament, K. 1997. *The Psychology of Religion and Coping: Theory, Research, Practice*. New York: Guilford.

Rizzuto, A. 1979. *The Birth of the Living God: A Psychoanalytic Study*. Chicago: University of Chicago Press.

Ryan, R., and E. Deci. 2001. "On Happiness and Human Potentials: A Review of Research on Hedonic and Eudaimonic Well-Being." *Annual Review of Psychology* 52:141–66.

Seligman, M., and C. Peterson. 2004. *Character Strengths and Virtues: A Handbook and Classification*. New York: Oxford University Press.

Smith, T. 2006. "The National Spiritual Transformation Study." *Journal for the Scientific Study of Religion* 45, no. 2: 283–96.

Strumpfer, D. J. W. 1995. "The Origins of Health and Strength: From 'Salutogenesis to Fortigenesis.'" *South African Journal of Psychology* 25:81–89.

2

Dancing Partners

Pastoral Care in Relational and Theological Perspective

Pamela Cooper-White

One of the most compelling images of God, from the fourth-century Cappadocian theologians, is the image of the Trinity as *perichoresis*, the complete, equal, and mutual interpermeation of the three persons or the dynamic dimensions of the Trinity.[1] Catherine LaCugna gives a beautiful, clear description, as follows:

> [P]erichoresis expressed the idea that the three divine persons mutually inhere in one another, draw life from one another, "are" what they are by relation to one another. Perichoresis means being-in-one-another, permeation without confusion....Each divine person is irresistibly drawn to the other, taking his/her existence from the other, containing the other in him/herself, while at the same time pouring self into the other.... While there is no blurring of the individuality of each person, there is also no separation. There is only communion of love in which each person comes to be...and at the same time...what God is: ecstatic, relational, dynamic, vital. Perichoresis provides a dynamic model

> of persons in communion based on *mutuality and interdependence*.[2]

Although technically not a translation for *perichōrēsis*,[3] the popular rendering into English of *perichoresis* as the divine dance is a compelling image for the dynamism, energy, and multiplicity-in-unity inherent in the symbol of the Trinity. As LaCugna writes, again:

> Choreography suggests the partnership of movement, symmetrical but not redundant, as each dancer expresses and at the same time fulfills him/herself towards the other. In interaction and inter-course, the dancers (and the observers) experience one fluid motion of encircling, encompassing, permeating, enveloping, outstretching. There are neither leaders nor followers in the divine dance, only an eternal movement of reciprocal giving and receiving, giving again and receiving again....The image of the dance forbids us to think of God as solitary. The idea of Trinitarian perichoresis provides a marvelous point of entry into contemplating what it means to say God is alive from all eternity as love.[4]

Perichoresis has been adopted in feminist theology as an image for "an ethics that upholds three central values: inclusiveness, community, and freedom. Since these ways of relating are the hallmarks of divine life, they should characterize the patterns of human persons in communion with one another."[5]

The image of the dance is not an image of an exclusive club or divine committee of three. The imagery of motion and spontaneity would seem to invite others—humanity, creatures, all living beings—to join in the "dance of all creation."[6] In Andrei Rublev's fifteenth-century icon, which depicts the Trinity as the three mysterious visitors to Sarah and Abraham under the tree at Mamre, the three figures incline democratically toward one another, but also there is a space at the table for us, as we gaze on the icon.

Elizabeth Johnson describes how the image of the Trinity is one that refutes all monolithic, totalizing tendencies of theology to define God: "At its most basic the symbol of the Trinity evokes a livingness in God, a dynamic coming and going with the world that points to an inner divine circling around in unimaginable relation...Not an isolated, static, ruling monarch, but a relational, dynamic, tripersonal mystery of love."[7]

The Trinity is, then, a spacious room—even a *matrix*/womb, in which multiple metaphors can flourish, honoring simultaneously the relationality and the multiplicity of God. Thinking in a bit more postmodern vein, the Trinity is an image that continues to empty itself of fixed essences, not cascading into a nihilistic nothingness of divine absence but rather an ever-shifting kaleidoscopic pattern. It is like a waterfall, *full* of light, color, and dancing shapes, that provides continual refreshment, a long cool drink for parched feelings and hardened thinking, cleansing for the perceived wounds and stains, cooling for fevered human hubris, and the occasional deluge for those who become too comfortable with the delights of any particular tributary of sacred ideology. Who would dare to enter into such dangerous, wet, creative contemplation? And yet, who would not be drawn by the beauty of such overflowing abundance? Moreover, as a pastoral theologian, who would not be drawn by the promise of growth, healing, and empowerment that springs from such a multiple image? What, then, are some implications for a relational pastoral theology?

A Trinitarian Pastoral Theology

If we are willing to explore these multifaceted efforts toward a multiple concept of God and a corollary construction of a mutual, co-constructive, cogenerative yearning *between* humans and the divine,[8] then we are led to a pastoral construction of human beings, consciousness, and its construction in mutual relations (potentially resonating with a variety of faith traditions, not just orthodox Christianity) and to an appreciation of this multiple, fluid relationality of both God and human persons as underpinning all relational approaches to pastoral praxis—through the spectrum of care, counseling, and psychotherapy.[9]

As we embrace a model of greater complexity and multiplicity of the human mind, this will lead us to a more complex and nuanced appreciation for the diversity and mutability of human persons in the way we understand pastoral care, counseling, and psychotherapy. What is *pastoral*—that is, what protects and promotes human growth, helps to heal psychic and interpersonal wounds, and may, at a psycho-spiritual level, even facilitate physical healing along the mind-body-spirit continuum—from this relational perspective, then, is not a vision of ultimate or reified *oneness* as in a homogenization of all "patients" (as objects) into a single uniform model of health and wholeness but rather the capacity for a pluriform and diversely just and loving human *creativity*. This creativity is grounded/surrounded/infused in the creative profusion, the incarnational desire and pulsing, living inspiration of the Trinity/loving God, which is the "source, wellspring and living water"[10] of mutual desire that bridges, through the very embracing of difference, toward the creative multiplicity of the other. This, then, becomes the new starting point for an emancipatory praxis of pastoral care, counseling, and psychotherapy, where the goal of care is to provide a space in which the person can be freed from the constraining myths of oppression (whether individual, intrafamilial, communal, or social and cultural) toward a freer exploration of her own multiform creative potential.

What might the three traditional aspects of the Trinity say, in a *non-essentialist* key, particularly as a source for a healing and liberative pastoral praxis, praxis with an ear toward metaphors that resonate with the pastoral functions of healing, sustaining, guiding, reconciling, and empowering? In my most recent book, *Many Voices: Pastoral Psychotherapy in Relational and Theological Perspective*, I have proposed the following Trinitarian language: *God as Creative Profusion*, *God as Incarnational Desire*, and *God as Living Inspiration.*[11]

God as Creative Profusion

GLORY be to God for dappled things—
For skies of couple-colour as a brinded cow;
For rose-moles all in stipple upon trout that swim;
Fresh-firecoal chestnut-falls; finches' wings;
Landscape plotted and pieced—fold, fallow, and plough;
And all trades, their gear and tackle and trim.
All things counter, original, spare, strange;
Whatever is fickle, freckled (who knows how?)
With swift, slow; sweet, sour; adazzle, dim;
He fathers-forth whose beauty is past change:
Praise him.

The English poet Gerard Manley Hopkins captures the multiplicity and fecundity of creation in this poem, "Pied Beauty."[12] Hopkins's nineteenth-century "father" language recedes in importance amid the swirling alliterations and the crunch of consonants that capture the wildness, unpredictability, and perfect imperfection, "dappled...fickle, freckled," of creation. The tenacity of life gives further evidence of the irrepressible nature of God's creativity. One of my own most powerful experiences of the realization of God's presence was in the Oakland, California, hills one late afternoon. I suddenly "saw," in a nonordinary way of seeing, the tremendous force and thrust and determination of the trees jutting out of the soft, seemingly precarious hillside soil and leaning vertiginously out over the landscape far below. The terrible scarring of those same hillsides by fire a few years later, and the rising again of tiny trees out of the seeds broken open by the ferocious heat of the fire, was a powerful sign of the force of new life, even resurrected life. What a deep symbol for the process of healing—from both loss and illness! Yet every day, if I pay attention, I am given the gift of reminders of those moments of seeing—in my urban setting in Philadelphia, and in among the historic walls of my Gettysburg home, I see it again: another tiny green spike or tendril, seemingly frail and tender, but with the force to gnaw and snake its way through concrete and brick, until it finds the sun and opens.

I love the fact that, even if I accidentally dig up a daffodil bulb in my garden while planting summer flowers and stick it in upside down, again by accident, it will figure out how to send its shoots down and around and up again, and in the spring, the daffodil will rise once more to animate and color its own tiny patch of winter-deadened space. Here is the unstoppable force of both tree *and* rhizome—on flat sidewalks, vertical walls, on the ridges and cliffs overlooking the San Francisco Bay or curled upside down in the dirt of my garden. Who can say where vertical ends and horizontal begins? Life, in all its fecundity, is three-dimensional, unruly, not bound by any compass but God's own greenward direction: Up! Out! Forward! Sideways! Heal! Grow!

God, then, *is* creative profusion, and the creation is no longer conceivable as a pristine product by a supernatural maker, but an irrepressible fecundity. This fecundity, this turbulent swarming of creation, it seems to me, is a much more healing, consoling, liberating, and empowering image for pastoral relations than a singular, authoritarian God the Father. To liberate the first "person" of the Trinity from a concretized identity as Father, or even Creator, opens the way to affirming the dappled, fickle, freckled multiplicity of the real human persons who come to us for care and healing. We are accepted, confirmed, loved in our complexities and contradictions. It is not the attainment of a shiny, polished perfection that will save/*salve* (soothe and heal) us but the increasing consciousness of our own intricacy—in Annie Dillard's words: "Intricacy is that which is given from the beginning, the birthright, and in intricacy is the hardiness of complexity that ensures against the failure of all life." Our own inner landscape, like the landscape as Dillard describes it, is "'ring-streaked, speckled and spotted,' like Jacob's cattle culled from Laban's herd."[13]

This theology has resonance with an expansive and noncondemning view of the human person as messy, multiple, in process, loved (in spite of and/or because of all his or her chaos), and therefore also loving. This is where all pastoral praxis has its beginnings and its endings: in learning to know and to love *all* the messy, conflicted, chaotic parts of ourselves, even as God has loved us from our beginnings "made in secret and woven in the depths of the earth" (Ps 139:14b) and in springing from that knowledge of being so deeply loved and growing in the capacity to love others. So the creation stirs in us and brings us into the awareness of God-with-us in our daily lives: God as incarnational desire.

God as Incarnational Desire

In all three aspects of the Trinity, God is love: the power of the erotic of life breaking through and insisting on newness, change, growth. This is true in a particular way as God is imaged in the second dimension of the Trinity—God willingly and lovingly present, *in* the flesh, fur, feathers, sea, and soil of the creation. The name *Emmanuel* (God-with-us) signifies God's own promise to be *with* us, even "to the end of the age" (Matt 28:20) and more, to be *in* us and in all creation. Just as perichoresis was used by the Cappadocians to describe the interpenetration of the three persons of the Trinity, perichoresis also applies to the relationship between God and the *world*. God is in us and we are in God—not on some disembodied or theoretical or "spiritual" plane apart from or above daily life but deep in our blood and our bones. As we walk forward in time and space, loving, working, watching, weeping, rejoicing, God is the whole energy of both justice and mercy, struggling forward through us and in us, in the historical movement of the world. God walks with us and in us, incarnate in history and intimately involved with us through the very human (and hence animal) experience of living and suffering in the body.

This is the miracle of incarnation, most clearly embodied for us, in the Christian tradition, in the life, passion, and resurrection of Jesus of Nazareth. The particularity of the astonishing revelation to the early Christians that *this Jesus* was God further tells us about what God is like. Jesus' character, as depicted over and over in the palimpsest of multiple Gospels and overlapping stories, was preoccupied with two central aims: to heal and restore to community those who were ill and/or outcast, and to reverse the social order, so that the oppressed would be liberated and the poor lifted up. In the belief that spread from the earliest eyewitnesses to the appearances of Jesus after his crucifixion, Christians even came to the astonishing conviction, read through the prophesies of Scripture and the messianic fervor of their times, that Jesus had been raised from the dead.

Whatever one believes about later dogmatic arguments about substitutionary atonement or the imagery of God sacrificing "his" son, a Trinitarian understanding of the cross points to the astounding assertion that the God who created the universe was so intimately bound up in the fullness of human experience that God allowed *God's own self* to experience excruciating torture and to die, and in so doing conquered death. Christians thus discern, through God's actions in the personality of Jesus of Nazareth, that God's own nature is to stand in solidarity with all who suffer and that God not only created the world but also offers a continuing promise of transformation from death to new life.

And this promise of resurrection is not only a promise about the end of our lives, but it is a promise that permeates all the deaths, the setbacks, the illnesses, and the losses we experience, big and little, with the hope that new life can and will come out of even the most desolate and wounded places in our lives. God, as revealed in the second dimension of the Trinity, comes to be known by us as the power of life—*eros*—which infuses our lives and our bodies with new energy, with zest for living, with healing for wounds and diseased bodies, and with hope for the future.

The Gospel narratives and Christian images of Jesus in the manger, in his mother's arms, and later on the road to Golgotha, on the cross, and in his mother's arms again in the Pietà also emphasize that God, like us, is vulnerable, is wounded. This is perhaps the greatest mystery, the incarnation. For Christians, there is no clearer depiction of God's vulnerability than that of God being born in a manger on a dusty straw bed, surrounded by the breath of curious animals and by frightened, uprooted human parents. And for Christians, there is no clearer depiction of God's woundedness than the image of God hanging and tortured on a first-century imperial Roman cross, betrayed and murdered by earthly powers and principalities. This is one of the more remarkable features of the Christian faith—that the God of the universe is not a God who lords over us but a God who participates in the bloody realities of concrete, fleshy living and dying. Further, God's vulnerability is not an illusion or greatness stooping to meet us, a condescension, as many classical traditions assert in order to preserve the greatness of God's sovereignty. This vulnerability is what God is, as God is revealed to us in the second dimension of the Trinity. And it is in and through such vulnerability, such at-oneness with the creation, that God continually acts to bring healing, justice, and transformation—new life!

This promise of transformation is at the heart of the pastoral enterprise. It heralds that change, however improbable, is never impossible. Much of what impedes growth, healing, and reaching out for new possibilities, for new life, is fear. A Trinitarian-informed pastoral psychotherapy holds out the belief that hope is possible and fear does not need to have the last word. The great spiritual writer and theologian Henri Nouwen posed the question, "How can we live in the midst of a world marked by fear, hatred and violence, and not be destroyed by it?" The message of the Gospels over and over is that, even at the times of our greatest fear and need, "Do not be afraid." In Nouwen's words, if we make the "house of fear" our permanent dwelling, we find our choices narrowed and our capacity for love constricted, until we can hardly breathe. Staying in our fear of change causes us to try to control everything and to become preoccupied with ourselves and our safety, until we may even come to hate others, because of threats we vaguely perceive. The rhythm of hope is the movement of pastoral care and psychotherapy—it is the movement out of this house of fear, this house of bondage, to a "house of love." If we internalize this good news, we will be led in the dance from fear and trembling to joy and freedom. This is the central aim of pastoral psychotherapy—not to be healed for our *own* contentment, or a solipsistic "self-actualization," but to be fully human, even as God-in-Jesus was *fully* human, which is to-be-for-others. As pastoral theologians, we cling to the belief that we can live again for others, in the power and the mystery of the risen life, which is Love.[14]

The incarnation, finally, is about God's desire. Not condescension, but love of the creation, draws God to us, "as close to us as our own breath," as Augustine is believed to have said. The promise of the incarnation, the promise of the transformation from fear to love, and from death to new life, lived vigorously, joyfully *in* the body, the promise of God's desire to be "as close to us as our own breath," leads in turn to the third aspect of Trinitarian imagery, that of the Holy Spirit as living inspiration, the ongoing energy that infuses and empowers the wonder of our relationships.

God as Living Inspiration

If the second dimension of the Trinity depicts God incarnate, the erotic living presence of the Holy in our embodied lives, the third dimension brings God to us in the very rhythm of our breath. The "Holy Spirit" is what we experience as the movement of God in our lives, simultaneously in us and among us, binding us together with one another and the whole created world. The Spirit has been variously thought of as breath, power, energy, wind.

Not coincidentally, human practices of prayer often involve a deepening and calming of the breath (whether intentionally or unintentionally through the physical relaxation that often comes with a shift in brain state during the focusing or clearing of the mind in prayer). The combination of calm, cleansing breathing and intentional focus on God, or bringing one's life, one's questions, one's feelings, one's problems before God, helps us to become more clearly aware of the presence of God/Spirit in us and in the various concerns and actions of our lives.

Not all forms of prayer are quiet and contemplative. Prayer may be any activity in which we practice awareness of the presence of God. This is the Benedictine rhythm of prayer and work, in which work itself becomes a form of prayer—going about our daily tasks, even seemingly mindless chores such as washing the dishes in a state of mindfulness of the presence of the sacred; as Thich Nhat Hanh described: "washing each dish as if it were a baby Buddha."[15] Whatever form it may take, prayer enhances our awareness of our relationship with God, which is always in motion, but not always something we attend fully. Prayer is the human practice of attending to the inspiration of the Holy in our daily existence, as lived in community.

Because the Spirit is not an isolated manifestation of the divine but conceived as one partner in the Trinitarian dance, the Spirit is in its own distinctive way yet another symbol of the *relationality* of God and of our life in and with God. As we breathe in, we know that we are not isolated. We do not live in bell jars;

we breathe in the entire world. And as we breathe out, if we are aware, we realize that we are reaching even with our breath beyond the confines of our own physical being. Our very existence affects others. Our very breath ties us to one another and to the planet. Even our breath, then, is unavoidably a matter of ethics. We cannot extricate ourselves from the very atmosphere in which we and all others live. Breathing reminds us that our very lives are intrinsically ec-static. We cannot live only for ourselves, but in and for one another, even as the Spirit swirls around and in and through us and all living beings in one great dance—a dance so great that it encompasses the entire cosmos and beyond.

The relational sign of the Spirit, then, is this motion of God, around and in and through, because it invisibly binds us together in one life, one community of creatures. Like it or not, believe it or not, we cannot help but participate in the dance of creation. And so our actions have consequences, not only for our own lives and those closest to us, but for the whole planet. The Spirit infuses all relationships, then, with God's own care, God's creativity, God's incarnational presence. We stand in relationship with this dynamic presence. The Spirit urges, whispers, prompts, and occasionally shoves us in the direction of God's priorities of love and justice. The image is a fluid one, like the air, not dominative and coercive but in-fluentia—always in-flowing. This flow of urgent love can be impeded, by human sin or by the thick scar tissue of woundedness, but can it ever be entirely blocked?

The pastoral relationship, then, encompassing the full spectrum of care, counseling, and psychotherapy, is no less fundamentally infused with this energy of God to help heal, grow, strengthen, and promote just flourishing of all persons and creatures. As with all relations among living beings, the pastoral relationship is characterized by a fluid intersubjectivity, where each partner in the relationship is simultaneously both "I" and "Thou" to both self and other and where meaning is co-constructed, not on either pole of the I-Thou duality, but in the "third space" that exists as a bridge of communication, a "potential space," to quote the British psychoanalyst D. W. Winnicott (1971)[16]—a place of possible but as yet unformulated understandings and a continuum of shared experience between them. In the pastoral relationship, given the asymmetry of roles between "helper" and "helpee," the psychoanalytic categories of transference (the helpee's subjective experience of the relationship and projections upon it) and countertransference (the helper's similar experiences and projections) become but one symbol of this dynamic interrelation, filtered through the separate subjective experiences and asymmetry of responsibilities of each partner.[17]

The psychoanalytic perspective adds the significant insight that this mutual relation never operates only at the conscious, interpersonal level of ordinary communications and transactions but encompasses the full range of unconsciousness in and between the participants as well and encompasses the "unformulated experiences"[18] and co-constructed meanings that lie only in potential, in the realm described by Christopher Bollas as the "unthought known."[19] This is the foundation of relational-psychoanalytic therapy. But in pastoral psychotherapy in particular, we are further convinced that we do this not merely by our own powers of reason or intuition but with the help of the pulsing, energizing breath of God dwelling in both partners in the therapeutic dance, and dwelling in the intersubjective space *between* us, which then opens up as a further space for God's creative profusion, God's incarnational presence, and God's living inspiration.

Countertransference and the Use of the Self

So what does this all have to do with what we do as pastoral caregivers, chaplains, and counselors? As I have written in *Shared Wisdom*, countertransference, or the "use of the self," is where all this high-sounding theory really comes into practice for us in some pretty concrete ways.[20] No one understands better than pastoral counselors and Clinical Pastoral Education (CPE)–trained chaplains how important the self is as an instrument or how impediments in self-knowledge can directly get in the way of the care we provide. It is at the heart of our pastoral counseling and CPE training missions!

To boil it down, the so-called countertransference is our subjectivity when we are in the helping role. In Freud's classical model, it was already understood as such. In the classical model, however, *subjectivity* was not viewed as a good thing. In the scientific belief system, in which Freud and most subsequent theorists were embedded, the helper was automatically conceived of as the expert who observed and knew and the helpee was the object to be observed and known. Objectivity was what was strived for. Subjectivity was devalued as containing contaminating elements of emotionality, irrationality, and unconscious acting out. Thus, in the classical model—including the classic training models of both CPE and pastoral counseling—countertransference has been taught and understood mainly as a *hindrance* to the helping process: something to be analyzed, so that it could be done away with or at least set aside while engaged in the work of helping.

In the relational paradigm, by contrast, subjectivity is *re*-valued as representing the whole spectrum of ways in which both one's own and the other's reality(-ies) can be understood. Relational subjectivity does not *exclude* our rational, thinking function,[21] but it *also* pays attention to our *affect* (or emotion) and our felt *bodily* sense as ways in which both self and other can be known. The relational paradigm also replaces the positivist one-sided relationship with something vastly more reciprocal. *Both* helper and helpee in this new model are *subjects*. They *both* observe and are observed, *both* know and are known. Even more exciting, I think, in this paradigm, is that what becomes knowable exists not only in each individual, but is made most fully accessible in the potential space that grows up *between* the two—already depicted early on in psychoanalysis by Carl Jung using the medieval image of the alchemical bath. Knowledge, including the rational, the emotional, *and* the embodied, is now understood as a shared and *co*-constructed pool in which the two participants are *equally* immersed, at both conscious and unconscious levels, in the "between" of their shared interaction.

Countertransference and transference (the helpee's conscious and unconscious views of us) become a continuum in this model, in which our mutual projections *onto* each other, and even *into* each other (which is called "projective identification"—when we begin to take in and behave out of what is unconsciously projected by the other onto and eventually into us) mutually shape our growing sense of understanding. Our focus, of course, is uniquely lopsided as professional caregivers, chaplains, and counselors on what we understand about the parishioners or patient or client, because in the helping relationship, unlike friendships, colleagueships, intimate partnerships, or parenting, the focus of knowing is always in the service of care and is not reciprocal in the same way.

From a theological perspective, such shared knowledge participates in the "infinite conversation" of which Buber wrote: "Extended, the lines of relationships intersect the eternal Thou."[22] In this model, we can see that as much or more is "going on" in the *middle* of the spectrum than at either end. In the relational model, insight or perhaps in its literal sense, *re-cognition*—thought that goes out and returns influenced, to be rethought again—flows back and forth between both participants. Glimmers of meaning may spark at any point along the spectrum at any time. Recognition may bubble up initially not only as a verbal thought, but often in the form of an emotion, or a bodily sensation, or a behavior—or even as a holistic flooding of all of our perceptions. Thus, the helper *uses his or her own self*, not only as a channel of information about his or her *own* knowledge and experience but equally as an empathic *receiver* of the *other's* affective state and the shared meaning that is emerging between them. This is the meaning of intersubjectivity in pastoral care: that we use all our senses to perceive not only what may be coming up inside of us that could be getting in the way of our understanding of the other, but also that we "tune in" more deeply and empathically with the other's experience. As such, it is a tool that can sensitize us even more profoundly to the sacred multiple truth, the *logos*, the "I am" of each person in our care.

Conclusion: Pastoral Theology and Praxis

A pastoral perspective oriented paradoxically, not just toward a singular "east" but toward a multiplicity of compass points and unfixed directions to a God conceived of as fluid, vulnerable, multiple, in motion, and in perpetual relation both with us and within us, emancipates us from constraining, static, monolithic notions of both God and human beings. A multiple/ Trinitarian and relational pastoral theology, it seems to me, is hospitable to a roomy conception of mind and self that makes new breathing space, space for each human person that can heal narrowness of vision and the constraining hardness of psychic scars in order to encompass an ever-widening capacity for relationality, both with other people and with and among the *inner* selves that inhabit the time and spatial dimensions of one's own lived life.

Theology and psychology meet in this pastoral third space between certainty and unknowability, where rigid hierarchies of both deity/humanity and consciousness/the unconscious begin to collapse, as we recognize that our creativity, art, and human nature itself, contain spheres of divinity and humanity, rationality and irrationality, knowability and unknowability, of abstract thought, emotion, and animal sense, both within ourselves and in our relations with one another and with God. In the words of T. S. Eliot's "Dry Salvages" from the *Four Quartets*:

> The hint half guessed, the gift half understood, is
> Incarnation.[23]

Notes

1. Discussion of *perichoresis* adapted and condensed from Pamela Cooper-White, *Many Voices: Pastoral Psychotherapy in Relational and Theological Perspective* (Minneapolis: Fortress Press, 2007), 76–82.

2. Catherine Mowry LaCugna, *God for Us: The Trinity and Christian Life* (San Francisco: HarperSanFrancisco, 1973), 270–71.

3. *Perichōreō* means "to encompass"; *perichōreuō* means "to dance around." Ibid., 312n94.

4. Ibid.

5. Patricia Wilson-Kastner, *Faith, Feminism and Christ* (Philadelphia: Fortress, 1983), cited in LaCugna, 272–73.

6. Line from John Arthur, "This Is the Feast of Victory for Our God," *The Hymnal 1982* (New York: Church Hymnal Corporation, 1985), Hymn #417, 418.

7. Elizabeth Johnson, *She Who Is: The Mystery of God in Feminist Theological Discourse* (New York: Crossroad, 1992), 192–93.

8. See ibid., 274–75.

9. The following trinitarian reflections are condensed from Cooper-White, *Many Voices*, 82–94. For further elaboration on the themes presented here, see chapter 2, "A Relational Understanding of God," in *Many Voices*, 67–94.

10. Borrowing from David Cunningham's trinitarian formulation in *These Three Are One: The Practice of Trinitarian Theology* (Malden, MA: Blackwell, 1998).

11. Cooper-White, *Many Voices*, 82–94.

12. Gerard Manley Hopkins, *The Poems of Gerard Manley Hopkins*, 4th ed., ed. W. H. Gardner and N. H. Mackenzie (London: Oxford University Press, 1967), 69, as cited in Cooper-White *Many Voices*, 893.

13. Annie Dillard, *Pilgrim at Tinker Creek* (New York: Harper's Magazine Press, 1974), 145.

14. Henri Nouwen, *Behold the Beauty of the Lord: Praying with Icons* (Notre Dame, IN: Ave Maria Press, 1987), 19, 20.

15. Thich Nhat Hanh, *Peace Is in Every Step: The Path of Mindfulness in Everyday Life* (New York: Bantam, 1992), 15.

16. D. W. Winnicott, *Playing and Reality* (New York: Basic Books, 1971), 41. For "potential space," see especially 106–10.

17. For a much more detailed discussion of transference and coun-

tertransference from a relational, intersubjective perspective, and its ethical implications for boundaries and care, see Cooper-White, *Shared Wisdom: Use of the Self in Pastoral Care and Counseling* (Minneapolis: Fortress, 2004), esp. chapter 3, "The Relational Paradigm: Postmodern Concepts of Countertransference and Intersubjectivity," 35–60.

18. Donnel B. Stern, *Unformulated Experience: From Dissociation to Imagination in Psychoanalysis* (Hillsdale, NJ: Analytic Press, 1997).

19. Christopher Bollas, *The Shadow of the Object: Psychoanalysis of the Unthought Known* (New York: Columbia University Press, 1987).

20. This section is adapted from Cooper-White, *Shared Wisdom*, 54–58 et passim. For a much more in-depth discussion of the concept of countertransference and the pastoral "use of the self," from both classical and contemporary psychoanalytic understandings, see chapters 1–3, pp. 9–60.

21. Even this might be challenged—the postmodern suspicion of rational cognition goes deep. See Cooper-White, *Shared Wisdom*, 214n75.

22. Martin Buber, *I and Thou*, trans. Walter Kaufman (New York: Charles Scribner's Sons, 1970), 114, 123 (n.b.: Kaufman translation reads "the eternal You").

23. T. S. Eliot, "Dry Salvages," *The Four Quartets* (1943; repr., New York: Harcourt Brace Jovanovich, 1971), 44.

3

Psychological and Spiritual Reflections for Visitors to the Sick

Robert J. Giugliano

> Someone I loved once gave me a box full of darkness.
> It took me years to understand that this, too, was a gift.
> —Mary Oliver

Maureen was diagnosed with breast cancer a number of years ago and had a mastectomy followed by radiation and chemotherapy, the usual and often effective treatment that is known to put the cancer into a permanent remission. We, my wife Muriel and I, have known her for going on thirty years, but it is only in the last few years that we have gotten close. She is sixty-two, Irish, sharp-tongued, unmarried, and deeply and lovingly surrounded by and involved in a large extended Irish family. She has phone calls and visits from her brother, his children and grandchildren, and her many, many cousins; in fact, the phone never stops ringing. She is known to tell Elaine, her favorite hospice nurse, "Tell whoever it is, I'm sleeping." Nevertheless she might talk to the caller, depending on whoever it is.

Her hospital bed is in the living room, and now she barely moves, sips tea from a straw, and has to have someone hold her now-occasional cigarette so she can get a good drag off it. The sharpness of her tongue and wit remain strong; she and Elaine are a good match playing off of each other. Maureen has pain and discomfort in her right eye. Elaine was on the couch and complained that her eye was now bothering her, "Everything I get, she gets," Maureen said, "I had a cold all last week and what do you know, so did she."

Her life is filled with devotion to God, the church that she loves with all her heart, and her father and mother, whom Maureen kept at home until her mother's death from Alzheimer's. Her family, O God, yes, her beautiful Irish family, her many priest and nun friends are now with her, in her heart and her memory, as well as they can be, as she lays in wait. She selected the readings and music, assigned the various tasks. The funeral service booklet's cover has a good picture of her and the date of her birth. "I only wish I knew when it was to be," she said, "so I could have them printed."

I resisted visiting her at home, which is only blocks away, when she got so sick after her last coming home from the hospital. I didn't much care for the fact that I was not visiting her as often as I thought I should or as often as I knew she might have wanted or expected me to. I asked for the grace of freedom from whatever it was that I was in the grips of that was preventing me from being present to my friend. After not visiting for a few weeks, I finally just went. Her door is always open. When I bent over and kissed her and weakly and guiltily said my, "Hi, Maureen, how are you?" she said, as we caught each other's gaze, "Oh, I have so wanted to see you." As a silent cry and tears welled up, I was moved by what she so warmly said, and by seeing the face of Christ and feeling the flame of his love in and through her, I received the grace I asked for. Resistance was replaced with eagerness to visit her. Now, I read Mary Oliver's poems, which she enjoys, make her a cup of tea, light and hold her cigarettes, and tell her I love her and that she is in my thoughts and prayers.

Anne, sweet, delightful, and pretty Annie, was diagnosed with cancer of the spine early in December 2006. Late that summer, as the days waned and fall approached with its golden beach days and longer shadows, she complained of back pain and went to a chiropractor at first. The pain worsened; she went to the local hospital, an x-ray was taken, and she was told she should start radiation therapy immediately, if only to bring some relief from the pressure that the tumor had on her spine. Her husband of almost fifty years, her dearest companion in love and grace, was stalwart beside her, as were her son and daughter, daughter-in-law, son-in-law, grandchildren, other relatives, and many friends. She was admitted to Sloan-Kettering in early January 2007; her family and friends stood vigil at her bedside 24/7. I always felt that I wanted to be with her. I loved her company, and we prayed together once. All she wanted was to go home and have hospice care there, but after having a mild heart attack, she never regained the strength to be discharged. She died on January 28, 2007, not more than eight weeks after the initial diagnosis.

Everyone, especially Anne, was at first in a state of disbelief. She was young, in her early sixties, alive, with a profound faith and spirituality that in some measure came from losing a college-age son, her dear David, in 1993. She had a sense of humor such that she could always be counted on to top Tom, her storytelling husband, who had a great delivery in the first place. Being with her during those days was a privilege, as she was being born into eternal life and as this life ebbed from her with every labored breath. Over the eight weeks, she gradually and peacefully gave up this life; she gave up being able to do all that she did as wife, mother, grandmother, aunt, and friend. She let it all go, as she was cared for by those she cared for in this life. One of the most touching moments was when my wife, Muriel, asked Anne if she would like her feet massaged. The memory of Muriel massaging Anne's feet with some fragrant lotion, while the pace of Anne's breathing settled down, has a deep and lasting Christ presence in it that I cherish. When I call to mind Anne singing the "Fields of Athenry," I am moved to tears and miss her; the grief of her husband and children is beyond words, as they hold her and their brother and son close in their hearts. The yearly Mass on their porch at the beach in memory of David is now an even more powerful and poignant expression of our faith, as we remember him now with his mother in the heart of God.

I offer these two stories of spiritual visiting because they illustrate a most important point: the one being visited, the patient, in his or her person, is a living sign and expression of the person of Christ suffering now in the world, in this life, through us, his sisters and brothers. The suffering body of Christ is living and present and calling out for care in those who are suffering throughout the world in all ways and in all places. To what then does this reality call us? How are we to understand our role as a spiritual visitor? Who are *we*, then, to the patient? Who is *patient*, then, for the visitor? How are we to relate to the patient? What are we to do with unpleasant feelings that arise from just being in the sick room with its particular sights, sounds, and smells and due to the personality and value differences between the patient and the visitor?

A Perspective on the Nature of the Spiritual Visitor–Patient Relationship

> Lord, my heart is not proud;
>   nor are my eyes haughty.
> I do not busy myself with great matters,
>   with things too sublime for me.
>
> Rather, I have stilled my soul
>   hushed it like a weaned child.
> Like a weaned child on its mother's lap
>   so is my soul within me.
>
> —Psalm 131:1–2

The spiritual visitor–patient relationship is a type of helping relationship. The visitor is there as a source of support, comfort, and assistance, taking the initiative to make oneself available for the patient. The visitor is the bearer of presence and open to receive the patient in the fullness of the patient's condition and its impact on the patient's sense of well-being, degree of acceptance of the diagnosis, and freedom to relate. The visitor is "there" for the patient in as complete and as appropriate a way as possible. Every specifically helping relationship, particularly pastoral counseling, psychotherapy, and spiritual direction has been seen as a reflection of and in the light of a good mother-child relationship. The primary characteristics or qualities of a growth-promoting mother-child relationship are: unconditional positive regard and love, openness to the full range of the child's emotional experience and expression, and being able to reflect back to the child a receptive understanding of the child's experience and feelings. A good-enough mother-child relationship is characterized by a sufficient degree of mutual emotional attunement, such that the child develops a solid sense of security and independence.

Some of the most remarkable research these days is on the mother-infant relationship and the effects of the relationship on the neurophysiological development of the infant. Simply stated, but with respect for the complexity of the issues involved: when the infant is cared for by a responsive, attentive, secure mother, who is able to fully receive her infant in such a way as to give that infant the experience of being in its mother's mind and heart, brain development is at its most effective and complete. The neuronal pathways having to do with the processing and regulation of emotion are developed in such a way as to contribute to the infant's developing a sense of security that enables it to explore the world.

The point of this digression is to suggest not that the spiritual visitor "mother" the patient but that the visitor reflect on what he or she actually brings into the patient's presence. In the Christian tradition, the mother-child relationship has powerful life-giving, mystery-evoking, incarnational and salvific meaning. The mother-child relationship, the Mary-Jesus relationship, enables God-taking-flesh, becoming one of us and intentionally subjecting Godself to the laws and experiences of human development. God comes into the world as an infant and is deeply wanted, warmly nourished at Mary's breast, held close in her arms, soothed in his crying by her tender care under the watchful gaze, guidance, and protective care of husband and father, Joseph.

D. W. Winnicott, a British psychoanalyst, was reported to have said in one of his radio talks to mothers and fathers, "There is no such thing as a baby. Show me a baby and I will always show you someone caring for the baby." And so, while it is the goal of the Christian spiritual life to become like Christ so as to bring God's unconditional love into the world, it is actually Christ and his mother, their loving, growth-promoting, and enhancing relationship that is incarnated in us. The spiritual visitor is the bearer of Mary and Jesus into the patient's presence—on the one hand, listening, empathizing, helping in practical ways, giving nourishment to the patient, and on the other hand, actively being present, anticipating needs, responding to requests, asking, as Jesus did, "What do you want me to do for you?" and in so doing touching the patient with God's healing presence and love by bringing Christ and Mary into the room.

Visiting the sick and dying is challenging. We may not want to be there for a whole host of reasons, from personality issues to feelings of revulsion, anxiety, anger, or sadness at the appearance of illness and disease on the face of the patient. But we, nevertheless, choose to respond to the call of this ministry and actively, with all deliberate intention, bring ourselves to the sick. Jesus and Mary are there for us as well, and in our prayer we can actively call on them to walk with us, to relieve us from our fears, so we can freely and fully be present to those we visit.

Health and Illness

"As long as you have your health, you have everything." What we have when we have our health is usually thought of as the integrity and wholeness of our bodies. Everything, all systems and organs, are working as they should, and discomfort and pain are not present, "thank God." But health also refers to more than freedom from physical disease or pain. Health is primarily a spiritual value, out of which one perceives and copes with the emotional, relational, physical, and practical challenges life puts before us. Seen in this way, health is not the opposite of illness; having a disease, being ill does not cancel out the sense of health and well-being but rather challenges it. Health is the capacity for living life in as complete and full a way as possible and the capacity for being able to respond, when challenged, in a proactive way so as to maintain a sense of well-being.

A disease refers to changes in the body from its normal and expected way of functioning. Having a disease, for example, hypertension or even cancer in its early stages, is not always accompanied by subjective feelings of illness, such as weakness, pain, or nausea. But knowing one has a diagnosis can change us completely and sometimes irrevocably. The first thing a diagnosis does is to tell us that we are not whole or complete, that something is "wrong" with us or we have "something" we shouldn't have. If there is anything a disease or condition does, it is to bring us to the realization of our limits, our not being completely in control of life and our very mortality. We are "earthen vessels," our life is fragile, and we are easily broken in body, mind, and spirit.

Reactions to Being Diagnosed

The following is a schema for understanding reactions to being diagnosed or to becoming seriously ill. These reactions are characteristic ways of adapting to being ill as well as states of mind and heart that are experienced from time to time during the phases of illness. This section will be written from the perspective that the disease in question is a very serious and/or life-threatening one. It is meant to be not an exhaustive explication of the psychology of illness but rather a checklist of points for reflection and consideration for the spiritual visitor and a frame of reference for appreciating and understanding what the patient may be experiencing and going through.

In the Beginning

The very first reaction to knowing that one is faced with a serious health condition is shock, disbelief, and anxiety. In the beginning, denial may also be present and it may often be a good reaction, as it helps to manage what may be overwhelming anxiety and worry. In denial, we may minimize the seriousness of the condition while we muster the personal and social support resources to deal with all that has to be dealt with at this time: getting accurate information; knowing the questions to ask; understanding medication, surgery, and any other treatments; knowing what we can do to ameliorate symptoms and to contribute to managing the illness. There is a lot to know and do in the beginning stages, not to mention keeping doctors' appointments straight. If the spiritual visitor is involved with the patient at this time, being of practical and instrumental support is a great help and an opportunity to be a calming, peaceful presence for the patient. The visitor is there for the patient and can anticipate some of the patient's needs: Do you need a ride to the doctor? Do you want me to stay with you at the doctor's office? Can I call your relatives? or, Is there anything I can do for you?

As the patient deals with the details of having a serious illness, the initial shock, numbness, disbelief, and denial begin to wane, and the patient is face-to-face with the reality of the challenge. There is a continuum of responses to this reality, from refusal to face the situation and continued denial, through anxious and depressed acceptance, to complete and humble acceptance. Each of these can be considered to be not only characteristic or typical ways of responding for some people but also feeling states that the patient can spiral into and out of, depending on mood and sense of vulnerability.

Desolation

St. Ignatius Loyola in his *Spiritual Exercises* sheds light on the states of spiritual consolation and desolation that accompany us in our spiritual development and on our journey to an intimate relationship with God. One of the hallmarks of spiritual desolation is the sense that God is absent, not to be found in the usual experiences of prayer, private or liturgical, or in other experiences that may be associated with God's presence, such as gazing at an infant or the moonlit sky or the sunset or a flower. Whether the patient has a developed relationship with God or not, the news of a serious health problem may very well bring the patient into spiritual desolation. This desolation is more often than not a sense that one has been abandoned by God. Not only is God absent and gone away, but the patient may very well have a sense that God has done this to him, perhaps as a test like what God did to Job. And, if God did not do it directly, then God certainly allowed it to happen. Ignatius recommends that a person in desolation meet the desolating spirit by spending more time in prayer. This may be the last thing the patient feels like doing, since in prayer we meet our deepest and most painful feelings and concerns. Being angry with God may act as an obstacle to sharing one's feelings with God. Prayer may be difficult at this time when one's attention is so easily distracted and disturbed by increased feelings of self-consciousness and body awareness. It is difficult to get away from that which is causing all the worry in the first place. Then, the body itself becomes the object of increased attention and the patient may become hyperalert to every sensation and ache.

Refusal

The person who refuses to accept the reality of his health situation is the one who fights against himself rather than the illness. If he prays at all, the prayer is focused on the illness, the pain, and the distress it causes and on having God remove all this. The underlying attitude is one of nonacceptance of reality; paradoxically, this type of prayer increases distress, because the person is always looking for relief and doing so increases attention to the body and its symptoms. One of the hallmarks of this type of adaptation to illness is noncompliance with medication and treatment and the outright refusal to do anything to change lifestyle, when such changes are important to remaining as healthy as one can so as to more effectively cope with the illness. For example, losing weight, exercising, and eating healthily for patients with heart disease, diabetes, or hypertension, and not smoking for those with lung problems are lifestyle changes that can contribute to increased feelings of well-being and improved coping. There is also a tendency, for those who cope in this way of refusal, to isolate themselves from others and to keep their feelings to themselves. Such interpersonal and emotional isolation does not reduce stress but rather increases it.

For at least two reasons, it is difficult for the spiritual visitor to be with the edgy, angry, withdrawn, and sometimes overtly hostile person. It is unpleasant to be in the presence of someone who is bitter and resentful to begin with, and communication tends to be only one way—the visitor is subject to a barrage of complaints and negative emotions. Second, one does not feel particularly supportive in a relationship like this, since the patient is not receptive to the supportive presence of the visitor. Just the visitor's presence is a reminder to the patient that he is subject to a health situation that he does not have any control over—that he is in fact a victim. There are some people who get some psychological benefit out of having others dote on them and plead with them to be more cooperative with medications, treatment, and lifestyle changes. While the person with emphysema, for example, may not be outwardly angry, hostile, or resistant, continuing to smoke while being reminded by everyone that it is not a helpful thing to do is an opportunity for passive expression of aggressive feelings. The visitor may feel that he is not being of any good help and that the visit is a waste of his time and his personal spiritual resources. This may be so, because the visitor may not receive any appreciation or sense that he or she was helpful or that the visit had any value to the patient. Taking these feelings and experiences to prayer is important for the visitor, so that he or she can grow more fully in the likeness of Christ and be able to be fully present and "stay awake" for the patient.

Anxiety and Depression

A step closer to humble acceptance of the reality of one's health situation and challenge is to be caught up in anxiety, worry, and depression. Usually, there is an increase in preoccupation with bodily sensations and feelings, such that everything becomes a symptom and a cause for further anxiety. There may be a "what's the use anyway" attitude that results in a halfhearted compliance with treatment, medication, and lifestyle changes. Not finding a sense of peace, calm, or security within the self, the patient may develop demanding and dependent relationships with caretakers, whose presence and ministrations bring about a sense of relief. The depression and anxiety may themselves be of such intensity as to affect sleep and appetite, and the only relief is received through antidepressant and antianxiety medications.

The basic stance of the spiritual visitor is, of course, to be present, to listen to, and to engage the patient, who more than likely will gain relief from talking about her or his situation. These patients usually have the capacity to engage the visitor, and as such the visitor can engage them in a discussion of prayer and thereby encourage the patient to spend time in prayer. If the patient is open and willing, praying with the patient may be very helpful. Since the patient's prayer is of the "take this cup from me" type, there is room for movement out of worry and depression into acceptance.

Humble Acceptance

The person who is able to face the reality of serious and life-threatening illness with a sense of humble acceptance is the one who is then able to move closer to God in prayer and to enjoy the spiritual and psychological fruits of that closeness. This person is willingly and eagerly proactive on his or her own behalf and so is actively engaged with treatment and lifestyle changes, which are designed to improve one's sense of health and well-being. The humbly accepting patient is not simply passive but rather actively engaged in knowing as much as can be helpful and in doing all he or she can to benefit from treatment and lifestyle changes. Such a person is able to engage in the discipline of whatever treatments and lifestyle changes the illness may require and is open to receiving the presence and support of family, friends, and visitors. Relationships with others tend to deepen, as the patient shares experiences and feelings during this challenging journey, which then encourages others to share in a like manner. There is an intimate reciprocity in these exchanges as well as in the prayers of an accepting patient, during which the need for God's compassionate embrace, care, and concern is sought and received.

The one who humbly and prayerfully accepts illness brings forth the loving presence of Jesus. In this way, the patient and the spiritual visitor become graced gifts for each other, and the time spent together becomes a kind of *kairos* time, a time beyond time. During *kairos* time, the presence of God is living and active. As Paul Claudel is reported to have said, "Jesus did not come to explain away suffering or remove it. He came to fill it with His presence."

Suggested Readings

Benson, H. 1996. *Timeless Healing: The Power and Biology of Belief*. New York: Simon & Schuster.

Cohen, R. M. 2008. *Strong at the Broken Places: Voices of Illness, A Chorus of Hope*. New York: HarperCollins.

Oliver, M. 2006. *Thirst: Poems by Mary Oliver*. Boston: Beacon Press.

Sulmasy, D. P. 2007. *A Balm for Gilead: Meditations on Spirituality and the Healing Arts*. Washington, DC: Georgetown University Press.

4

Life as a Shimmering Shadow

Life, Loss, and Death Thereafter

Neil J. McGettigan

The music of Camille Saint-Saëns in the *Carnival of the Animals* is meant to capture in its melodies the nature and character of the various animals it depicts. So the beautiful theme for the swan is a slow and lyrical interpretation of its serene movement, as it glides without effort over the water. The musical theme, in a ballet interpretation, is known as "The Dying Swan," and the music lends itself to the graceful movement of a prima ballerina, who seems to glide in air toward a final fluttering end in peaceful death. The interpretation is true to the nature of a swan in its gentleness and its tranquility of movement, and it is also a breathtaking expression of human beauty and artistry in performance. While we are awed with the beauty, we are at the same time swept up into a pool of inner emotional response to the thought of death itself, the same death, whether for the swan or for the ballerina we see on stage.

Sad though it is to contemplate the reality of death, we are still caught up and enraptured by the haunting experience of that interpretation of the music. Throughout great artistic endeavors, there are many depictions of death, experienced in different ways, often tragic, at times dreadful, heroic, violent, or even peaceful. But, so far as we know, it is true to human nature alone to be aware of death. It is that same awareness of death that makes it possible for us to wonder about its meaning and ask ourselves what death leads us into. Is the awareness and the wondering about death a curse of human nature or perhaps its great blessing?

Why some people live and die in one way and other people live and die in a different way is probably beyond explanation. In the title of her book *Necessary Losses*, Judith Viorst states bluntly that human life is not negotiable without loss. Her confident assertion derives from statements, as she says, not only "from Freud and a wide range of other psychoanalytic thinkers but on many of the poets and philosophers and novelists who have concerned themselves—directly or indirectly—with aspects of loss."[1]

From that point of view, we learn that the manner of dealing with the realities of loss to a great extent determines the manner in which the individual person chooses to live and to die. Within the psychoanalytic tradition, it is firmly established that the pain of loss, in varying degrees of intensity, reenacts the pain of what Viorst refers to as the "Original Loss" and describes as "the loss of that ultimate mother-child connection."[2] Reliance on her personal experience and on stories of loss shared with her by people, famous and ordinary, emphasizes that all our losses are "indeed pervasive," and though experienced differently by every person, there are certain losses that all of us must face and none can avoid.

If, as Viorst notes, "psychoanalytic thinkers" agree that birth is the first human experience of necessary loss, it is commonsense thinking that death is the last human experience of necessary loss. Linking the two as the beginning of loss and the end of loss does not trivialize all the losses in between, but more importantly, it leaves unanswered the greater question. What is the loss that in our *human being* needs to be regained or satisfied and seems never to be satisfied in life? Within a psychoanalytic context, the loss of "oneness with mother" is a plausible answer, so far as the phenomenon of birth needs an answer. However, it does nothing for the unexplainable and unredeemable loss for us in human death.

A psychoanalytic context tells us that death is the "ultimate loss," and it is the same for every other living creature. It gives us no help with the more perplexing loss, that is, the loss of being who we really are when, as human beings, *we know that we are*. In a religious context, that reality of human existence is recognized as an immortal soul. Existence as an individual human being requires a biologically necessary loss of "oneness" in birth in order to be an individual "some-one" able to desire oneness—the oneness with mother that was a necessary loss in order for anyone to be born both biologically and psychologically. The reality seems to be that a necessary loss in human existence is ultimately unexplainable and a veritable paradox.

Moreover, what is a paradox of loss in the phenomenon of human birth takes on an additional paradoxical perplexity concerning the reality of loss in the phenomenon of human death. Neither phenomenon explains loss. The paradox yields itself to the form of a riddle, and in so doing initiates a need for an intuitive understanding of loss that is in excess of ordinary reasoning. A paradox puzzles human reasoning and leaves it puzzled; a riddle gives up on human reasoning in favor of human intuition in order to satisfy our need for understanding. The psychoanalytic context of Viorst, however, tries to create a rational solution to the paradox of human life and death but ignores this perplexity in its context of human reasoning. Instead, it offers an artificial intellectual framework for both life and death simply as loss, but necessary loss in both beginning and end.

To what consequence does that lead? Toward the end of her long exploration of the many necessary losses that living life entails, Viorst expresses a desire for someone to teach her what she calls in her penultimate chapter, "The ABC of Dying." It is the place where she brings to completion the saga of the life journey that begins, as she says, with initial separation in birth and ends in what she designates as the "ultimate separation" of death.[3] Where to turn to learn that lesson is surely the most important decision that a person will make in life. As her presentation of thoughts and comments indicated from the outset, Viorst turned to and learned largely from the psychoanalytic tradition. And in her summary, the upshot of all the learning from that tradition seems to be this: life begins in separation and ends in separation.

As we all do, Viorst includes also what she learned from experiencing both loss and gain in her own life and what she has learned from poets and philosophers and from the lives of those she loved and admired. And in the most succinct statement of what she learned, she says, "losing is the price we pay for living." It may appear, as to many thinkers it does appear, that nothing more can be said. Viorst adds, nevertheless, a consoling reminder that all our losses and gains "are inextricably mixed" and "there is plenty we have to give up in order to grow."[4] In other words, as I interpret her meaning, loss in life can be explained and compensated for by gain, because the losses in life enable psychic or spiritual growth.

The inner growth of psychic life, however, to which Viorst alludes in this reference to growth, is logically subject to the same degree of loss and separation that is inevitable in organic life and is, in consequence, a scant consolation, unless we can find sufficient reason or explanation for the necessity of loss in the inner growth of psychic life. It leaves the mind to question: why is there necessity for psychic growth and toward what destiny do we live and grow? That is why, so Freud concluded, many delude themselves with the "universal neurosis" of religion.[5] It needs to be said, too, that it is also why so many are consoled by religion and why they live differently and die differently because of religion. It appears to me, then, that the nature of growth in life remains a matter of importance not to be so easily dismissed, and whether or not it has purpose and endures through to immortality is a matter of even far more importance and less easily dismissed.

Nor does Viorst dismiss either task. What Freud dismissed as the illusory religious image of immortality can be replaced, so she reports, but not in the neurotically religious manner that Freud belittled. It can be replaced by other contexts "in which we can summon up for ourselves images of after-death continuity," other contexts that can provide "other ways of imaging immortalizing connections and continuities."[6] Consolation from the pain of loss in life may be found in a smorgasbord of choices that she offers as alleged pathways to immortality: religion, living on through nature, leaving behind words and actions that impact the future, progeny, and finally perhaps, a transcendent experience. My review of the list of "contexts" suggested sees none of the contexts, except for religion, as either an "immortalizing connection" or any kind of worthwhile consolation after death. All such things are ethereal; they will become loss.

For what purpose we grow and for what destiny we live remain unanswered to my satisfaction simply by reference to *psychic growth*. That answers the *fact* of life with the *how* of life. It answers no purpose for life and requires a search for an answer in another place. Under the constraints of the impeccable logic for which Freud is noted, the psychoanalytic tradition is compelled either to leave unanswered the question of "why life and loss are what they are" or to confront the human dilemma of "why even bother to continue to grow in life through the pain of loss." What is left to gain in *psychic growth*, when in death there is nothing more to lose? Each one of the five "consolations" of loss cited by Viorst in her list of "immortalizing connections and continuities," except for religion, does to my mind still retain the character of a loss, and as such offers no perceptible gain. With its traditional and blatant promise of immortality, however, religion at its core characterizes immortality as gain and, indeed, not the ultimate loss but the ultimate gain.

The dead-end view of our journey of life from a series of separations to a final separation of which there are no more receives a thorough investigation in an erudite study by Sandra M. Gilbert. The preface to the book, which she entitles *Death's Door*, explains the etiology of her work. It originated as a desire to show that "the fate of the elegy as a genre has been significantly affected by the cultural forces that have constructed what Wallace Stevens called 'the mythology of modern death.'" She continues to say "and in doing this, I expected to explore the revisionary laments with which poets have for more that half a century responded to both 'modern death' and modern modes of mourning."[7]

What Gilbert expected to be a study in her familiar area of poetics "broadened into an examination as much of contexts as of texts." Her own final text became a critique that she said was "in some sense experimental" and began to entail "the techniques of different genres (autobiographical narrative, cultural studies, literary history)," because she felt a need to include something more than the products of poetic imagination. In her words, Gilbert explained the additions as "an effort to ground my investigation of the poetics of grief in the complexity and richness of what, for want of a better word, I'll name the 'real.'" That effort to get to the "real" meant, so she says, "not only analyzing the lamentations that mourners utter when they find themselves stranded at death's door but also exploring the rapidly changing beliefs and customs that shape such lamentations as well as my own experience of such beliefs and customs."[8] Let us poetically call it like hearing the lion's roar at death's door.

The subtitle of the book, *Modern Dying and the Ways We Grieve*, underscores the inseparability of death and grief, those collateral components of loss. It also implies a cause-and-effect relationship of loss with respect to death and the grieving aftermath. Instead of being only the professional work of scholarship she had anticipated, Gilbert discovered that the book became personally elegiac and autobiographical in its own right, because of the reflections on grieving she felt compelled to include. She explained the compulsion as a need to mourn the loss of her husband, an unexpected and apparently unnecessary loss through medical malpractice.

> I think I felt driven to *claim* my grief and—almost defiantly—to *name* its particulars because I found myself confronting the shock of bereavement at a historical moment when death was in some sense unspeakable and

> grief—or anyway the expression of grief—was at best an embarrassment, at worst a social solecism or scandal.[9]

In addition to the loss of her husband in death, Gilbert felt deprived of the necessary grieving that is a natural component of her loss. The "historical moment" that has no rational explanation for loss cannot tolerate the reminder that loss is real and unavoidable.

Of special significance and pertinence to my point is the fact that the research of Gilbert becomes a résumé of responses made by modern poets and artists to the harsh realities of death and grieving without ostensible religious reference or interpretation. Throughout the study, she intersperses a mix of historical, philosophical, literary, and artistic forays into the mystery of death and offers her own reflections on the experience of loss. In consequence, her memoir becomes somewhat of a prose elegy following the unexpected death of her husband. At times, it contains hints of a personal protest against "the specific procedures for grieving that seem to be distinctively 'modern,' and sometimes even unique to the millennial moment we inhabit." In the list of cultural changes that contextualize this modern way of grieving, Gilbert cites first "the crises bred by the disintegration of redemptive religious faith."[10]

The title Gilbert chose, *Death's Door*, makes a forthright statement of the inevitability and futility of death. It implies a bland and matter-of-fact conclusion that life is simply a journey through a door to nothingness. This impression is reinforced by the author's selection of a painting by the French artist, Georges Rohner, used for the cover page. His painting depicts a bare room with an open door that leads toward another open door and presumably into a series of others, the end of which is a blank wall or unrecognizable something or more implicitly, nothing. Of course, the cover art is open to different interpretation. But in her final chapter, Gilbert offers her explication of another painting called "La Victoire" by the French artist, René Magritte. She selected it to be the frontispiece to the book, and the ambiguity that the painting represents is a more subtle repudiation of any certainty of life after death.

The final pages of the book, moreover, are devoted to her analysis of an architectural proposal submitted to be an appropriate memorial for "ground zero" after the 9/11 tragedy in New York City. The meaning she derives from the memorial is bleak and in keeping with the poetic expressions that abound in the book. In her interpretation, the memorial is a concrete expression of loss, and a loss that is ever without closure.

> But obviously, no matter how we struggle to achieve "closure," death's door didn't, can't and won't close. Indeed, the truism that death's door is always open has been the argument of this book. Although the Church once closed or at least glamorized that portal, it's now almost always at least ajar.[11]

Gilbert correctly infers the meaning of the proposed structure as a statement of loss. Designed to fill the empty space where the twin towers once stood, the memorial will be a constant reminder of their absence. The architects describe their intention that it will be "a space that resonates with the feelings of loss and absence." Within the ambience of a "field of trees," there will appear "two large voids containing recessed pools." A cascade of water continuously feeds the pools, but gazing into them reveals nothing but "large voids, open and visible reminders of the absence."[12]

Much more explicitly than the paintings or the memorial do, Gilbert makes these same points within the book through her study of poets, both lyric and elegiac, whose sentiments concur with this fatalism. In the long run, her research amounts to an announcement of the discrediting and demise of religious belief, what contemporary poetry in its treatment of elegiac responses to loss considers to be useless and unreliable religious belief. No longer credible, the consolations of religion offer no release from the pain and suffering that accompany loss in life.

However difficult it may be to accept loss, adjustments to it can become a step forward in life and possibly an opportunity. Very likely, professional dancers experience the poignancy of loss more painfully and prematurely than any other group of artists. When that loss comes to them, when denial and self-deception are no longer able to overcome the testimony of pain and self-appraisal, the honest admission of its arrival may seem to be equivalent to the ending of life itself. In a way, it is an end to life, to the only life the dancer has ever known and loved. The average "death" to that life for the dancer happens at thirty-four years of age and even sooner if injury occurs, and it often does.

For most of us, aversion to any thought of death may remain even into the final years of life. It cannot be totally removed from awareness, however, except by some form of mental or psychological disorder. It can be resisted and relegated to the deepest recesses of the unconscious, until something happens that places it into the forefront of concern. It comes in its favorite masquerade as loss—loss of things that are precious, such as youth, beauty, strength, health, independence, love, family, friends, and all those things we expected to have forever. Loss appears in a subtle disguise that only hints at the reality of its fullness and sometimes in a "fell swoop" that is remarkably dire. Loss can be mildly disruptive and it can be totally incapacitating.

Physical losses are routine in life as aging progresses. But physical loss, whether routine or by accident, can become in special circumstances intense almost to the point of death. In a report on the traumatic effect of termination of dancers' careers, *The New York Times* (October 21, 2007) introduced its subject as a "Dance Transition." In the life of a dancer, the inevitable moment of transition is when the dancer must accept a dreaded loss, the moment when the dance is over and the curtain is falling for the last career performance on stage.

Beyond the ordinary, dancers possess exceptional physical stamina, suppleness, and grace, even at the point when they must acknowledge they are no longer capable of sustaining the ardors of dance routine and performance. No matter when it comes, at that dreaded moment that seemed so far off in the enthusiasm of youthful beginnings, they may still excel in physical fitness, but it is not enough to satisfy the profession or to satisfy themselves. So it is that, for professional dancers, the time of transition is painful. It is excruciating loss.

So a New York journalist, Abby Aguirre, relates in the echt language of dancers who tell her what it means for them to come to terms with the end of a career in dance. Her article describes emotional responses of dancers, who have appropriated words of grief to describe the experience of ending their careers in dance. "Love, death, loss, devastation: these are the terms dancers tend to apply to 'transition,' dancer-speak for retirement since Career Transition for Dancers, a nonprofit service organization, was established in 1985."[13] The author says that for dancers it is such an intimate and personal crisis that they are reluctant to share it with those who will not understand.

> Ask a dancer to describe the feelings stirred by the idea of leaving the stage, and you might be forgiven for wondering if you have posed a far more personal question.
>
> "You're losing your first love."
>
> "It's a death."
>
> "The loss is pretty devastating"[14]

The gentle word *transition* does not convey the impact of retirement for dancers, and it happens to them without any academic study or experience in any other endeavors behind them. In fact, to help dancers with the practical consequences of transition was the motivation for which Career Transition for Dancers came into existence. A desire to help dancers in their need to "go through a period of mourning" and to prepare them for the future inspired Edward Weston, the founder of Career Transition, to set up its headquarters in Midtown, New York City. Shortly thereafter, the New York City Ballet and the Alvin Ailey School partnered with

Fordham University to provide opportunities for dancers to earn college degrees and to give them hope for the future.

Hope for the future does not come easily for the dancers. They continue to struggle with the loss, because the loss is not complete. Dancers report that they are still dancers in mind and spirit. In their minds, the dance endures, and breaking away is intense and may be not entirely possible. In group sessions with therapists and mentors, dancers try to come to terms with the reality of transition and what it means for them in the future. One dancer described how her spirit still draws her to the flow of graceful movement even after a severe hip injury took her off stage.

> "I go down to these playground rings at Riverside Park," she said.
>
> "There are 10 rings in a row. I start from one end, grab the first ring and swing to the next, and then to the next. I get going fast, and when I'm going fast, I turn midair and grab the next ring from the other direction, so I can go back and forth. I get this force going and do these turns, one ring to the next. People say, 'you look like you're dancing.'"[15]

We can agree that she is dancing, dancing once again as best she can. Some dancers are able to reiterate her sentiments in words that are appropriate to their own experience, as did Daryl Fowkes. After sixteen years of a career in dance and four years of "transition," Fowkes is acutely aware of how the dance is still a part of him. "The thing is, after four years my brain is still that of a working dancer. I still eat and sleep like a dancer…in my head I'm still a dancer."[16]

For others apparently, words are not adequate or the feelings of loss are so intense and complicated that words cannot be found to express them. That was the case for a former Rockette, while a seminar leader was trying to help the group of dancers "to think positively" about all the valuable assets of reliability, discipline, and perseverance they had acquired through their long years of training and dancing. Because the hurt of loss is impervious to healing by explanation, the "dancer" within overpowered her thoughts and compelled her to interrupt, announcing that she was "having a terrible time."

> "People don't understand that being a Rockette entailed more than kicking my legs. I was a Rockette my whole life and then—." She broke off. "I feel like an outcast, like all the energy has been drained out of me, like I'll never find anything else that—." After another painful thought she could not complete, she said simply, "It's very, very hard."[17]

Is it possible for the dancer to explain the loss or for us to understand it? It is no more possible to understand what the loss of dance means to the dancer than it is to heal the loss by explanation.

Granted that we have no complete understanding of why loss is necessary in the first place and only limited consolation in understanding that it is just an inevitable part of ordinary living. But for many people, religious conviction is a source of inner strength and comfort when they face that inevitability. For instance, many can and do understand that the object of our love in human relationship is not something to be possessed forever, and they accept that loss, because they also understand human love to be somehow an explanation analogous to the mystery of God as love. Recourse to rational explanation about human love as a phenomenon does little to resolve our perplexity in the experience of loss except to clarify the logical truth that without love there is no reason to experience loss and likely no actual experience of it.

Despite strong religious conviction about "a loving God" and perhaps even more so because of the conviction, the standard question that arises is: why must we endure loss at all, why must it be so? The most that can be said without contradiction is that religious conviction about love and its loss matters and makes a difference. It matters more when it is shared and given meaning in ritual. Usually this is true when family and friends who share the loss are able to lend support by sharing their basic convictions about loss and death and participating in common rituals that give meaning to those convictions, such as sitting shiva or gathering for a wake or funeral service. How can we decide whether the ritual makes the meaning or the meaning makes the ritual?

From her research into all aspects of the grieving process as it has developed and changed over time, Terese A. Rando concluded that familial and social features of contemporary life have made the experience of loss more complicated and difficult. Among the changes, she notes the diminishing importance of religious values and rituals during the experience of loss and considers the change in the modern way of life to be a serious deprivation of consolations that in the past made the process of loss less painful and provided healing for the suffering that accompanies it.[18] The title of her book, *How to Go on Living When Someone You Love Dies*, makes a concise statement of the need to address the consequences brought about by suppression of traditional rituals of grief and bereavement. It is one of many such books and manuals written to address that need for readers who have not themselves abandoned religious belief and understanding and are able to find comfort and relief in it.

Religious faith does make a difference and offers what skeptics call simply an anodyne to the pain of sadness and despair in the face of loss. Other authors have not been so much interested in artistic statements about the enigma of death as they are in the grief that accompanies loss and the healing that grieving can provide. They face the reality in the everyday experience of loss and grieving. Carol Pregent tells just one story in her book about loss, her own very unusual story. It is a story of loss, a loss that, when we hear of it, we want to say, it should not be. A parent, who gives birth and raises a little girl until the child becomes strong and beautiful, just stepping through the threshold of love as a young woman, should not be also the mother who must care for and comfort her child as her child approaches death. It should not be. Carol Pregent did care for and comfort her daughter, but she also learned from her daughter all during the sickness and up until her death.

Her daughter Lisa knew about loss from the point of view of someone who had just seventeen years to learn how to accept it. A virulent form of cancer taught her that her life would be short. Lisa learned abruptly that things change and will never be the same, just when she had begun to find joy in them and call them her own—her keepsakes, her friends, her family, and even the beauty she began to see in herself and the boyfriend who loved her for it. At seventeen, she knew how to give up one by one the things she had just learned how to love, things precious to her and given to her to have for too short a time. To give up a dream of leaving home for college, to realize a gradual loss of ability to travel with friends to new places and adventures and, eventually, to be never again with them to share those memories are the losses that afflict people with the ordinary passing of time, but they came to this unusual young girl at an "out of the ordinary" time.

Still a teenager, Lisa had to accept the loss of those things with special meanings that teenage girls cherish and her teenage friends very likely continued to keep close by, as she did for herself as long as she could. But the passing of time for her was rapid and the special meanings of those things slipped too quickly away. Lisa, it seems, wanted to spare her mother the anguish of worry about her keepsakes. It may be, as well, that she wanted simply to tell her mother that her child had grown up enough to understand and to accept that loss is part of life. As Pregent tells the story of one of the last heartbreaking things she had to do for her daughter, she reveals not just the sadness she feels in her heart for Lisa but her astonishment at the maturity of her child.

> She had a small collection of meaningful things on a stand beside her bed. Included in this carefully selected memorabilia was a picture of her boyfriend, the letter he

> had written to her, and a picture of a tear he had drawn. This latter was a skillfully drawn, many faceted gem-like presentation of a teardrop; and in it he had written, "There is much more to a tear than meets the eye" (more wisdom from youth). This day Lisa said to me, "Mom, take all this stuff and put it in the bottom drawer of my desk." "Oh Lisa," I replied, "are you *sure*?" She nodded her head. "He's not coming back"—more letting go in her life, pain added to pain. He had not visited her once since she had been bedridden; no word of why. I assume he was afraid. We all were. But he was young, and he hadn't bargained for such a heavy burden when he asked a pretty girl out so many months ago. I collected her belongings and put them away.[19]

During the last weeks of her daughter's life, Carol Pregent received a gift from her child. Lisa did not plan to give her mother a gift and did not know how much her mother would treasure it as a gift. Neither did she know that it would be a gift to everyone who might someday hear her story. She just wanted to tell her mother how she was feeling and to let her know that, with all she had to give up, she still had something that she was able to hold on to and something that would see her through all her unimaginable losses in the days ahead.

> "I've been thinking, mom," she said. "People have told me that faith is believing something till it happens—kind of like, believing it so hard that it makes what you want to come true happen." I listened intently, as she spoke half to me and half to herself. With a far away look in her eyes she continued, "I think that real faith is when nothing is going right, and you know it will not happen the way you want it, and then you believe anyway....Doesn't that sound like faith, mom?" "Yes, Lisa, that sounds like faith to me." Later Lisa's mother adds

> these unspoken words of remembrance to her child, "Yes, my baby girl, that is faith."[20]

For Pregent, the story of Lisa's death was not complete until she could add those words of assurance for her "baby girl" to hear. She wanted her beloved daughter, even after death, to hear her words of appreciation for the gift of wisdom Lisa had left her mother.

So close to death and so aware of its certainty, Lisa did not give up her faith. Sickness forced unbearable loss on Lisa, but it could not take away her faith. For this young teenager, the words she spoke expressed a full lifetime of faith, a faith that was her strength for acceptance of a reality of loss in death that so many of us with long years of living fear to think about but know must come. Her faith enabled Lisa to accept the death to come for her, no matter how unwelcome, but her grief was a different kind of burden, a relentlessly increasing burden of all her losses—her letting go, one thing after another, of all that was precious and dear to her.

That faith in a meaning and purpose to her life, even a life too full of loss for its brevity, was an assurance that Lisa did not lose even as she approached "the ultimate loss" of death. As Carol Pregent and her husband lay on either side of the frail body between them on the night that Lisa died, their teenage daughter used the breath she struggled to take in to speak to her father in a feeble voice. In her weakness and because she was "restless and disturbed," her struggle seemed to come from a desire "to communicate something which she no longer had the capacity to do." But as Lisa was dying, she still wanted to speak to her father, but only the first word "Dad" escaped her lips.

> Dad was the last word Lisa said. She said it quite a few times—maybe five, maybe seven—I'm not sure. It was such a struggle for her to speak each time; but she seemed to be overcome with the need to say something. Something that will forever remain unspoken.[21]

In her recollection of what was taking place, Pregent tells us that, although her daughter no longer tried to speak, "she continued to struggle with something" and that she also "remained restless and sighed deeply."

Then, to relieve her child of the anxiety of trying to hold on to life, her mother whispered to her, "It's all right, Lisa. Just let go, it will be all right." Continuing her effort to comfort her child, she encouraged Lisa with the promise that after death "it will be so beautiful when you get there...it will be so wonderful, so wonderful we can't even imagine"; and, heaving a great sigh, the child relaxed and ceased to struggle. Although Lisa could no longer speak, she could still hear the words her mother spoke: "Lisa,...do you believe that it's going to be wonderful when you get there?" Without words of her own to speak, Lisa was able at last to express her faith in the purpose and meaning of her short life. Lisa nodded her head twice in agreement with her mother.[22]

To any woman who reads the memoir of Carol Pregent and who has given birth to her own child, it will be easy enough to feel all the losses in the story—not just those for Lisa, the "little losses" of things and the "necessary losses" of sickness and death but also all those for Pregent with the loss of her child. Death to the child is also death to the mother. It is the story of many losses interwoven into one. It may be clear to some as well that the faith of the mother became interwoven into the faith of the child.

In fact, living through a prolonged period of anticipatory loss as it moves toward the outcome can have an impact on faith and on the entire process of grieving in the aftermath of loss. C. S. Lewis gives a heartfelt but troubled account of its unique torment. The title of his memoir, *A Grief Observed*, invites interpretation. Was anticipation of the loss of his wife to cancer so unbearable a torment for Lewis that he found it easier to cope by objectifying his grief in the title? Or was it merely his way of guarding his privacy and obscuring his identity, as he intended by publishing under a pseudonym? In his memoir, he provided an undecipherable clue: "I must have some drug, and reading isn't a strong enough drug now." Lewis adds another admission that "by writing it all down (all?—no: one thought in a hundred)," he believed that he could "get a little outside it."[23]

Whatever mix of motivations prompted his memoir of loss, in the writing of it Lewis uncovered a confusion of feelings buried within him. It became in effect an opportunity for a deeper entering into a bond of love with his wife and a more wrenching experience of their separation. During the time of her approaching death and while he became aware of how anticipation of her worsening pain and suffering intruded into every remaining day of their life together, he also learned to cherish every moment of time with her.

Recollection of those precious memories and reawakened feelings deepened the torment of loss that Lewis endured but also strengthened his appreciation and desire for the love from which the torment came. Being caught up in the baffling and wondrous mystery of loving carries with it the cost of knowing that, according to whatever we believe about separation in death, love will be for us ultimately either eternal mystical bond or everlasting forlorn loss into nothingness. It is the same choice for all of us to make: eternal life and eternal love or no life and no love. "Better to have loved and lost than never to have loved at all," is in the long run little comfort, but it is all the wisdom outside of religious faith we have left to guide and inspire us.

Struggling as he did with this dilemma, Lewis vacillated between an utter despair of love forever lost and a rekindled hope of undying love. After the death of his wife and in the midst of confusion about his loss, the working through of that struggle in his personal diary or journal, which he eventually published, denoted a stronger than realized reliance on his faith in the assurance of love living on, even within the very grief of separation by death. Is it possible that to steep the human spirit more deeply into the experience of love exactly as it comes to us in our grieving brings with it a revelation of love's immunity to death? St. Paul shares his own revelation in "O death, where is your victory,

O death, where is your sting?"(1 Cor 15:55). That is not at all to deny the intensity of the sense of loss and its reality. But it may be instead to discover that an unflinching determination to face separation and loss for what it is and to face the grief, anger, despair, confusion, or whatever else accompanies loss and to discover that simply facing loss releases us from its bondage.

The outcome of any struggle to penetrate the mystery of human love and the puzzle of its loss in death will be, of course, as variable as the uniqueness of the persons who experience the love and the loss. Perhaps respecting the uniqueness of our private responses and leaving us to find whatever meaning will suit us, Lewis leaves the outcome of his own struggle open to speculation. In the uncertainty of his revelations, there is a possibility for us to find a meaning of love overcome by death and a possibility to find a meaning of love triumphing over death, or there is the possibility of something entirely different.

> When I lay these questions before God I get no answer. But a rather special sort of "No answer." It is not the locked door. It is more like a silent, certainly not uncompassionate, gaze. As though He shook His head not in refusal but waiving the question. Like, "Peace, Child; you don't understand."[24]

That is how Lewis reports the outcome of his struggle to find a meaning for the loss of his wife in death. He is left without understanding but not without meaning.

From that point, Lewis considers the traditional Christian theological teachings of "the fruition of God" and "reunion with the dead" and finds them to be "blank cheques."[25] Those theological certainties of an afterlife in which we are promised the possession of God and happiness with departed loved ones for an eternal afterlife are not immediately accessible to him and do nothing to relieve the pain of his separation. And yet something does give him relief and hope and renewed faith. Lewis says it was a vague experience that gradually gave him some confidence and did so without making any sense at all—not any sense that can be put into words. He informed us only that "one moment last night can be described in similes; otherwise it won't go into language at all." Even as a simile, the account of his experience is imprecise.

> Image a man in total darkness. He thinks he is in a cellar or dungeon. Then there comes a sound. He thinks it might be a sound from far-off waves or wind-blown trees or cattle half a mile away. Or it may be a much smaller sound close at hand—a chuckle of laughter.[26]

Whatever the experience happened to be, real or imaginary, it affected Lewis to the extent that his sense of connectedness with his wife was restored in a way that he felt difficulty expressing. The jottings in his journal become meanderings and are almost kaleidoscopic in nature, wavering between "two widely different convictions" pressing on his mind: that judgment in the afterlife will be "inexorable" and "even more painful" or that "all shall be well and all manner of thing shall be well."[27]

When his journal refers to the experience later, he calls it "that impression which I can't describe except by saying that it's like the sound of a chuckle in the darkness." The inexactness of the experience made it lack the credibility of evidence, but to Lewis that was of no importance.

> Even now, I won't treat anything of that sort as evidence. It's the quality of last night's experience—not what it proves but what it was—that makes it worth putting down. It was quite incredibly unemotional. Just the impression of her mind momentarily facing my own. Mind, not "soul" as we tend to think of soul. Certainly the reverse of what is called "soulful." Not at all like a rapturous reunion of lovers. Much more like getting a telephone call or a wire from her about some

> practical arrangement....Yet there was an extreme and cheerful intimacy. An intimacy that had not passed through the senses or the emotions at all.[28]

The experience of the intimacy was more important to Lewis than any need for evidence. Despite the absence of emotion in the contact, which he qualified as "whether real or apparent," in the experience of that sense of connection "the intimacy was complete" for him once again. Nevertheless, there remained an ambiguity concerning the resolution of his struggle with faith, and he felt uncertain about whether to think of the nature of God as intelligence or love. Knowing that "the best is perhaps what we understand least," he was at last able to set the problem aside as "probably another of the nonsense questions" that only death will answer.[29]

In addition to his extraordinary career as a renowned university professor and highly successful writer, Lewis became famous as a theologian and apologist for the Christian religion. In lectures and broadcast presentations, he tried to make the essential teachings of Christianity understandable and acceptable to ordinary people and to inspire them to believe. He knew the questions and knew the answers, until he discovered that some questions have no answers, and still he wanted them to have answers—answers able to be put into words to make them understandable and acceptable. He taught the answers of faith as if they were only answers to be learned. And he struggled to learn the answers of faith rather than to live them. In the experience of loss, eventually, he began to know the difference between the *knowing* and the *living*. For Lewis, and it may be the way of things for everyone, loss was a test of faith. This is the difference he discovered.

> The reason for the difference is only too plain. You never know how much you really believe anything until its truth or falsehood becomes a matter of life and death to you. It is easy to say you believe a rope to be

> strong and sound as long as you are merely using it to cord a box. But suppose you had to hang by that rope over a precipice. Wouldn't you then first discover how much you really trusted it?[30]

Long before Lewis gave up his demand for evidence in order to accept his belief that an eternity of reunion with his wife will really happen, the message in the Letter to the Hebrews disabused them of expecting anything more than faith as proof. This assurance that "faith is the assurance of things hoped for, the conviction of things not seen" (Heb 11:1) nullified for us as well any expectation of an intellectual breakthrough or "brainiac" discovery of a solution to the mystery of loss and death.

The answers about faith and loss that Lewis was searching for were in another place within him and not to be found just in his thinking. But he resisted and to no avail turned his efforts instead to torturous bouts of thinking. "Feelings, and feelings, and feelings. Let me try thinking instead," he said. The "horribly high" stakes of losing his wife were able to shake Lewis, during this time of grief, out of what he called his "merely verbal thinking" and his "merely notional beliefs," because he had to be "knocked silly" in order to make them real and to make sense of it all. From the pain of loss, he revived his faith. As a man who endured the torment of loss and his intellectual confusion, Lewis was able to say: "Only torture will bring out the truth. Only under torture does he discover it himself."[31] Perhaps, only in loss does loss explain itself.

There is no loss without a someone to know the loss, to feel it, to suffer it. The effort to explain loss through the phenomenon of "the psychological birth of the human child,"[32] to use the famous phrase of Margaret S. Mahler, is necessarily tautological. That is to say that, in so doing, we say loss generates loss, and it is no real explanation. An oft-quoted statement of St. Augustine is closer to the truth and to logical conclusion and sees loss as the reality of our creation in the mystery of God's being: "You have made us for yourself, O Lord, and our hearts are restless, until they rest in Thee" (*Confessions*, I, I, p. 21).

And so, our experience of loss leads us to desire God and to seek release from loss and the only solace from death in possession of God in eternity. In a Christian context, and of course one radically contradictory to an exclusively psychological perspective, death is overcome by life. Indeed, St. Paul is bold enough to announce the triumph, "Where is your victory, O Death? Where is your sting?" (1 Cor 15:55). Another step is required to give adequate explanation. Beyond the boundaries of the science of psychology (if you distinguish between them), it calls for explanation of philosophical or theological concepts. This is what Lewis clings to and hints at, as he remembers his final moment with his beloved.

Painful thoughts of loss and separation drove Lewis to put his experience of them into the words of his journal. His final thoughts tell of the dying words of his wife. They were her words of faith. "I am at peace with God," she said and spoke them not to her husband but to the chaplain. Wrapped in a smile, she left for her husband only one thing as a token of her love, something for him to ponder. "She said not to me but to the chaplain, 'I am at peace with God.' She smiled, but not at me. *Poi si torno all' eternal fontana.*"[33] Where his thoughts then led him, Lewis does not say. He preferred that we should be left instead to our own thoughts. He tells us she turned and smiled into the unknown. The quote from Dante Alighieri that he employs to express his feelings invites us also to wonder what took place at that moment. The words say, "perhaps she turned toward the eternal fountain." Her gaze into the unknown made her smile, and we are left to ask: Did she smile into an unknown of love lost forever? Did she smile into an unknown of love eternal?

Notes

1. Judith Viorst, *Necessary Losses* (New York: Simon & Schuster, 1986), 17.
2. Ibid., 34.
3. Ibid., 304.
4. Ibid., 325, 327.
5. Sigmund Freud, *The Future of an Illusion* (New York: Liveright, 1955), 76.
6. Viorst, *Necessary Losses*, 321.
7. Sandra M. Gilbert, *Death's Door: Modern Dying and the Ways We Grieve* (New York: W. W. Norton, 2006), xviii.
8. Ibid., xxii.
9. Ibid., xix.
10. Ibid., xxii–xxiii.
11. Ibid., 462.
12. Ibid., 462–63.
13. Abby Aguirre, "Tentative Steps into a Life after Dance," *New York Times*, October 21, 2007, Arts and Leisure, 24.
14. Ibid.
15. Ibid.
16. Ibid.
17. Ibid.
18. Terese A. Rando, *How to Go on Living When Someone You Love Dies* (New York: Bantam Books, 1988), 5.
19. Carol Pregent, *When a Child Dies* (Notre Dame, IN: Ave Maria Press, 1992), 71–72.
20. Ibid., 72.
21. Ibid., 15.
22. Ibid., 16.
23. C. S. Lewis, *A Grief Observed* (San Francisco: Harper, 1989), 10.
24. Ibid., 69.
25. Ibid., 70.
26. Ibid., 64.
27. Ibid., 65.
28. Ibid., 73.
29. Ibid., 74–76.
30. Ibid., 22–23.
31. Ibid., 36–38.

32. Margaret S. Mahler, *The Psychological Birth of the Human Infant: Symbiosis and Individuation* (New York: Basic Books, 1975).

33. Lewis, *Grief Observed*, 76.

References

Aguirre, A. "Tentative Steps into a Life after Dance." *New York Times*, October 21, 2007, Arts and Leisure, 24.

Augustine. *Confessions*. Translated by R. S. Pine-Coffin. New York: Dorset Press, 1986.

Freud, S. *The Future of an Illusion*. New York: Liveright, 1955.

Gilbert, S. M. *Death's Door: Modern Dying and the Ways We Grieve*. New York: W. W. Norton, 2006.

Lewis, C. S. *A Grief Observed*. San Francisco: Harper, 1989.

Pregent, C. *When a Child Dies*. Notre Dame, IN: Ave Maria Press, 1992.

Rando, T. A. *How to Go on Living When Someone You Love Dies*. New York: Bantam Books, 1988.

Viorst, J. *Necessary Losses*. New York: Simon & Schuster, 1986.

5

Illness and the Quest for an Adult Faith

John J. Shea

The adolescing self "tends to image God in a still-growing way."

Introduction

In this presentation for caregivers I want to talk about illness and the ways it can relate to adult development and adult faith. The illness I want to talk about is serious illness, the kind of illness that makes us question what life is all about. Arthur Frank (1998) talks about this kind of illness. He calls it "deep illness." We will look at the different forms this deep illness takes and at ways of listening to the stories that the seriously ill tell. With deep illness as our focus, next we look at an article by Paul Andrews (1981) that provides a developmental perspective on serious illness and another way for caregivers to listen to what the seriously ill person may be experiencing. Then, after looking at how we image God, especially as we ourselves develop and mature, we hear the story of "Elizabeth," a woman whose imaging of God was profoundly challenged by serious illness. This presentation ends with a summing up of the relation between illness and faith.

Arthur Frank and "Deep Illness"

The understanding Frank has of serious illness is as illuminating as it is profoundly human. In his way of thinking, "illness is 'deep' when perceived as lasting, as affecting virtually all life choices and decisions, and as altering identity."[1]

Frank recounts his own experience of heart attack when he was thirty-nine years old. He went for a long jog, getting ready for a race, when suddenly his pulse sped up. He stopped running, went to lean on a car, and then passed out. Afterward, he tried to forget what had happened, but something would not let him do that. "My mind wanted to forget it. My body said no. Something was wrong; something had changed, seriously."[2] He saw his family doctor, who thought there was probably nothing to worry about, but ordered a cardiogram just to be sure.

> A week later he called to tell me it showed I had had a heart attack. He seemed uncertain of the medical details, but I hardly heard him; I was lost in a sudden and profound change. In the moments of that call I became a different person.[3]

Frank draws a helpful distinction between disease and illness. Talking about disease reduces the body to its physiology, to a breakdown that can be made objective in some way and that can be measured. As he puts it: "in disease talk my body, my ongoing experience of being alive, becomes the body, an object to be measured and thus objectified." Illness, for Frank, is something quite different. "Illness is the experience of living through disease. If disease talk measures the body, illness tells of the fear and frustration of being inside a body that is breaking down. Illness talk is a story about moving from a perfectly comfortable body to one that forces me to ask: What's happening to me? Not it, but me."[4]

So what is "deep illness"? "Deep illness may be critical or chronic, immediately life-threatening or long term."[5] It may have different levels of impairment and these may fluctuate, but the illness itself is "perceived as lasting" by the person.

> For as long as one is deeply ill, there is no end in sight. Deep illness is lived in the certainty that it will be permanent and the fear of this permanence. Some of the deeply ill have every assurance that they will be ill for the rest of their lives. Others have some chance of recovery, possibly a good chance, but illness is deep as long as any light they can see at the end of the tunnel is at best flickering.[6]

Usually when we are faced with "deep illness" we think, of course, of the possibilities of recovery. But, says Frank, "If recovery is taken as the ideal, how is it possible to find value in the experience of an illness that either lingers on as chronic or ends in death?" Frank believes that we need to pay attention less to recovery and more to renewal, and as he says: "Renewal is a shared process."[7] Too many ill persons are deprived of any real conversation or dialogue about their illness. On the one hand, the deeply ill person needs to be able to share his or her experience with a caregiver. On the other hand, there is no dialogue on the experience of the illness if there is no one—often the caregiver—who is empathic enough and able enough to listen to the story of the ill person and to enter into a mutual relationship with him or her.

For Frank, the caregiver is the listener to the story of the ill person, a vital role, if healing and renewal are to take place. But is there anything that can be said about the story that allows the caregiver to share in the deep illness of the storyteller? It is at this point that Frank makes another extremely helpful contribution. He proposes "three recognizable narrative structures" that many stories of serious illness have. There is "the restitution story," "the chaos story," and "the quest story," each with a unique structure for the teller and each story calling for unique responses from the listener.

The Restitution Story

The restitution story "tells of getting sick, suffering, being treated, and through treatment being restored to health." This is the story that most of us tell and most of us want to tell, because it is a success story. Disease is "an enemy and cure is a version of conquering that enemy." This is the kind of story that is "expected and encouraged" by the medical community and the kind of story that is often told with extreme relief by the ill person. The problem with the restitution story is when it can no longer be told. When the restitution story is not true, those still seriously ill are "isolated in their suffering" and "can achieve no critical distance from their pain."[8]

The Chaos Story

This kind of story is just the opposite of the restitution story and tells of "deepest illness." In the chaos story, "disability can only increase, pain will never remit, physicians are either unable to understand what is wrong or unable to treat it successfully." Typically, in this kind of story, trouble multiplies and events are compounded. The illness begets a seemingly endless downward spiral of work-related problems, family problems, social problems, insurance problems, financial problems, or housing problems that seem to have little solution. "To talk from the position of chaos is to be unable to render one's life story as a story with any narrative ordering." This kind of story is very hard to listen to. As Frank observes: "The chaos story that cannot become a story induces claustrophobia in the listener because of its lack of any distance from immediate events. Chaos talk is submerged, gasping for air, and it soon leaves the listener gasping."[9] But listening is all the more important here. Listening honors the suffering.

The Quest Story

In the quest story, illness is understood as "a condition from which something can be learned (though not in a didactic sense) and this learning can be passed on to others." As Frank sees it: "Quest stories are being told when the teller claims new qualities of self and believes illness has been responsible for these changes. Quest stories are about illness leading to new insights." There is not a sense of "gladness" that the illness happened, but there is a sense of "giving up the old self," accepting life "unconditionally," and finding a new and perhaps fuller sense of self. Quest stories "look not to restitution but rather to what can be reclaimed in life," and because they do, they can be hard to listen to. If the quest story involves "finding a grateful life in conditions that the previously healthy self would have considered unacceptable," this challenge of acceptance and deeper meaning may be there for the listener as well.[10]

With all three kinds of stories—the restitution story, the chaos story, and the quest story—Frank makes it a point of stressing the importance for the caregiver of "just listening." He stresses that "*people tell the stories they need to tell in order to work through the situation they are in.*" He also believes that "change cannot be hurried."[11] The point of entering into the conversation and listening to the story is not to fix it, but to honor it. Change cannot be directed by the caregiver, but it can be nurtured:

1. by holding the "sincere belief that the story you are hearing *needs no change*";
2. by helping the ill person "*hear exactly what story* she or he is telling";
3. by helping the ill person know that "they are living *a story that is theirs to tell.*"[12]

Paul Andrews and "Developmental Tasks of Terminally Ill Patients"

In a rather profound article, Paul Andrews (1981), writing as a hospital chaplain, uses the eight-stage developmental framework of Erik Erikson (1963, 1964, 1968, 1980) to understand how a person might respond to having a terminal illness. At whatever stage of development the person may be—for example, someone in his or her early twenties and perhaps negotiating Erikson's identity stage (stage 5)—the disease may make it necessary for the person to rework the previous four stages (trust, autonomy, initiative, and industry) already negotiated and then work "at an accelerated pace" on the three stages (intimacy, generativity, and integrity) still remaining.

As we get ready to look at how Andrews uses the stages of Erik Erikson (see figure 1, my synopsis of Erikson's stages), five things are helpful to keep in mind about them:

1. All the stages are based on what Erikson calls the "epigenetic principle," a "ground plan," in which each stage has "a time of special ascendancy," until all the stages are negotiated in order to form "a functioning whole."
2. Each stage, therefore, lays the foundation for the stage or stages to follow, meaning that each stage is dependent on the stage or stages that preceded it.
3. "Identity" is Erikson's central notion in the stages, so that all the stages, as successfully enough negotiated, represent development in identity.
4. There is a strength or virtue (see figure 1) to be developed at each stage, and this strength is what allows the person to continue developing.
5. In addition to the need for "identity," the stages are animated by an inherent human need to realize wholeness or "integrity."

Figure 1: Erik Erikson—Stages of Development

Age	Task	Some Characteristics
0–1	Trust vs. mistrust	A time of *taking in*; "the attitude to be learned at this stage is that you can trust the world in the form of your mother"; a mutuality is set up; outer good becomes inner certainty, outer evil becomes inner discord; trust of the mother begets trust in one's own body—that it is okay to have bodily needs. A favorable ratio of trust to mistrust begets the virtue of *hope*.
1–3	Autonomy vs. shame and doubt	A time of holding on and letting go; the toddler develops his or her autonomy ("I am me") by learning a sense of control, what to hold on to and what to let go of, in "cooperation" and "willfulness"; doubt comes from loss of control and shame from being exposed and feeling there is something wrong with who I am. The virtue to be developed is will power.
3–6	Initiative vs. guilt	A time to *make like, to play* in a purposeful way (child thinks of being "big"); initiative and sexuality develop here; the boy is "phallic intrusive" and the girl is in a "catching" mode; the *superego*, that is, "the great governor of initiative" is developed to control both fantasy and action with guilt. The virtue to be developed at this stage is a sense of *purpose*.
6–Puberty	Industry vs. inferiority	A time to *make things*, to go to school and learn the skills needed for the culture; industry is "being busy with something" and learning to "do a job," and with that it is acquiring the tools and the techniques of the culture in a world shared with others; the danger is developing a sense of inadequacy and inferiority. The virtue to be consolidated is *competence*.

Continued

Age	Task	Some Characteristics
Puberty–Adulthood	Identity vs. identity diffusion	A time to *be oneself* by developing a "reasonably coherent sense of self" that has "sameness" and "continuity" that make possible a personal, sexual, and social identity; adolescence reworks mistrust, shame, doubt, guilt, and inferiority in a quest for identity, and identity ushers in adulthood; with identity I am able, as Freud said, "to love and work"; adult *conscience* is developed here. The virtue to be developed here is the strength to relate to others in fidelity.
Young Adulthood	Intimacy vs. isolation	A time *to lose and find oneself in another's intimacy* is "the ability to fuse your identity with someone else's without fear that you are going to lose something yourself," and it is "the capacity to commit oneself to concrete affiliations and partnerships and to develop the ethical strength to abide by such commitments, even though they may call for significant sacrifices and compromises"; the danger is isolation, "to be absorbed in oneself." The virtue here is *love*.
Mature Adulthood	Generativity vs. stagnation	A time to *create* and *take care* of the next generation; in addition to having and raising children this includes "productivity" and "creativity" in other areas; the danger is stagnation, "turning the drive for generativity in on oneself, so that one begins to treat oneself as a child, building up one's whole life as if one were one's own child." The virtue here is *care*, "the enduring concern for what has been generated by love, necessity, or accident."
Old Age	Integrity vs. despair	A time *to be through having been*, a time of *acceptance of what was and had to be*; integrity has to do with owning one's life, with "adjusting to the triumphs and

old age disappointments involved with living," with being "happy and content with the fact that one is," with integrating ultimate concerns; the danger is despair because there is no time to start over. The virtue that allows us to pass on is *wisdom*, that is, "a detached concern with life itself in the face of death itself."

Let us look now at Andrews's (1981) appropriation of Erikson's stages from the perspective of someone who is twenty-three years old and has just been given a diagnosis of terminal cancer. Let us say that a young man—we can call him Tom—has been negotiating Erikson's stage 5, Identity vs. Identity Diffusion. What might be happening to him now that he has received this diagnosis and is in the hospital?

Trust vs. mistrust. It would not be surprising to find Tom renegotiating this stage of development. Fear is overwhelming and survival is at stake. The questions for Tom are: Whom can I trust? Can I trust the doctors? Can I trust my family and friends to be there for me? Can I trust what people are saying to me? Can I trust the diagnosis? Can I trust my own body? Can I trust God? For a time, at least, there may be "incessant speculation about whom and what to trust."[13]

Autonomy vs. shame and doubt. As Andrews notes: "The disease's process and hospitalization will present chances for the person to reexamine earlier decisions about autonomy and shame." Having the disease and being diagnosed as having cancer may be experienced as shameful. So the questions for Tom are: Can I be me in this process? Can I hold some autonomy, as I face what is happening to me? "Fevers, isolation, odors, bedpans, attention to intake and output, ostomy care, and being dependent on others can contribute to a feeling of embarrassment or shame." How do I deal with these feelings? Can I believe that "I am different and distinct and important" in these circumstances?[14]

Initiative vs. guilt. If initiative and sexuality develop together, they should be expected here. "This is a stage of identifying with staff members—especially those of the opposite sex. It is a time of cooperation and for many an initiation of friendship ventures toward the staff." There may be a lot of guilt over these initiatives, especially if rejection is experienced. At this time there may be anger at authority figures for what is happening; at this time there may be a lot of anger at God for allowing the illness to happen. "Often there is a theme of suffering as punishment for past evil deeds."[15] So the questions for Tom may be: Can I initiate a relationship with the nurses? Am I guilty for getting sick? Is God punishing me for what I have done?

Industry vs. inferiority. Industry is, of course, initially a school-age task, but it surfaces now in a new way, because there is a lot to learn about the illness, the diagnosis, the terminologies, the procedures, and the projected outcomes. Tom may need to ask such questions as: How did I get this illness? What can I learn about the diagnosis? Why this treatment? What is this procedure for? The virtue at this stage is *competence.* Tom may be trying to become competent in his disease, and he may need the doctors, the nurses, and other hospital staff to give him enough of the information that is important for him to learn.

Identity vs. identity diffusion. Identity issues were the issues that Tom was working with at the time the illness was first diagnosed. Who am I? Who am I for others? What do I want to do with my life? What are my values? With the terminal illness these question surface in a new way. "Am I a sick, well, or dying person?" So much is now changing. As Andrews says: "There is understandably great confusion and uncertainty of identity with the diagnosis, treatments, and transitions." Tom is asking again: Who am I? Who am I for others? Others, especially others who relate in mutuality, can be very helpful here. "Family and staff can help the person who struggles with the identity versus confusion task by taking a rehabilitative approach. They can provide support and at the same time encourage the person to examine, affirm, and perhaps reshape identity."[16]

Intimacy vs. isolation. "The person who is diagnosed as having terminal illness is faced with decisions about who will be allowed to share the inner recesses of the life." Although Tom, at age twenty-three, may have been just beginning to negotiate the issue of whom to share life with, he will need to do it now. He will have to ask: "Will anybody be allowed in? Will only certain thoughts or moods be shared and others locked away? Will being singled out for death become a sentence of punishment and solitary confinement?" And again, the empathic caretaker will be very important. "Only those who recognize intimacy as self-disclosure and acceptance can bear the helplessness of being around the often unchangeable process of dying."[17]

Generativity vs. stagnation. Although Tom has not reached the natural time of generativity, the time "of establishing and guiding the next generation," as he might have done as a parent or through a career, he will need to focus his energy on something beyond himself. The questions he needs to ask himself are: Is there something I need to do for others? What do I want to give myself to? Is there something important for me to give to the community? And again, caretakers are important. "Staff and significant others can reinforce positive decisions to refocus priorities and to live purposively whatever time is left."[18]

Integrity vs. despair. As we see in figure 1, "integrity has to do with owning one's life." This is what Tom is called to, even though that life may be far shorter than he ever imagined. The wholeness to which Tom is called will "temper the sadness of leaving." The questions Tom needs to ask at this final stage are: Can I own my life as my own? Is my life "what it was and what it had to be"? Can I accept my life as I lived it, and can I accept death? And is there an identity I have in God that transcends death? Again, the caretakers are very important. "The person who has chosen despair or bitterness can be encouraged to consider reconciliations or restitution. Forgiveness and acceptance—especially of self—are key components to choosing integrity."[19]

John Shea and Adult Faith

Given the description of deep illness and the possibilities for renewal offered by Arthur Frank, and given the developmental description of dealing with terminal illness developed by Paul Andrews, what can we say about the relationship between serious illness and faith in God? The question of how these two profoundly human experiences—illness and faith—interact with each other is often the most important question that the seriously ill ask themselves. In fact, it is often the most important question that caregivers and a host of other people come to ask themselves. How does serious illness challenge one's relationship with God? And if we ask this question, can we ask it from a perspective of renewal, human growth, and development? In other words, might the God one images in "the restitution story" be quite different from the God one experiences in "the quest story"? Might the God one encounters in reworking Erikson's *initiative vs. guilt* stage be quite different from the God one may experience in the *integrity vs. despair* stage? Does how we image God need to change and grow as we change and grow?

John Shea (2005) is interested in understanding the way we image God for three very important reasons. First, our imaging of God captures our *relationship* with God; religion, as we live it, is not about God, but rather about our *relationship with God*. Second, if religion is not about God but about the relationship we have with God—the self and God together—then religion can be understood as something that is developmental; "the self and God together" is a living relationship experienced as able to change and grow. Third, if living religion, "the self and God together," is developmental, then the way we image God is inherently developmental; we can talk about an imaging of God that is, perhaps, still coming to be mature or adult (adolescing faith), and we can talk about an imaging of God that is mature or adult (adult faith). In other words, if we, as individual persons, are meant to grow up and become adult, then our imaging of God is meant to grow up and become adult as well.

There are two basic developmental paradigms of how the self is able to relate to God. There is the paradigm of *adolescing faith*, in which a self that is still coming to adulthood tends, in a still-growing way, to image God and, therefore, tends to image a "Superego God," an imaging of God only partially developed. Then there is the paradigm of *adult faith*, in which a self that is "a reasonable coherent whole" is able at least to image God in a more complete way.[20]

Adolescing Faith

Let us look briefly at the paradigm of *adolescing faith* with its adolescing self relating in incomplete or fettered imaging to a Superego God. This is, of course, the beginning of faith for most of us.

Adolescing Self

The adolescing self is by definition a self on the way to adulthood. As such, it has two overall characteristics that are always found woven together. This self is a *still-forming self*, a self still growing, still coming together, still on the way to its own coherence. And this self is a *still-dependent self* because, as long as it is still forming, it remains dependent on significant others and the culture for how to be and relate to others.

Fettered Imaging

Until we become adult, all of our imaging of reality is fettered, incomplete, less than whole in some way. An adolescing self, that is, a self that is still forming and still dependent, has a still-forming and a still-dependent way of imaging reality. Fettered imaging is simply adolescing imaging, the imaging that comes directly from the still-forming and still-dependent adolescing self.

Three interwoven strands at the core of fettered imaging directly affect our imaging of God. They are *fantasy*, *relating in transference*, and *the logic of objective knowing. Fantasy* makes reality into whatever the adolescing self decides that it should be. It protects the adolescing self as it faces the wonders and fears of an unfolding world. Fantasy "fills in" what is missing, so that experience can make sense. Coming from the wishes, fears, and innocence of the adolescing self, fantasy tends to substitute, says Paul Pruyser "tolerable fictions for intolerable reality."[21]

Relating in transference—which is akin to fantasy—is a still-forming and still-dependent way of relating to others. The adolescing self experiences the other person as an object for satisfying his or her own forming and dependency needs. Growing up relationally, says Karin Stephen (2000), is a process of "overcoming transference." Mario Jacobi observes:

> It is a fact that in a relationship which we term transference, the Thou as another whole subject hardly does exist as such. The other person is an object for my own needs, desires, fantasies and fears. The other does not have reality as a whole subject but is somehow the carrier of the projection of my own psychic reality. The other person is experienced as a part of myself and is not a Thou in his or her own right.[22]

When we relate to God in transference, we know and depend on a God created, at least to some extent, by our own projection and maintained for our own ends.

The logic of objective knowing, although much more than an adolescing phenomenon, becomes important as the self comes to understand the need for unbiased observation, objectivity, and a scientific approach to reality. This logic says two things:

1. *What is real is empirical*, that is, what can be known lies in a concretely observable world of sight and sound and sense, so that knowledge can be demonstrated and verified;

2. *What is real is objective.* What can be known is "out there in the real world," separate from the knower and the same for all to observe.

Applying the logic of objective knowing to God, an adolescing self might say, for example, "God is not just a figment of my imagination. God is not just some subjective feeling. God is real. God exists. God is out there, an objective part of the real world." As the self continues to grow, it may find itself needing to relate to reality in ways that are more personally meaningful but, until that time comes, this logic of objective knowing easily fetters the reality of God. In fact, all three strands of fettered imaging, until they are engaged, struggled with, and eventually left behind, leave us imaging a Superego God.

SUPEREGO GOD

The God an adolescing self with its fettered imaging relates to is a Superego God. This God is—and really could only be—a God not yet fully formed, a God still incomplete, a God not yet whole. This God comes to us in any number of different forms, yet it has some rather definite characteristics that can be accurately described.

1. *The Superego God is a Supreme Being.* This God is, as Thomas Merton describes it, "a God who is simply 'a being' among other beings, part of a series of beings, an 'object' which can be discovered and demonstrated."[23] Although an immensely powerful object that is "over against" us, the Supreme Being is part of an ordered system that is ultimately logical, objective, and contained. And although an unchangeable reality utterly different from us, this powerful Supreme Being is often quite human and parental—able to protect us from harm and evil.
2. *The Superego God is a God of Law.* In what is possibly its most prominent characteristic, this God is perceived to

be an absolute authority, commanding what must and must not be done. If the Superego God is divine law, then the adolescing self relates to this God through obedience to the law. While often patient and acting with considerable restraint, the God of Law is often found to be a God of Guilt, evoking terrifying fear and capable of unleashing tremendous judgment and powerful condemnation.

3. *The Superego God is a God of Belief.* The right beliefs easily become the essence of faith, and, therefore, the adolescing self possesses the Superego God by holding the right beliefs. We "become convinced," says Mark Taylor, "that the essence of religious faith can be objectively defined in formal doctrines and discursive teaching presented by priests and professors. From this perspective, the task of the believer involves, at most, the mastery of objective doctrine and teaching."[24]
4. *The Superego God is a God of Dependency and Control.* It is the God of Dependency and Control—this Supreme Being with all its power, this God of Law with its commands of what must and must not be done, this God of Belief with its propositions about what must and must not be accepted as true—that the adolescing self both depends on and is controlled by. The God of Dependency and Control is at once a God of Providence and a God of Domination.
5. *The Superego God is a God of the Group.* The place where the Superego God lives, moves, and has its being is in the group. The God of the Group is, for all practical purposes, a gathering of adolescing selves around the all-powerful Supreme Being at its unseen center. The God of the Group is a powerful, hierarchical, and closed system. Only in and through the group can the adolescing self find out how to know and to follow the Superego God.

John J. Shea

Adult Faith

Now we can look at the paradigm of *adult faith* with its adult self able at least to relate in full or unfettered imaging to a Living God. This adult faith is a description of the fullness of what our relationship with God can be.

Adult Self

An adult self is a fully formed, interdependent self, a self that functions in mutuality as its own whole. No longer still forming and still dependent, the adult self is an undivided, integral whole that needs to relate to whatever is other in a mutual way. "Crucial to a mature sense of mutuality," observes Judith Jordan "is an appreciation of the wholeness of the other person."[25] The adult self has six essential characteristics:

1. The adult self *is a body-self*. An adult self "finds its anchor in its own body."[26] The body is owned by the self, and the self is comfortable in the body. Marcel describes fidelity, hope, love, and communion as mature embodied realities. And Freud's famous dictum "to love and to work" can easily be seen as presupposing the wholeness of the body-self.
2. The adult self *is founded in feeling*. Feeling is the felt, meaningful aliveness of the body-self and the sense of this self in relatedness. It is in the intimacy of feeling that the body-self is available to itself, and it is in the intimacy of feeling that the body-self is open to others and to the world.
3. The adult self *has a sense of depth*. Some see this depth as the place of "soul," because the essence of the human is there. Some call this depth the "heart," because it is a living center of striving and courage. Some understand this depth as the locus of the "spirit," because aliveness, purpose, and resolve are celebrated there. All that is most personal to the adult self is both revealed and concealed in the depth.

4. The adult self *has clear boundaries*. Clear boundaries make for the delineation, coherence, and wholeness of the adult self. "There is," says Jung, "no personality without definiteness, wholeness, and ripeness."[27] With clear boundaries, the adult self, a body-self with feeling and depth, has its own dimension and place in its mutuality with whatever is other.
5. The adult self *exists in intimacy*. Intimacy is the feeling and depth of the body-self welcoming the feeling and depth of the other. The boundaries of the adult self are, paradoxically, quite penetrable. It is the very penetrability of these boundaries—evidenced in such qualities as openness, availability, self-forgetfulness, understanding, and love—which makes intimacy possible.
6. The adult self *is its own responsible process*. "To be responsible," asserts Richard Niebuhr "is to be a self in the presence of other selves, to whom one is bound and to whom one is able to answer freely."[28] In fact, my ongoing sense of myself actually depends on my ability to respond to what is other. In adulthood, the responsible self and the call of the other go together.

Unfettered Imaging

The adult self is able to image reality in a way that is whole, complete, and without constraint. While the imaging of reality in the still-forming and still-dependent adolescing self is a fettered process of imaging, the imaging of reality in the adult self is an unfettered, integral process of imaging. It is no longer embedded in elements of fantasy. It is no longer distorted by relating in transference. It is no longer confined by the logic of objective knowing. Unfettered imaging is our unique process of imaging reality that comes directly and completely from the adult self, allowing us to experience things as they really are. It gives us what Kenneth Bragan describes as "a reality untainted by preconception or by distortion."[29]

Living God

The God an adult self is able to image in unfettered imaging is a Living God. This God is a transformation of the Superego God, a God fully formed, complete, and whole. Like the Superego God, the Living God comes to us in any number of forms, yet it has some definite characteristics.

1. *The Living God is a God as Thou.* This God as Thou, a transformation of the Supreme Being, is an encompassing and unique reality, which the adult self is able to encounter freely, intimately, and in integrity. As Charles Kao says, "I and Thou are integrated and yet differentiated,"[30] and the experiencing of this God resonates in the feeling and depth of the body-self. The God as Thou is an experience of salvation, an experience of healing and of being brought into some greater wholeness.
2. *The Living God is a God of Love.* This God of Love, a transformation of the God of Law, is an encompassing and unique reality, which the adult self is able to relate to freely, intimately, and in integrity. The God of Love is very profound. It resonates in the feeling and depth of the body-self as experience of salvation, an experience of healing and of being brought into some greater wholeness.
3. *The Living God is a God of Mystery.* The God of Mystery is an encompassing and unique reality, which the adult self is able to encounter freely, intimately, and in integrity. Often, the God of Mystery is utterly profound, and the adult self finds itself responding to it in wonder and awe. This God of Mystery, which resonates in the feeling and depth of the body-self, is an experience of salvation, an experience of healing and of being brought into some greater wholeness. The God of Mystery points to "a reality which is experienced but whose inexhaustible depths and breadth our powers can never encompass."[31]

4. *The Living God is a God of Freedom.* This God of Freedom is an encompassing and personal reality, which the adult self is able to encounter freely, intimately, and in integrity. The God of Freedom may be quite disarming, and the adult self may find that it wants to respond in a kind of self-surrender or openness. The God of Freedom, which resonates in the feeling and depth of the body-self, is an experience of salvation, an experience of healing and of being brought into some greater wholeness.
5. *The Living God is a God of Community.* The God of Community is an encompassing and personal reality, which the adult self is able to encounter freely, intimately, and in integrity. Often the God of Community is deeply authenticating and enlivening, and the self finds itself so much at home that it wants to give back to this God all that it is receiving. The experiencing of the God of Community, which resonates in the feeling and depth of the body-self, is an experience of salvation, an experience of healing and of being brought into some greater wholeness.

Elizabeth

Elizabeth has been a high school teacher for many years. She had a long struggle with a very serious form of cancer in midlife. But until that time—really up until she was in her forties—she suffered from a scrupulosity that crippled her sense of herself and crippled her relationship with God. This is her story of imaging God in excerpts from *Finding God Again* (Shea 2005).

I don't know if I remember an early image of God. I just remember the distinct point where my faith went from a complete childlike aspect to a rules relationship with God. At the age of seven, I became very rules conscious. At a time when it should have been a happy time, it became a time of me thinking of God as this person that has these rules and these regulations. I was always looking for the right rule. And that followed me right through life. There was a complete reversal of childlike trust. I was always scared that I was doing the wrong thing.

Before I was seven, I considered myself normal. Normal in the sense that I don't remember having any problems with the scrupulosity I have had all these years. Grade school was about all these rules, rules for this, rules for that. "These are the rules, and if you don't obey them, you're gonna be punished." God was the law and the rule, and if you didn't follow it, you're guilty and you're sinful. The whole thing worked on you so. I was guilty all the time. I was racked with guilt for years. I was afraid all the time, afraid to do anything wrong. I was afraid to think for myself. Even when I knew what was right, I would always have to have somebody in authority say it was right. I don't think I ever lost that. It was horrible.

I remember too, like an image of a trusting father. The Good Shepherd comes to my mind. You know, somebody-taking-care-of-His-flock kind of thing. Yeah, and I was the child and He was the father. But I think that was in the background, a background image. But in front was the rules thing that kept me from really realizing that the background person was there. I mean, that God would be there to show me what I needed to do, that I would have a more trusting attitude instead of ending up with so much fear.

Getting cancer, that was the crisis. Actually, I have had cancer twice. The first time was about eight years ago, and I just tried to hide it, you know, "I'm gonna get over this, and I'm not gonna die." It was that kind of thing, and then I got better. The second time it was more serious. They sent me home to die. Later, when another doctor finally decided to operate on me, I was in the hospital almost six weeks. The first time, I think I was just angry. The second time was a different realization, a completely different realization. It brought me to an aloneness, a complete and utter aloneness—it's hard for me to talk about it. I knew that everything on this earth is kind of like nothing. And it felt like there wasn't anybody there for me.

Then, when I went through the operation and all the recovery in the hospital, I thought that I had been purged spiritually. I thought that it didn't matter that I didn't have my own basis for religion. And then, you know, I wasn't scrupulous, and I wasn't worried about the rules. There were more important things to think about. But it wasn't true. The experience in the hospital was very healing, and a number of really beautiful things happened to me there, between the doctors and me and different members of the staff. But it still didn't relieve me of the scrupulosity or any of that. As soon as I started to heal physically, then those old feelings started coming back. And that's when I knew that I needed to be healed spiritually. If I wasn't going to die right away, then I had better figure out how to live.

The difference is therapy. When I went through therapy, everything in the room changed. I was dealing with all those things I could never let myself feel. I was angry at myself for what I did to myself all those years, angry that I wasn't empowered enough to be able to change, or speak up, or be personally responsible. Therapy was a kind of empowerment, I'd say, a personal empowerment for myself. And that affected my religion, because if I couldn't be this total person who was empowered, how could I totally empower myself to believe in God? How could I have a close relationship with God, if I wasn't personally empowered myself? So I think it was more of a change in my personality, and that affected what I believed spiritually. My relationship with God would have to be totally personal and not something based on the authority of somebody else. It was what I felt inside of me that I was trying to deny for all those years, I think. The more you bring it out, the more, I think, it's a blossoming of your own personal spirituality. Your relationship with God comes out more as you develop as a person, as you mature.

I experience God through other people and through my feelings. I have intuitive feelings, or something, in connection with other people and myself and God. That's like what prayer is for me now. Prayer was, well, before it was rote, and earlier in life it was rote and petition, asking for things but never really feeling like a center. And now prayer is more of a feeling and a center. I don't usually ask for anything. I usually ask that I'm open to God's will and that He shows me what He wants me to do. So it's sort of like more of an openness and a pouring, like opening my hands and saying whatever. And it's more of a trusting. It's intuitive, and I don't know, but it feels more spiritual. I don't have to go anywhere to find God. I think He's everywhere. I think He's in every relationship and I think that He's all around me. Almost always in working with the problems of my students, I can feel His presence. I feel peaceful now, peaceful and calm.

Summary

What can we say about serious illness? Serious or "deep" illness is a normal part of life. It is very important for the seriously ill person to be able to tell the story (the restitution story, the chaos story, or the quest story) in order to stay connected with life. Serious illness often challenges our imaging of God in very significant ways. It may lead some of us to stop believing in the Superego God. It may leave some of us petitioning the Superego God, praying for restitution or for an end to the chaos. It may draw some of us to embark on a spiritual quest in which self and God are transformed together. It may usher in for some of us an experience of the Living God (adult faith), a God of relationship, deeply felt, intimate, and transforming.

What can we say about listening to the seriously ill? We can say that this listening often is wonderfully validating for the ill person. We can say that it is very helpful to understand the kind of story that is being told (Arthur Frank) and to understand what may be happening developmentally to the person who is telling the story (Paul Andrews). We can say that it is the integrity (adult self) of the listener—the caregiver—that allows him or her to relate in mutuality, honoring the story without needing to change it. And I think we can say that it is the adult faith of the listener that may help the seriously ill person grow in his or her own faith, if that needs to happen.

Finally, what can we say about the wholeness of the self before God? Again, it is an integral self (adult self) who is able to recognize the wholeness of the other, including the wholeness of God (Living God). And it is the wholeness of the self, at the end of life, that allows us to accept life as it was and had to be, to accept the approach of death, and to find the wisdom that comes from the presence of the Living God. We are called to be one with a God as Thou, a God of Love, a God of Mystery, a God of Freedom, and a God of Community.

Notes

1. A. W. Frank, "Just Listening: Narrative and Deep Illness," *Families, Systems & Health* 16 (1998): 197.

2. A. W. Frank, *At the Will of the Body: Reflections on Illness* (Boston: Houghton Mifflin, 1991), 9.

3. Ibid.

4. Ibid., 12, 13.

5. Frank, "Just Listening," 197.

6. Ibid.

7. Frank, *At the Will of the Body*, 2.

8. Frank, "Just Listening," 200, 201.

9. Ibid., 201, 202.

10. Ibid., 203, 204.

11. Ibid., 206.

12. Ibid., 209–10.

13. P. Andrews, "Developmental Tasks of Terminally Ill Patients," *Journal of Religion and Health* 20 (1981): 244.

14. Ibid.

15. Ibid., 245.

16. Ibid., 246, 247.

17. Ibid., 247, 248.

18. Ibid., 249.

19. Ibid., 249, 250.

20. See J. J. Shea, *Finding God Again: Spirituality for Adults* (Lanham, MD: Rowman & Littlefield, 2005).

21. Paul W. Pruyser, "Lessons from Art Theory for the Psychology of Religion," *Journal for the Scientific Study of Religion* 15 (1976): 1–14.

22. Mario Jacobi, *The Analytic Encounter: Transference and Human Relationship* (Toronto: Inner City Books, 1984), 64.

23. Thomas Merton, "To Ripu Daman Lama," in *The Hidden Ground of Love: The Letters of Thomas Merton on Religious Experience and Social Concerns*, ed. William H. Shannon (New York: Farrar, Straus and Giroux, 1985), 452.

24. M. C. Taylor, *Journeys to Selfhood: Hegel and Kierkegaard* (New York: Fordham University Press, 2000), 62.

25. Judith V. Jordan, "The Meaning of Mutuality," in *Women's Growth in Connection: Writings from the Stone Center*, ed. J. V. Jordan et al. (New York: Guilford, 1991), 82.

26. Paul Ricoeur, *Oneself as Another* (Chicago: University of Chicago Press, 1992), 319.

27. Carl C. Jung, "The Development of Personality," in *The Collected Works of C. G. Jung*, vol. 17 (Princeton, NJ: Princeton University Press, 1981), 171.

28. H. Richard Niebuhr, "The Responsibility of the Church for Society," in *The Gospel, the Church, and the World*, ed. K. S. Latourette (New York: Harper & Brothers, 1946), 114.

29. K. Bragan, *Self and Spirit in the Therapeutic Relationship* (London: Routledge, 1996), 81.

30. C. C. Kao, "Maturity, Spirituality, and Theological Reconstruction," in *Maturity and the Quest for Spiritual Meaning*, ed. C. C. Kao (Lanham, MD: University Press of America, 1998), 45.

31. J. N. King, *Experiencing God All Ways and Every Day* (Minneapolis, MN: Winston, 1982), 29.

References

Andrews, P. "Developmental Tasks of Terminally Ill Patients" *Journal of Religion and Health* 20 (1981): 243-52.

Bragan, K. *Self and Spirit in the Therapeutic Relationship*. London: Routledge, 1996.

Erikson, E. H. *Childhood and Society*, 2nd ed. New York: Norton, 1963.

———. *Identity and the Life Cycle*. New York: Norton, 1980.

———. *Identity: Youth and Crisis*. New York: Norton, 1968.

———. *Insight and Responsibility*. New York: Norton, 1964.

———. *Toys and Reasons: Stages in the Ritualization of Experience*. New York: Norton, 1977.

Frank, A. W. *At the Will of the Body: Reflections on Illness*. Boston: Houghton Mifflin, 1991.

———. "Just Listening: Narrative and Deep Illness." *Families, Systems & Health* 16 (1998): 197–210.

Jacobi, M. *The Analytic Encounter: Transference and Human Relationship*. Toronto: Inner City Books, 1984.

Jordan, J. V. "The Meaning of Mutuality." In *Women's Growth in Connection: Writings from the Stone Center*, edited by J. V.

Jordan, A. G. Kaplan, J. B. Miller, I. P. Stiver, and J. L. Surrey. New York: Guilford, 1991.

Jung, C. G. "The Development of Personality." In *The Collected Works of C. G. Jung*, volume 17, 167–86. Princeton, NJ: Princeton University Press, 1981.

Kao, C. C. "Maturity, Spirituality, and Theological Reconstruction." In *Maturity and the Quest for Spiritual Meaning*, edited by C. C. Kao, 41–52. Lanham, MD: University Press of America, 1998.

King, J. N. *Experiencing God All Ways and Every Day*. Minneapolis, MN: Winston, 1982.

Marcel, G. *The Mystery of Being*. 2 volumes. Chicago: Regnery, 1960.

Merton, T. "To Ripu Daman Lama." In *The Hidden Ground of Love: The Letters of Thomas Merton on Religious Experience and Social Concerns*, edited by W. H. Shannon, 451–53. New York: Farrar, Straus and Giroux, 1985.

Niebuhr, H. R. "The Responsibility of the Church for Society." In *The Gospel, the Church, and the World*, edited by K. S. Latourette, 111–33. New York: Harper & Brothers, 1946.

Pruyser, P. W. "Lessons from Art Theory for the Psychology of Religion." *Journal for the Scientific Study of Religion* 15 (1976): 1–14.

Ricoeur, P. *Oneself as Another*. Chicago: University of Chicago Press, 1992.

Shea, J. J. *Finding God Again: Spirituality for Adults*. Lanham, MD: Rowman & Littlefield, 2005.

Stephen, K. 2000. "Relations between the Superego and the Ego." *Psychoanalysis and History* 2 (1): 11–28.

Taylor, M. C. *Journeys to Selfhood: Hegel and Kierkegaard*. New York: Fordham University Press, 2000.

6

Illness and the Paradox of Power

A Spirituality of Mortality

Kieran Scott

We need an approach to loss, illness, and death that is both religious and educational. This essay will address the first part of that duality. Such an approach, I propose, has to come to grips with the dynamics of human power. Power, then, is the hermeneutical lens through which I will view the issues of loss, illness, and death. At the outset, let me say, what is true for the individual in this regard is true for the nation.

In a letter to the *New York Times*, Tom F. Driver, professor emeritus at Union Theological Seminary, wrote:

> "For a very brief time after 9/11 we North Americans had a chance to learn from our pain. One of its lessons might have been how much we are like others in our vulnerability, our suffering and our flawed leadership. Since we were getting a flood of messages of sympathy and solidarity from around the world, we might have learned from them how to turn pain into compassion and wisdom." "Instead," Driver continues, "we used 9/11 to bolster our own feelings of 'us versus them,' our illusory

> dream of invulnerability and our search for enemies rather than friends. This mentality, a blend of machismo and militarism, has given us bloody Iraq, tempts us to nuke Iran and requires us to look under every rock for dangerous foes." "Given this mentality" he writes, "we will find them." (September 14, 2007, A20)

When I read this, Lord Acton's judgment came to mind: "Power tends to corrupt, and absolute power corrupts absolutely." However, what is true for the nation is just as applicable to the individual.

In Leo Tolstoy's *The Death of Ivan Ilyich*, Ilyich is a successful lawyer and respected judge in Czarist Russia: a man near the peak of his power. Suddenly, he is confronted with the imminence of his own death at the age of forty-five.

After months of painful reflection, induced by his own illness, he is forced to face the truth about his life. "What if my life, my entire conscious life," Ilyich asks himself, "simply was not the real thing?" The life he has built for himself, he suddenly realizes, has been a lie, an illusion, a potential life, not an actual one. Ilyich didn't know what he really wanted in life. What was his problem? For Tolstoy, worldly ambition was Ilyich's problem. It was his attachment to and preoccupation with specific images of success that closed him off to intimations of a better way.

First, Ilyich was fascinated with the power of his office. He reveled in the power of his judgeship—how he controlled and diminished others to enhance himself.

Second, Ilyich was driven by blind social ambition. He longed to be accepted by the social elite of St. Petersburg. He wanted to be with the in-crowd, those that counted. He thought it would elevate his status and significance in public. What it did, in fact, was blunt his moral sensibilities...and lead him to die without having lived a real life.

Ilyich discovered this in the last moments of his life. While thrashing his arms in pain, he unexpectedly caught hold of his son's hand. Immediately, his preoccupation with his own pain dissolved. He was delivered from the illusion and unreality of his former life. He saw the light...is converted...his life is redeemed. But he would not live to act on his new revelation. What was revealed to him was the nature of an authentic life and his vocation to live it. Loss, illness, and death can put one in touch with such authenticity. The key, however, to unlocking its secrets is discovering the paradox of human power.

The Paradox of Power

James Baldwin wrote that Americans are not very good at paradox. They tend to categorize, simplify, and separate reality into polar opposites: black/white, straight/gay, life/death, us/them, and so forth. Paradox is, on the other hand, an apparent contradiction. It is one of the hallmarks of human maturity, and, according to John Shea (2005), where we may find God again. Religious traditions, with their sacred texts and representative iconic figures, disclose for us the paradox of human power.

Power for many of us is a dirty word. Liberal Christian theologians are ambivalent, if not downright suspicious, about it. It seems to cut moral corners and run roughshod over people. It seems to operate so different from love. Liberals tend to want to get rid of it. But this only leads to impotence. Power is ubiquitous. It is as ubiquitous as persuasion or friendship. It is an inescapable dimension of human relations. It is fluid, flowing through the entire network of group life. It is what Daniel Finn (2007) calls "the software of daily life." Its reality must be attended to if it is to play a part in the transformation of the world. Power, like so many important words, has two almost opposite meanings. When political "realists" (from Machiavelli to Foucault) talk about power, they have a very clear meaning in mind. Power means the exercise of force; power in this context means to coerce and dominate, to control unilaterally by force or violence.

Thomas Wartenberg (1990) offers a "field theory of power." His conception of power is based on the notion of a magnetic field.

Power is present and functions through a field of influence or "networks" of power (Foucault). Like a magnet, it alters the social space surrounding it. It alters the opportunities, the options, faced by those whom power affects.

Wartenberg (1990) identifies three types of power: force, coercion, and influence. These forms exist in relationships. Their primary location is "in the ongoing, habitual ways in which human beings relate to one another" (165). They are part of the software of organizational life, family life, school life, and the life of the church.

Force is a physical intervention by a human agent to prevent another (human or nonhuman) from doing something. For nearly everyone, it is a daily occurrence in our lives—from forcing open a can of vegetables, to forcing snow from your sidewalks. As a one-directional act against humans (and nonhumans), force is always questionable. It may slide into violence. However, it is not by nature immoral. Parents prevent children from running into the street. Force may have to be used to stop a would-be rapist. And, force may be necessary to restrain an incompetent or criminally dangerous human being. In each case, however, force has to be carefully rationed and morally analyzed.

Coercion is the second form of power. According to Wartenberg (1990), it occurs when a human agent is able to affect another significantly. Coercion exerts pressure on the other to get him/her to act in a desired way. What distinguishes coercion from mere force is the threat, or in fact, the effect of a successful threat. Because of the threat of the first human agent, the other decides to alter what he/she would otherwise do. Coercion is a restriction on the freedom of another. It does allow for innumerable degrees of exercise from psychological intimidation to water boarding. However, like force, it is also not by nature immoral. We can distinguish between good and bad coercion. But transparency is critical here for those with power who want to be moral.

The third form of power is influence. As Wartenberg (1990) puts it: a human agent influences another when one's communication leads the other to "alter her assessment of her action-environment in a fundamental way" (105). This influence can occur through persuasion based on rational argument, on personal trust, on expertise, or on a combination of argument and trust. So influence is a form of power when it alters the other's action-environment. Wartenberg claims that this form of power is more stable than either force or coercion, since the other willingly does what she does (110).

A book that received quite a bit of attention and praise a few years ago was Joseph Nye's *The Paradox of American Power: Why the World's Only Superpower Can't Go It Alone* (2003). Nye distinguishes between "hard power" and "soft power" in thinking about the power of the United States in the world. The language quickly became absorbed into international discussions. Hard power is the military option. Soft power takes the form of cultural influence. Nye's two kinds of power are simply two kinds of force. The distinction between hard and soft is only a minor issue of degree in the exercise of power. However, Nye never gets to the real paradox of power. His hard and soft powers coerce people in a one-way exercise of force. In a corresponding fashion, Wartenberg's force and coercion are similar to Nye's hard power, while influence (as a form of power) is equivalent to soft power. Here, once again, the paradox of human power is absent.

The real paradox of human power is that power can be almost the exact opposite of force or control. Power can also mean receptiveness. It is an invitation to cooperation. People hanker for an expression of power that is mutual and communal. Etymologically, the word has the same root meaning as possible, passive, or potential—"the capacity for action." Humans are born with the capacity, that is, the power, to be receptive. Here, to receive can be the greatest human power. The paradox of power is that power begins in vulnerability or passivity. But, ironically, it is our human receptiveness or passivity that is our strength. We are able to exercise control of our surroundings by ideas and language. St. Paul writes, "for power is made perfect in weakness...for whenever I am weak, then I am strong" (2 Cor 12:9–10). The paradox at the heart of human existence is that receptivity, and our responding to it, is more powerful than simple coercion. Of course, we humans can easily forget our own strength and resort to using force against others when threatened. Force may be the best available option, the best available form of power sometimes. But force should not be equated with power or thought to be the main form of human power. Force, in fact, is the sign that human power has failed. Human power, on the other hand, resides in listening and responding. This receptive mutual exchange leads to cooperation and enhances the power of each. Human life becomes richer the more that receptivity to others is exercised. To paraphrase Lord Acton's statement: power, in this form, tends to heal and reveal, and absolute power, in this form, heals and reveals absolutely.

A Spirituality of Mortality

Nowhere is the paradox of human power revealed and tested more than in loss, illness, and death. People who glory in their possession of power may find they are living in a delusion; the first heart attack may bring them to reality. The very young, the very old, and the sick are the ever-present reminders that human life is surrounded by dependence.

But the possibility exists that suffering and illness can make us callous, bitter, insensitive, angry, and imbalanced. It does not always lead to moral intelligence and insight. It can also motivate the snipers who killed the students at Virginia Tech and Northern Illinois universities.

There is another way of relating to illness, however—a redemptive way, a transforming way, the way of, what I call, a spirituality of mortality. Suffering can make a person (go) deep. It can direct one to an inner core to bring it all together. We see this in great people—Nelson Mandela and Mother Teresa. Both saw the deep secret of life, suffered a lot, and came out serene on the other side. From a Christian perspective, the secret of life is the cross of Christ: it is the brokenness of Jesus on the cross. Inside of brokenness, inside of pain, inside of humiliation is the key to understanding life. Accepting and incorporating the reality of suffering and death into our lives is the inner light. It is the needed hermeneutic. The cross does that for us. It is a school of humility.

Dorothee Soelle (1975), writing in the context of worldwide suffering, asserts that humans learn through suffering. Suffering makes one more sensitive to the pain in the world. It can teach us to put forth a greater love for everything that exists. "As with all historical experiences," Soelle writes, "there are various possibilities for relating oneself to suffering. We can remain the people we were before or we can change. We can adopt the attitude of the 'knowing one,' of the clever person who saw it coming...but we can also find our way to the other attitude, that of learning." Soelle continues:

> In a certain sense learning presupposes mystical acceptance; the acceptance of life, an indestructible hope. The mystics have described how a person can become free and open, so that God is born within the depths of his soul; they have pointed out that a person in suffering can become "calm" rather than apathetic, and that the capacity for love is strongest where it grows out of suffering. (126–27)

For Soelle, this learning in and from suffering brings a form of liberation. Those who learn in suffering, who use the experience to overcome old insights, who experience their own strength and come to know the pain of the living, are beginning the exodus.

What great spiritual writers do essentially is to introduce us to ourselves. They shine a flashlight inside us. They are religious psychologists. They disclose the inside of our human experience...what we have been running away from all our lives, namely, our own mortality. John of the Cross observes that receptivity to our suffering and mortality can make sense of everything. It can lead to an inner serenity. However, nothing can be learned from individual human suffering unless it is worked through. But how do we humans do that?

Two contrasting examples offer case studies in how, and how not, to do it.

David Rieff (2008) offers an intimate and vivid account of his mother's, the writer Susan Sontag's, final illness and death. Sontag was diagnosed with breast cancer in 1975, at age forty-two. She survived the draconian treatment, only to develop uterine cancer in the late 1990s. Again she survived, and again she developed a new cancer. She died in 2004. Three decades of having cancer, waiting for it to recur or being treated for it might be a catalyst for some for religious contemplation or philosophical reflection. In Sontag, it brings out the rebellious adolescent. Each battle and victory strengthens her appetite for life and her conviction that she was immortal.

Rieff (2008) questions whether, on some level, his mother thought she was too special to die. "She believed in her own will," he writes, "and grandiose though it may seem, in her own star. My mother came to being ill imbued with a profound sense of being the exception to every rule" (74). Her life-organizing principle was: she could accomplish what she could will in life. That same belief made it impossible for her to accept that her fatal illness was not another circumstance she could master.

During her last nine months, Sontag embarked on an all-out campaign to cure an incurable disease. As chronicled by her son, David Rieff, she underwent a bone marrow transplant that failed, recurrent hospitalization, dire infections, wild mood swings, and gruesome mental and physical suffering. In the midst of this dreadful ordeal, there was a desperate Internet search for more and better treatment. She never admitted she was dying. Even her family, friends, and physicians were unwilling or unable to help her accept the inevitable. Rather they were cast in the role of cheerleaders. Their job was to enthusiastically endorse her struggle, always to be optimistic and supportive and never, ever, to talk about death. Rieff, in the role of head cheerleader, writes: "What she wanted from me was an adamant refusal to accept that it was ever possible that she might not survive" (74). Sontag believed, in her own secular and agnostic way, from the day she was diagnosed that she could once again best the odds, not through New Age beliefs, but through new science.

Biological death is not the worst of happenings. It is something to be accepted when all the signs point to its appropriateness. We need an approach to death that is necessarily a religious one. Sontag's answer is a confirmation of the bankruptcy of Western enlightenment.

A more realistic, pragmatic, and yet philosophical and religious response is offered by Eugene O'Kelly in his book, *Chasing Daylight* (2006). O'Kelly, a fifty-three-year-old American chief executive of the accounting firm KPMG, was diagnosed with inoperable brain cancer in May 2005. *Chasing Daylight* is a commonsense guidebook on how to die. O'Kelly sends the message: stop and smell the roses, enjoy every sandwich. O'Kelly had been a controlling, orderly, privileged, and powerful businessman. He sometimes felt like an eagle on a mountaintop. Then, to his astonishment, the mountain disappeared after he learned he had three brain tumors. Suddenly he rethought his living and dying from the ground up.

O'Kelly describes discovering the world around him—nature, connection with loved ones, living in the moment as if for the first time. He searched for ways to savor what was within his grasp without yearning for the impossible. His religious faith was a significant assistance to him in his quest. The book describes O'Kelly's medical decline: his vision began to dim, his handwriting deteriorated, simple tasks became onerous. "One thing at a time" became the motto and instruction. He wondered what it would take to make healthy people slow down...and live. Eugene O'Kelly died a "good" death on September 10, 2005. He glimpsed elements of the meaning of an authentic life. However, he had also come to realize that to live is to die: life at the center of things includes the acceptance of death.

Daniel Callahan, of the Hastings Center, has sought to explore the folly of what he calls the "gospel of medical progress," namely, the idea that medicine brings the good news of liberation from death and dying. He claims it is an empty promise of an infinitely postponed mortality and a modern form of idolatry. Callahan reminds us that suffering caused by illness and death can be reduced but never, never overcome. The best medicine can do is to be committed unequivocally to care. In his book *The Troubled Dream of Life* (1993), he writes that most of us cling to "illusions of mastery" of our own bodies, our own health, our own future. Life becomes a quest for autonomy, independence, and control. This search for independence puts death out of mind (but not out of sight), leaving almost no place in public discourse for a meaningful discussion of suffering, decline, and death as inevitable companions in life. Death, from this perspective, is defeat, a cruel destroyer at the end of life. Callahan is not morosely obsessed with mortality (although his Irish background may color his perspective!). For him, caring is at least as important as curing. But he is convinced that the "flight from dependency," suffering, and death is a "flight from humanity." Human life, fundamentally, incorporates interdependency and brokenness. We need to be receptive to that human reality. Herein lies the unique power of humans.

Christianity, Judaism, and Islam each affirm the uniqueness of the human. Humans are the best at suffering, they declare. We can foresee our own deaths, and suffer not only in dying, but also in thinking about dying. Other animals can suffer painful deaths, but only humans get the news six months, nine months, eighteen months in advance, so that we can start experiencing the long process of dying. Humans are able to exercise control of these circumstances by inner reflection. With a spirituality of mortality, they can discern that suffering and death are the tragic center of all of life's schemes. They are what David Tracy calls "boundary experiences" or "limit-situations" that disclose to us our basic existential faith (or unfaith) in the very meaning of life.

Charles Taylor writes:

> The connection of death with meaning is reflected in...the way in which facing death, seeing one's life as about to come to an end, can concentrate the issue of what we have lived for. What has it all amounted to? In other words, death can bring out the question of meaning in its most acute form. This is what lies behind Heidegger's claim that an authentic existence involves a stance of Sein-zum-Tode, being-toward-death. (2007, 14)

This confronts us with ultimate questions and concerns. The rest of life seems petty, strange, and foreign now to this authentic world. This is the point where we experience the religious dimension of life.

So the cross can be either a riddle or a redemptive symbol. Mystics have described how suffering and dying can have transformative possibilities (Ruffing 1994). They can be our tutor:

1. releasing us from our own self-interest;
2. reorganizing our lives around a transcendent center of meaning;
3. becoming open and receptive to the birth of God within;
4. uniting our suffering to the redemptive suffering of Christ;
5. enlarging our compassion for the suffering of others in the world.

In Christian theological terms, dying like this, in communion with all, means dying "in Christ." But to die "in Christ" is also to rise "with Christ." One is freed from limited communion for greater communion. The Christian and Jewish term for that is *resurrection*. Resurrection, then, is a negative, or more precisely, a double negative term. It affirms life by negating the negation of life. In other words, life is affirmed in spite of real death. As William Butler Yeats wrote, "All changed, changed utterly: A terrible beauty is born." That is the paradox of power at the center of the Christian Gospel.

References

Callahan, D. 1993. *The Troubled Dream of Life*. New York: Simon & Schuster.

Driver, T. 2007. Editorials/Letters. *New York Times*, September 14, 2007, A20.

Finn, D. 2007. "The Catholic Theological Society of America and the Bishops." *Origins* 37, no. 6 (June 21): 88–95.

Nye, J. 2003. *The Paradox of American Power: Why the World's Only Superpower Can't Go It Alone*. New York: Oxford University Press.

O'Kelly, E. 2006. *Chasing Daylight: How My Forthcoming Death Transformed My Life*. New York: McGraw-Hill.

Rieff, D. 2008. *Swimming in a Sea of Death: A Son's Memoir*. New York: Simon & Schuster.

Ruffing, J. 1994. "Physical Illness: A Mystical Transformative Element in the Life of Elizabeth Leseur." *Spiritual Life* (Winter): 220–29.

Shea, J. 2005. *Finding God Again: Spirituality for Adults*. Lanham, MD: Rowman & Littlefield.

Soelle, D. 1975. *Suffering*. Philadelphia: Fortress Press.

Taylor, C. 2007. "The Sting of Death: Why We Yearn for Eternity." *Commonweal* (October 12): 13–15.

Tolstoy, L. 1981. *The Death of Ivan Ilyich*. New York: Bantam Books. Originally published in 1886.

Tracy, D. 1975. *Blessed Rage for Order*. New York: Seabury Press.

Wartenberg, T. 1990. *The Forms of Power: From Domination to Transformation*. Philadelphia: Temple University Press.

Yeats, W. B. 1956. "Easter, 1916," in *The Collected Works of W. B. Yeats*. New York: MacMillan Pub.

Part II

Psychological Dimensions of Life, Loss, and Death

7

The Psycho-Spiritual Implications of Illness and Injury

Pamela Cooper-White

As pastoral caregivers, we know that there is an inextricable connection between our bodies, minds, and spirits. That *psychē* is the Greek word for both mind and spirit is a truth we know well. The following discussion, then, will address the psychological implications of illness with particular attention to two dimensions: first, the impact of illness and injury on a person *psychologically*; and second the spirit-mind-body connection from the perspective of pastoral theology and the psychosomatic aspects of illness.

The Psychological Impact of Illness and Injury

We all get sick sometimes. Often, if the illness is uncomplicated enough and short-lived enough, we can basically shrug it off—perhaps even enjoy a few sick days home under a blanket with a cup of tea and a good mystery novel. But many occasions of illness or injury have a much greater emotional impact on us: if the illness or injury is particularly acute (sudden) and disruptive, if the illness or injury results in a chronic condition that causes a permanent alteration of our choices and behaviors, if the illness or injury is fatal or we have reason to believe it could become fatal. All these things can cause us to experience illness both as trauma and as a form of loss.

It is, therefore, always crucial to ask the question: *What is the meaning we are making of our illness at a given time*? For various reasons, the meaning is crucial, even for the same illness. The same illness in one person could be understood as a challenge or hurdle to overcome, in another as a crisis to be weathered, and in yet another as a reminder of a parent's or grandparent's disease process that calls up all kinds of family-of-origin issues; for another the same illness becomes a matter of guilt because it prohibits the person from meeting certain responsibilities, or for another, a matter of abruptly facing mortality.

Many years ago, in a seminar sponsored jointly by Harvard Divinity School and Harvard Medical School, I did an interview-based study of patients at the Massachusetts General Hospital Hand Clinic. My subjects were people who had sustained serious hand injuries and were postsurgical rehab patients. Although my sample was small and the results of the study can only be considered anecdotal, it became very clear to me in talking to these men and women that there was a distinction between what they would characterize as "pain" and as "suffering." Pain did not necessarily correlate with these patients' degree of perceived suffering. While some patients reported a high degree of physical pain, their suffering was less than some other patients, because they were able to articulate a quality of hopefulness about their situation. For others, this was reversed. The more damaging the injury was perceived to their sense of self or to their livelihood or the more emotionally distraught or hopeless the patients felt, the more they suffered, even if their pain was less. The lesson to be learned from this—which we probably all can validate in our own experience—is that the *meaning* we make of illness and injury, including the level of hope versus despair or devastation we experience, has a significant impact on our experience of *suffering*. Also, as other studies in the literature have suggested, the meaning we make of our illness or injury may also have a direct impact on our physical prognosis.

Especially for patients who experience their illness or injury as a significant psychological loss or even trauma, then, it may be helpful to frame the psychological support we can give in terms of the normal processes of *grieving*. There are quite a few models of grieving. For example, William Worden has articulated four "tasks of grieving":

1. to accept the reality of the loss;
2. to work through the pain of grief;
3. to adjust to the environment in which the deceased is missing;
4. to emotionally relocate the deceased internally and move on with life.

In Worden's theory, a benchmark of healing is being able to think of the deceased without pain (sadness, yes, but not wrenching pain or physical symptoms).[1]

Another theory I teach in my classes is Thomas Attig's "relearning the world," that is, naming all the "worlds that are impacted and must be relearned by an individual after a major loss," including: the physical surroundings; adjustment to the absence of the deceased; relationships to fellow survivors (rearrangement of family system and roles); relearning our selves (our sense of identity, role[s], autobiography), our place in time and space (closeness and distance; clock and calendar), and our spiritual places in the world (relationship to God, goodness, meaning); and finally relearning our relationship with the deceased.[2]

Probably the most familiar theory in the literature of thanatology is Elisabeth Kübler-Ross's stages of dying: shock, bargaining, denial, anger, and acceptance.[3] These "stages" have been frequently applied to the grieving process by Kübler-Ross and others,[4] but it is my view that, though not necessarily in such a fixed sequential order, they are actually more applicable to the various feelings that arise in anticipation of one's own death or the death of a loved one and they are not as helpful in understanding the process of grief after the loss.

The theory I find to have the most immediate descriptive power for the grieving process comes out of the branch of psychoanalytic object relations theory called Attachment Theory. At the time of a death or major loss, the deceased is gone from our external world, but is still strongly cathected, that is, continues to live on inside of us as an object of continuing intense emotion and attachment. Freud in his *Mourning and Melancholia* stressed the importance of the process of turning inward for a time during grief, until the reality of loss can be accepted and the inner representation of the lost loved one can be integrated into the experience of life beyond the beloved's death.[5] Attachment theorists have elaborated on this process. In particular, C. M. Parkes articulated "Four Phases of Grief," which track the normal stages through which this gradual internal processing of loss can take place.[6] I believe these stages can also be applied to understanding how we incorporate our experiences of illness and injury, particularly when those experiences involve a sudden, chronic, or fatal illness:

1. *Shock and Numbness*. This is the initial phase, in which we simply cannot cognitively process what has happened to us, and it takes us some time to assimilate the new reality into which our illness or injury has thrust us.
2. *Searching and Yearning*. In this phase, the inner reality has not yet caught up to the external situation. In bereavement, this may take the form of someone who believes she or he is still glimpsing or smelling the perfume of or receiving communications from the deceased person. There are certainly cultural and religious variations on how we interpret these phenomena, but at least one psychological explanation involves the projection of the inner object onto the outer world, where the actual loved person is no longer present. In the case of illness or injury, this might resemble

the stage of denial in Kübler-Ross's stages, in which we continue to believe we are still the person we were before the illness or injury and try to behave as if nothing has changed. But what is really happening is that our inner sense of self has not yet caught up with the new reality and the ways in which it may be limiting us or slowing us down.

3. *Disorganization.* This phase resembles depression and actually feels worse than the first two phases. The recognition of this is important, especially in a society and a culture where we are often only granted a few days of bereavement leave from work, and the general stoic culture of North America expects us to "buck up" and move on with our lives within a few weeks; however, in bereavement the disorganization phase generally peaks as long as five to nine months after the loss. With illness or injury, this is the stage of disillusionment, in which we fully confront the losses that the illness or injury represents in our lives. As we adapt to this new reality, we may experience more overt sadness and grief, anger, despair, confusion, or a variety of other negative emotions.
4. *Reorganization.* This is the final stage in Parkes's theory, and it represents finding a "new normal." This is not at all the same as denial and putting on a cheerful front. It is a newfound way of coping with whatever the illness or injury has introduced into our lives for however long we may need to accept it.

To the extent that we, as pastoral caregivers, can recognize and help individuals through these various phases of grief in relation to illness or loss, we may become more sensitized to the meanings that the illness has for them. This will also restrain us from jumping into either a "fix-it" or a problem-solving mode with the person, or sinking with them into a kind of parallel hopelessness or anger. This sensitivity is also a useful tool in recognizing our own countertransference, both at the level of the *actual* loss this person's illness may represent to us as we relate to the patient and our feelings about that and also at the level of our own fear of frailty, injury, vulnerability, and mortality. We need to raise this fear to the level of consciousness so that we do not project our own anxieties onto those in our care or allow our anxieties to impede our emotional availability to them.

The Spirit-Mind-Body Connection and the Psychosomatic Aspects of Illness

Turning to the spirit-mind-body connection and the psychosomatic aspects of illness in both traditional Western medicine, generally, and traditional Western psychiatry, specifically, we will now address the field of psychosomatic medicine, which has historically been treated with suspicion and marginalized as a research discipline. We can trace the movement of psychosomatic medicine in North America back to the 1920s when Adolf Meyer, professor of psychiatry at Johns Hopkins, called for a "subordination of the medically useless contrast of mental and physical." This movement took off in the 1930s, resulting in the first issue of the *Journal of Psychosomatic Medicine* in 1939. But of course it has ancient roots, all the way back to the "father of medicine," Galen, in the second century CE with his interest in the "passions or perturbations of the soul," and in the middle ages with Maimonides' observation, for example, in the twelfth century that "passions of the psyche produce changes in the body that are great, evident, and manifest to all."[7]

The movement took off in the psychiatric world as well in the 1930s, especially with Franz Alexander and Flanders Dunbar and was reinforced by the recognition of the mind-body link evident in war veterans returning from overseas with "combat fatigue" and what we would now recognize as post-traumatic stress disorder. It peaked around 1950, as Theodore Brown has noted in his historical review of psychosomatic medicine. It even made it to Broadway in the lyrics of *Guys and Dolls*: "A goil could develop a cough!" In the

1960s, however, the field began to decline. As psychoanalytic models were eclipsed in general psychiatry by more attention to both behavioral and pharmaceutical models, the focus on the "meaning" of illness and the possible unconscious psychogenesis of disease and injury fell by the wayside. Nevertheless, some very good work continues in examining the effect of stress, particularly on the heart, endocrine, and immune systems of the body, although this work attends more to conscious, behavioral phenomena than to the unconscious or to a psychodynamic perspective.

The ups and downs of psychosomatic medicine have had less impact on our fields of pastoral care and counseling, however. From our own pastoral perspective, a holistic approach to health and illness has always been bedrock. The same year that saw the first issue of the *Journal of Psychosomatic Medicine* also saw the publication of Anton Boisen's *The Exploration of the Inner World* and his introduction to pastoral theology of the idea—based in no small part on his own experience as a psychiatric patient—that the human person should be understood and cared for as a "living human document" of higher priority in diagnosis and treatment than our favored theories and texts.[8] Bonnie Miller-McLemore more recently adapted this to an even wider, more intersubjective and communal feminist model as "the living human web."[9] This interconnectedness of mind, body, and spirit and of persons in relationship with one another is at the heart of our pastoral identity and practice. Because the integration of body, mind, and spirit is foundational to our identity as practitioners, we are naturally more receptive to the idea that not only how we feel physically can affect our minds and souls but that the condition of a person's thoughts, feelings, and spirituality can also have an impact on physical health.

This holistic perspective, like any perspective, can of course be misused. While we understand that thoughts and feelings can sicken patients both mentally and physically, this should never be a rationale for blaming them for their disease. Some cancer patients in particular have reported feeling "kicked while they were down" by well-meaning practitioners and articles that suggested that they brought cancer on themselves by having a "type C" personality or failing to be assertive enough or failing to process their feelings enough, and so forth. While a holistic awareness of body, mind, and soul may be helpful in encouraging healthy living and even—with some caution—the prevention of illness, we must also recognize that we live in a culture that is prevention and self-protection focused to a fault. Life, as the Buddhists articulate best of all the world's religions, will always involve suffering. We cannot ever perfect our minds or emotions or souls to the point where we can avoid suffering. Our very humanity is defined not by being disease- or wound-*free* but by how we cope and by what grace we allow joys, suffering, and all into our lives.

Pastorally therefore, as compassionate listeners we must remain sensitive and available to the meaning that individuals *themselves* make of their suffering. Some may identify an underlying disordered pattern of thinking or feeling, a loss of balance in their lives, or even, in some faith traditions, an implication of sin that is bound up for them in their loss of well-being. But that is something that is sacred to each individual's process and is unique to that person. It is ours neither to suggest nor to impose nor to judge. At our intersubjective best, we become the compassionate ears that "hear" the ill person "into speech," to quote Nelle Morton.[10] Then, as pastoral caregivers, we will be present to whatever meanings and whatever feelings arise, and we will serve as witnesses to God's loving care in the midst of suffering in whatever form it may take.

Notes

1. William Worden, *Grief Counseling and Grief Therapy*, 2nd ed. (New York: Springer, 1991).

2. Thomas Attig, *How We Grieve: Relearning the World* (New York: Oxford University Press), 108–21, 163ff.

3. Elisabeth Kübler-Ross, *On Death and Dying* (New York: MacMillan, 1970).

4. Elisabeth Kübler-Ross and David Kessler, *On Grief and Grieving: Finding the Meaning of Grief through the Five Stages of Loss* (New York: Scribner's, 2005).

5. Sigmund Freud, *Mourning and Melancholia*, in *The Standard Edition of the Complete Psychological Works of Sigmund Freud*, ed. and trans. James Strachey (1917; repr., London: Hogarth Press, 1966).

6. C. M. Parkes, *Bereavement: Studies of Grief in Adult Life* (New York: International Universities Press, 1972).

7. All quotations in this paragraph, as well as the historical information, are from Theodore Brown, "The Rise and Fall of American Psychosomatic Medicine," presented to the New York Academy of Medicine, November 29, 2000. Available online at http://www.human-nature.com/free-associations/riseandfall.html.

8. Anton Boisen, *The Exploration of the Inner World* (New York: Harper, 1952).

9. Bonnie Miller-McLemore, "The Living Human Web: Theology at the Turn of the Century," in *Through the Eyes of Women: Insights for Pastoral Care*, ed. Jeanne Stevenson Moessner (Minneapolis: Fortress Press, 1996), 9–26.

10. Nelle Morton, *The Journey Is Home* (Boston: Beacon Press, 1985).

8

Loss and the Unraveling of Life

Neil J. McGettigan

A man's reach must exceed his grasp,
or what's a heaven for?

—Robert Browning

From a point of view that eventually finds its way into all rational human awareness, we must acknowledge that loss is the very fabric of human life, or to put the matter plainly, loss is what life is all about. In the precise language of dictionary meaning, loss as a noun is "probably a back-formation" or a shortened word form that is derived from the past participle of the Old English verb "losian," which has for its first meaning "to perish."[1] Simple deduction leads to an understanding of loss, then, as the state of having arrived at the end stage, the culmination of the act or process of perishing, that stage being more aptly called *destruction* or *ceasing to exist.* This apparent etymological affiliation with "losian" further identifies loss in its rudimentary and most stark meaning as death. For that reason, to my mind, loss is actually an unraveling or an unstitching of life, and life and loss are inextricably linked until the unraveling in death is complete.

It follows that human life, at least biologically, is nothing more than a winding down, or in reference to Shakespeare's metaphor about sleep reprised in the title of this article, an unraveling of human existence to the point of destruction or of not being.

With the help of poetic language to bespeak his facile imagination, Shakespeare praises "sleep that knits up the ravell'd sleeve of care, the death of each day's life...."[2] That is to say, sleep thus serves us as a temporary "stop gap" within the lifelong process of perishing and allows us by sleep to knit things up again and to restore, at least for a day, the energy of life.

With this insight, moreover, the poetic genius of Shakespeare gives us in *Hamlet* an additional and valuable bit of wisdom to ponder. He injects this thought about the healing and restorative power of sleep through an image that has been a fascination for me since it first made me wonder while reading the passage. At one and the same time, his metaphorical connotation of sleep as "healing" juxtaposes itself and invites another connotation, a connotation of death as the "big sleep" or the final sleep of life. And the wondering leads me now to focus on the constant need for sleep as the anodyne for loss that is able to knit up the "ravell'd sleeve," the sleeve that now metaphorically stands in for the span of life from birth to death. As we are so well aware, the zest of life, the energy, the joie de vivre of every day wears life down, and it needs to be renewed again and again. Sleep may knit it up again for a new day, but the unraveling is inexorable until, as Hamlet asks himself, "in that sleep of death, what dreams may come?"[3] Or is it just as likely, no dreams at all?

The ruminations of Hamlet can easily invite us to share his depressive assessment of human life. Might the anger and frustration of the "melancholy Dane" infect us with the same despair of life that ended in the fate of the rejected Ophelia, singing her woes to the willow tree before drowning herself from madness, or was it sadness? How do we avoid or overcome the desperation that follows knowing the bald fact of human mortality—without a reply yet? What personal response is available to lift us up above negativity and to find meaning and purpose in the unalterable phases of life's unraveling? Since poetic imagination can convey truth deeply and powerfully and often also more truthfully than plain language, a wild flight of my own imagination asks me to employ a likeness to music in a frail attempt, if not to fathom the mystery, then to at least alleviate despair about the impermanence and fragility of human life.

From my more whimsical and less severe point of view, it is possible to use a figure of speech, a simile, and to think of loss as an aspect of music that is part of its nature and exactly responsible for its beauty. And loss may be so in human life and exactly responsible for its beauty. Loss in life may be likened to a few musical notes that gradually contribute to a melody, a rapturous melody or theme of life. In music, each note alone is not music at all, and by itself a single note can never become a melody. It is necessary that each note must perish so that the music can live. Taken all together, these bits and pieces of sound vanish, but as they do, something more than any one of them begins to come into being. Philosophers like to say that, as human beings, we seek meaning in life. Can this be like the way that each day of human life, as it passes, gives meaning and brings into existence something more than it is in itself? Do all the days of life have meaning and establish for us an emotional introduction or prelude to the inevitable experience of death, something final and unknown and perhaps more wondrous in meaning than anything life until then has had to offer?

Death is the last note sounded in life, the last and very final loss, of which there are no more. But is there a melody? Is there a song that sings? To be sure, each note of music already sounded is part of something more than itself and the melody does not live, does not come into being, until the single note loses voice and perishes. Is it not, though, still within the melody that was "in the making"? In the same way, just as intertwining themes in a musical prelude do not deliver full emotional resonance until they unfold within the dramatic development that follows in an opera or in a symphony, so too all the meanings of loss in life, great and small, build together into a final crescendo of meaning, a realization that enables us to see life itself as loss. It is a realization that intrudes into awareness, no matter how bitter or sweet it is to accept or how obstinately we try to avoid the truth.

Weak and inadequate and never complete in meaning art may seem to be, but it says much more than simple words communicate. Music and painting and poetry and dance and every other genuine expression of art, however simple, have power beyond plain understanding and tell us what we cannot know in any other way. Together, they can be even more compelling. The artistic imagination of William Butler Yeats, for example, communicates an elusive experience of poetry, music, and dance as they become blended into one sense of beauty and truth. His poetic creativity in a single endeavor gives music and body movement in dance a unique meaning that defies simple and plain explanation. At the same time, the beauty of his poetic art tells us what we recognize to be utterly and thoroughly true. Consider, for example, our perplexity in the truth we discover in the beauty of the dance.

> O body swayed to music, O brightening glance,
> How can we know the dancer from the dance?[4]

The words at once delight and dumbfound us for meaning and startle us with truth. Dancer and body and music become some other thing, and only in the poetry do we begin to understand the truth that some other thing has come to be.

This is another truth. Every moment of time passed, every single breath taken, every heartbeat spent not only moves us forward in life but also removes us farther away from life. In view of this truth, what convictions, philosophical, spiritual, or religious can help us deal with that reality? Is it possible that our thoughts and feelings about the reality of human existence, about what life really is, can be a benefit and even help us live life better? If we listen to the wisdom of the great teachers of the past, in some way or other they insist on the absolute necessity of dealing with the truth about death and the absolute futility of attempting to avoid it.

Although this truth is a routine fact in all great wisdom teachings, it receives an emphasis in Buddhism that may seem almost morbid or even macabre. Almost contradictorily, serious reflection on the inevitability of death is advocated by the Buddha as not only admonitory but also beneficial for achievement of the "art of being truly alive." Equally difficult to perceive at first is the contention in Buddhist teaching that, rather than holding us in the grip of fear and apprehension of death, the practice of "maranasati" or "death awareness" is actually the path to liberation and Nirvana. As an introduction to this practice of reflection, Larry Rosenberg assures us that "the shining light of death can liberate our life." He explains that the practice is not for everyone and is helpful only when the person is ready for it. Nevertheless, it is best considered sooner rather than later because, as he says, so far as death is concerned, the time is now.

> Death is not waiting for us at the end of the road. It is walking with us the whole time. We are fascinated by disaster epics, like the story of the Titanic, but the truth is we are all on the Titanic, right now. We just image it's a pleasure cruise, just as the people on the Titanic did. At the same time, we harbor a huge amount of unfelt fear about sickness, aging and death, and that fear robs us of vitality, partly because we expend so much energy avoiding and repressing it. Bringing up this fear and facing it...is a great enhancement to our lives. Really facing death enables us to appreciate and make the best use of our life in a whole new way.[5]

None of this is a revelation for anyone beyond childhood. In the practice of death awareness, however, the five contemplations that are presented for frequent reflection in Buddhism are nonetheless formidable.

1. I am subject to aging. Aging is unavoidable.
2. I am subject to illness. Illness is unavoidable.
3. I am subject to death. Death is unavoidable.

4. I will grow different, separate from all that is dear and appealing to me.
5. I am the owner of my actions. Whatever I do, for good or ill, to that I will fall heir.[6]

Despite the foreboding tone of the practice, in Asian countries it has been venerated for centuries as the highest form of reflection. "Of all the footprints," the Buddha said, "that of the elephant is supreme. Similarly, of all mindfulness meditation, that on death is supreme."[7] In the Buddhist tradition and in keeping with an expectation of the final achievement of Nirvana, consolation at the time of death appears to be rooted in the notion of contact with a "Fundamental Mind," which is not subject to death and is the basis for the experience of a kind of transcendence that moves beyond death and is independent of it.

However beneficial these meditations may be regarded in ancient tradition, they remain ominous to the Western frame of mind. Mostly they are fearsome. And in the passage from *Hamlet* that is largely the impetus for an elaboration of these fears that paralyze Hamlet, Shakespeare provides a description of what has become the prevalent modern attitude of aversion to the thought of death as a reality in life. In what is without question the most famous soliloquy in all of his plays and one of the most dramatic moments in the history of the stage: William Shakespeare prompts Hamlet, while grieving over the loss of his father and raging over the guilt and lascivious relationship of his murderous uncle and his adulterous mother, to ruminate on the mystery of death. In this desperate moment, Hamlet contemplates taking his own life as a way to escape the ponderous obligation of a dutiful son to revenge the death of his father, but he cannot act. His anger and despair bring him to the verge of self-destruction, and he can do nothing. He can do nothing because he fears the outcome, the mystery of what lies behind that irreparable step. He ponders the imponderable.

> To be or not to be, that is the question:
> Whether 'tis nobler in the mind to suffer
> The slings and arrows of outrageous fortune,
> Or to take arms against a sea of troubles,
> And by opposing end them. To die, to sleep—
> No more—and by a sleep to say we end
> The heartache and the thousand natural shocks
> That flesh is heir to. 'Tis a consummation
> Devoutly to be wished. To die, to sleep—
> To sleep, perchance to dream. Ay, there's the rub,
> For in that sleep of death what dreams may come,
> When we have shuffled off this mortal coil,
> Must give us pause. There's the respect
> That makes calamity of so long live.[8]

The passage prompts us as well to wonder about what lies behind the veil of that inevitable event in life. Is that the final answer to the great question? Will death itself be but a kind of dream, an unending dream or, as some say, a drifting away into nothingness? Shakespeare exploits the dramatic impact of death's inscrutability but, sharing the limitations of every human being, can provide for us no adequate answer to the question. Instead, Hamlet decides that it is better for him to be a coward and to suffer "the slings and arrows of outrageous fortune" rather than to end it all. And we are left to our own ruminations.

So it seems to be then, that in this metaphorical explanation of what life is, we discover it to be a never-ending process of having and giving up, possessing and losing, until there is nothing more to lose and the regaining happens not again. Very likely, we will never get in our understanding beyond whatever bits of understanding we can derive from metaphor. Still, we may find in this metaphor of sleep, that knits up the unraveling, a glimpse into the mystery of life and its partner death. We may catch a glimpse of it in what we know in the everyday experience of loss. Loss as the unraveling of life is, perhaps, all that can sum up for us what life itself in the long run has for its ultimate meaning. Late or soon in life, the inevitability of loss intrudes into awareness and shatters the delusion of life always being the same.

This episode in the life of a very young child introduced her to the painfulness of loss all too soon. But late or soon, are we ever really ready to know the pain? Nine-year-old Shelby had just been sent to bed at the end of a terrible day. It was a terrible and sad day for a little girl. It was a day that she could not completely understand and did not want to accept. Her grandmother—my sister—had just died.

Shelby was frightened and did not want to be alone. She saw the little rocking chair that she had used during visits to her grandmother's house, where it always seemed to be waiting just for her. As she sat in it close to her grandmother, she would rock gently and feel warm and comfortable and loved. Now here it was in her own room, placed there by her mother, who had thought it would be a comfort for Shelby to have it with her through the night. But it was not a comfort there in the shadows. It just made her feel more alone and more sad. The sadness and the loneliness drove the little girl out of bed, and she ran crying into her mother's room and into her arms.

I was there when Shelby ran into her mother's room. I stood dumbfounded and helpless at the sight of the girl. It was not a surprise for me to see Shelby crying as she jumped into her mother's bed and was smothered into her arms. It was a terrible day for all of us, and we all still cried, at times only silent and dry tears as grown-ups often do. But it was the unexpected feeling of helplessness that pulled me, too, deep down like a dead-weight anchor to a place where I, like Shelby, did not want to be.

I did not want to be in that place where there are no complete answers and where we have to face the mystery of life and death without answers. We do, of course, have answers to give, kind and tender and loving words that we believe, and we want the words to give comfort and heal the hurt. Those were the words that

Shelby heard from her mother, but they did not heal the hurt, because they cannot heal a hurt that will not ever really heal.

"Shelby dear," her mother said, who had her own painful grief to cope with. "Nana isn't suffering anymore and she is in heaven now but she still loves you. And she will always be with you and love you and care for you." Then there were no more words. Nothing there in the room, except the scream of a little child who had to cry out the truth, the only truth a child can really understand and will ever really know. "Mommy, I know Nana's in heaven, I know. But it will never be the same!" The words pierced my own heart and held me in a moment that I wanted to run away from. I wanted to escape the recognition of undeniable and unalterable truth. "But it will never be the same." My sister had died. What was before will be no longer—it is gone forever and faded into the past, not to be regained.

It will never be the same. That is the truth of loss, and it is the meaning of loss in life, and, in truth, loss is ever a part of life. Ordinarily, loss is what we speak of in the event of death, when we want to commiserate and offer sympathy for a loss. It is a formal recognition of the sadness and grieving that leaves survivors bereft and "at a loss" when death removes someone beloved and cherished from their lives. In that understanding, the notion of loss is directed toward an external deprivation, as if some "outside" thing has been taken away. The notion is accurate but limited, because it does not include the full range of our human experience of loss.

Perhaps instinctively we resist wanting to think, to know, or to admit to ourselves that by its very nature loss is that ineluctable dimension of life itself. To live now is to move away from now to another now to come or even not to come. It is the inevitable and unpredictable reality of existence. Human experience of loss, then, unless denied, thwarted, or suppressed, will include the full range of psychic awareness. It will be a realization that life itself is an ongoing diminishment of our human being. It is loss in that sense that can be called "the unraveling of life."

Before Shelby had run into that room, it had been quiet, just adults talking softly about the important things that needed to be discussed, decided on, and done. In the quiet, I was able to think about everything I had to do. But it was the stark reality of a new and painful truth too soon forced into the awareness of a child that riveted my attention and forced me into submission to another truth. It will never be the same for me, I am no longer the same, I am diminished and at a loss.

I was less. I was without, without—and I did not know how to complete the thought and to say what I was without: without my sister, the "Nana" whom Shelby grieved; without my sister to be there for me, to call me by name, to listen to me when I spoke. That certainly was true. But, what was it exactly that I had lost? I know that I *had* lost, and in a sense, I *was* lost, or as we sometimes hear it said was "at a loss." The "I" that was could never be the same again. Was it my own childhood realization, deepened and hidden, that was then at once awakened within me, aroused because it was the awful truth that had to be called forth—a truth I had to face as the only explanation for what life now meant for me? Because we know who we are and what we have, we must also know who we are in life will not always be so and what we have in life we will not always have. It will never be the same. Human life is inexorable change and loss.

There is a touch of irony in this bitter fact of life. We are called to engage in life and many do so happily. Answering the call to be fully alive, we can be active in the most intense and exhilarating experiences of life that it is possible for us to know. Ironically, the more satisfying and rewarding life becomes for us, the more painful and wrenching will be the loss of what it is. Those who are able to feel most deeply the thrills of life are able to feel most deeply the loss of those thrills. Gifted artists and performers, who have worked to reach the high points of achievement, become aware that the peaks of life are ephemeral. The peaks of life are destined to pass on as soon as they come, because with the waning of excellence, they must go.

George Bernard Shaw, who lived to a ripe old age, is thought to have lamented the loss of his youth by praising youth as such a glorious and wonderful thing to have that it is a "shame to waste it on the young." Inclined as we may be to agree with Shaw that youth is a precious time of life, we may still not begrudge the young their youth. Instead we can be happy with them, because they have it to enjoy. Nor do we believe that Shaw wanted to grasp youth away from the young but rather to make all of us appreciate it more. So it is in Buddhist meditation that realization of loss in life enables us to be more alive to life, and regret for what has come and passed distracts from what is now and whatever is yet to come.

One of the British poets who ushered in the pessimism of the twentieth century, A. E. Houseman, obsessed more about what life takes away from us than about what life can give to us. His "spiritual journey" led him from paganism to deism and finally to atheism and left him with no thought about loss in life except its inevitability. So dismal was his outlook on life that one critic described him as a poet "who wrote blithely about murder and suicide, personal betrayal and cosmic injustice."[9] Like Hamlet, who thought of death as a "consummation devoutly to be wished" but had no stomach for suicide, Houseman thought of death as release from the troubles and woes of life. In one of his most famous poems, "To an Athlete Dying Young," Houseman praised death in the splendor of youth, because it cheated time of the privilege of stealing youth away. In the poem, a young athlete who made his town proud and happy as winner of a race is carried home in triumph "shoulder high" amid cheers. Not long after, and still in the beauty of his youth, an untimely death brings the athlete once again "shoulder high" when he must be carried along "the road all runners come" to his final resting place in the town cemetery. For whatever the reason of his untimely death, still the athlete was a "smart lad to slip betimes away," before the laurel of his victory crown withers, "withers quicker than the rose."

Houseman's view of the finality of death and hopelessness of life is evident in his description of the ultimate destiny of the young man, to be set down at the threshold of his new home in the cemetery, where he will forever be a "townsman of a stiller town." A more explicit statement of the futility of human striving can be detected in the sentiment Houseman uses to end the poem. An early death spares the athlete the need to experience more grievous loss, loss of triumphs and renown, implicitly the only rewards of life. Thus the young lad will avoid this worse fate and "will not swell the rout / Of lads that wore their honors out." He will never be deprived of his honors and never be a runner who can no longer run or whose "renown outran him" and his fame died "before the man." Was the poet overly negative about the process of human aging and the necessity of loss that is the natural part of living? Is death indeed, as Hamlet mused in his contemplation of suicide, "a consummation devoutly to be wished?" For some individuals who see life as worthwhile only in its fullness, loss, apparently hard loss of any kind, causes life to be so bereft and void that life itself is no longer bearable.

Ernest Hemingway, who knew and admired the skills of the matador dodging with ease and grace the ferocity of an enraged bull, celebrated life in all its fullness and exulted in human courage in the face of danger and even death. *For Whom the Bell Tolls*, one of his greatest novels, was a tribute to the courage of those who fought for freedom in the Spanish civil war. Courage in war and of the bullfighter in the face of death he could admire, but what about courage in the face of loss? Is loss, loss in life and the grieving that accompanies it, so unbearable that it terrifies even the brave? For a man who has much, there is much to lose. In his life Hemingway had much to lose, not only the vigor of his youth and manly good looks but also the waning of his creativity as age approached. Whether or not this was a preoccupation of Hemingway's, who can say? He did in his writing grieve vicariously for the loss of courage and grace as well as the loss of beauty and youth and romance. No need for him to be advised by the poet John Donne's injunction, because he knew it in his mind, and as time passed he felt it in his own aging and in his bones. Hemingway and Donne together rang the same church bell and proclaimed the same funeral message: loss and its companion death await everyone who walks the earth.

> No man is an illand, intire of its selfe; every man is a peece of the Continent, a part of the maine;
>
> ...
>
> And therefore never send to know for whom the bell tolls; it tolls for thee.[11]

Was it even more so that for Hemingway any waning of his inimitable precision of language and narrative genius as well as the lost vigor of youth with its courage and grace were to him a reality as of death itself? Was life then for him no longer life but the same as death? Was such a life to him more dreadful than death? Complaining about his struggle with manic depression, he said "If I can't exist on my own terms, then existence is impossible....That is how I've lived, and that is how I *must* live—or not live."[12] Death came to him peremptorily before his final decrepitude and by his own hand with a gun from his prized collection of guns, guns that also represented for him his celebrated prowess as a hunter of prey on African safari. Unreasonable resistance to giving loss and death itself a rightful place in our estimation of life exacts a heavy toll.

In the 1939 film *Stagecoach*, the actor John Wayne, idealized as a popular paragon of manly valor in the face of adversity, uttered the laconic phrase "a man's got to do what a man's got to do." The words became a trite but venerable colloquialism for either mocking or adulating the stalwart and fearless manliness depicted in what Hollywood called the "action hero," whose courage never falters nor prevents him from performing his duty. A "real man" will do what is necessary, no matter how hard it is, and a real man is what Ernest Hemingway considered himself to be. He did all the things indicative of what a "real man" wants to do, traveling to exotic and dangerous places, fishing and hunting big game on safari in Africa, and in his lifetime rising to the pinnacle of wealth and fame and success in his profession.

Hamlet was deterred from self-destruction by "the dread of something after death, the undiscovered country from whose bourn no traveler returns"; and Shakespeare attributes the dread seemingly to the fear instilled in Hamlet by conscience, which "does make cowards of us all." Like all authors telling a story, Shakespeare can inject any hint of a reason that suits his fancy for explanation, but real life does not give up its answers easily. Imbedded somewhere in the life of Hemingway, an adventurer, a man of action who did not flinch facing fear, lies a reason to explain why he decided to rush toward death and meet it head-on. And somewhere imbedded in the life of each one of us lies an explanation for what loss means for us and how we accept and live with it in life.

Joyce Rupp has an interesting approach to loss and speaks of loss in terms of a "goodbye." It is not only interesting but also informative, because it anchors loss in the quotidian of ordinary life experience. What could be more ordinary than our childhood experience, when we first learned to say goodbye to grandparents, who must return home after a visit at Christmas or at a first birthday party? Following after that elementary lesson of life come the many departures and leave-takings that fill our days and years always with a sense, either vague or distinctive, of something gone away from us, missing for awhile or perhaps even forever lost.

> What is a goodbye? It is an empty place in us. It is any situation in which there is some kind of loss, some incompleteness, when a space is created in us that cries out to be filled. Goodbyes are any of those times when we find ourselves without a someone or a something that has given our life meaning and value, when a dimension of our life seems to be out of place or unfulfilled. Goodbyes are all of those experiences that leave us with a hollow feeling someplace deep inside.[13]

Can all of our goodbyes in a way bear something reminiscent of the traumatic first loss of the closeness of mother that seeks a desperate comfort in the infant's transitional object? Are the tears of dear friends or lovers departing for what may be an interminable separation psychically related to the tears of the child left on that first day at school and separation from home? What is instructive in Rupp's approach is her insight that the "ordinary" and routine goodbyes of life are necessary and helpful experiences for psychic and spiritual growth. She notes also that, while losses are part of each day of life, they sometimes choose us and we sometimes must choose them. Regardless of choice, all leave-takings introduce us to the reality of life and are essential for spiritual growth.

There is a city in Northern Ireland that some of the Irish will call "Londonderry" and others will only call "Derry." It is a place that has known grief and loss, in turmoil and in death, and in many, many, many sad and happy goodbyes. It is the town where I began to understand and appreciate how some long ago goodbyes gave my life to me here so far away from where the goodbyes took place. Only there did I begin to feel the happiness and the sorrows that those goodbyes held.

A large sculpture in the center of the town of Derry depicts an Irish family in departure. It tells the story of goodbyes, the goodbyes of Irish emigrants leaving a poor and barren land to build a future in a land across the sea.[14] Each leave-taking was unique and all were the same—with the same sadness and the same happiness. The figures in the sculpture tell just one story, because it is only one goodbye for those who leave and those who remain. An elderly mother and father stand back together and alone, as a young family of husband and wife and their children move off ahead of them, off to a new life, leaving the past behind. The little boy clutches his fiddle and his mother's hand as they walk into the distance. Alongside them, his sister carries her books and clings to her father. They have one another and these few mementos to take with them into a new life leaving their grandparents behind. One small child faces forward with the eagerness and joy of leaving and the other looks back sadly to wave. From that glance backward, what will the child carry away? What will be the remnant of a last glimpse of the children for the grandparents to cherish in memory? The sturdy father and his son may recall the eagerness and joy of leaving. For them departure promised hope and happiness in the future, yet all goodbyes tell the same story of happiness and joy. We look upon one family in departure, and we know the story of it all.

When I was a child walking home from school, I delighted in the autumn leaves. They seemed to be waiting there for me in neat little piles along the sidewalks in West Philadelphia, where we lived. I indulged in the pleasure of crunching through them and sometimes in the mischief of kicking them high into the air, so that they scattered in all directions and glided gracefully to the ground. They might once in a while to my delight show off a glint of colors from the late afternoon sun. In the life of a child, the autumn leaves can be fun to jump into and roll around in and nothing more. They carry with them no thoughts or feelings or any other meaning but just to be there. That was a time when we did not know that the leaves are a loss.

We grow up to see the autumn leaves through a window pane, "those autumn leaves of red and gold," and now we know that it is not just another day that has passed but a time of life. A season has passed, another time of year gone by that will not come back again. From all the seasons gone by, we have gathered to ourselves bits and pieces of life that are with us still and never go away entirely, because when each one returns, it has a meaning of its own that returns to us in thought. Some meanings of the seasons are writ large in common memory and we share those thoughts and meanings in our most profound utterance, "For everything there is a season, and a time for every matter under heaven: a time to be born and a time to die..." (Eccl 3:1–2).

As a young girl eighteen years of age, my grandmother came from Ireland and stayed here in Philadelphia until her death, except for one visit late in life for a Eucharistic Congress in the

1930s, long after the death of her parents, to whom she had said her goodbye long ago. That is all the information I have about how Nana left her parents and brothers and sisters at home to join cousins who waited to greet her in Philadelphia. How she made the journey and when she made her arrival are lost in family history. Only a snippet of a clue remains for me to tell. My sister recalled being with Nana in her later years, when she lived with us as part of the family. Nana was unusually quiet at this one time they were alone together, and she was lost in reverie. It was her special time of year, she said to her grandchild, her autumn of the year, when she was preoccupied with "long thoughts." She said "long thoughts"—it was her Irish way of talking about the deep thoughts no words can say. The "long thoughts" she never put into words, but they were thoughts that took her back across the sea in longing, longing for what used to be.

Gerard Manley Hopkins was a poet who could find words for "long thoughts." With his exceptional style of poetry, he was able to find words for deep thoughts that startle us with meaning. A devoutly religious poet, Hopkins gave deeper meaning to the passing of the seasons into the time of falling leaves. In the first line of the poem, "Spring and Fall, to a Young Child," Hopkins addresses all of us in her name and brings us to know, in a way unknown to us before, that all our grieving in life is one sorrow united in human loss and human mortality. He brings us into the feelings of a child grieving over the loss of all the beauty birthed in spring and chides her and us gently for a childish sorrowing over the dying leaves. The leaves will return, and we will grow "colder" to the loss, because in a childish way we do not yet know what it is.

> Margaret, are you grieving
> Over Goldengrove unleaving?
> With your fresh thoughts care for, can you?
> Ah! As the heart grows older
> It will come to such sights colder
> By and by, nor spare a sigh

Though worlds of wanwood leafmeal lie;
And yet you will weep and know why.

The startling truth is that, "as the heart grows older," and we begin to become more intimate with all our grieving, only then can we know "sorrow's springs are the same." They are what they are, because all loss and the grieving for it is the same loss, no matter what name we give to it or no name at all. When words of the mouth fail us and the mind can tell us nothing, the spirit within us knows what it hears. And the heart tells us what it is we grieve for.

Now no matter, child, the name:
Sorrow's springs are the same.
Nor mouth had, no nor mind, expressed
What heart heard of, ghost guessed:
It is the blight man was born for,
It is Margaret you mourn for.[15]

There is a need within us to be connected, to be one. Some say a "holy longing" and others say simply "wanting bliss." The poet says it—"and yet you will weep and know why"—and life teaches us the truth for us to know, the truth that is there in life for us to learn. All our weeping is the same. From the first moment we lose hold of Mommy's hand to the last release of breath, all our weeping is the same.

Notes

1. *Merriam-Webster's Collegiate Dictionary*, 11th ed. (Springfield, MA: Merriam-Webster, 2003).

2. William Shakespeare, *Macbeth*, Arden edition, ed. Kenneth Muir (London and New York: Routledge, 1992), act 2, scene 2, p. 54.

3. William Shakespeare, *Hamlet, Prince of Denmark*, ed. Constance Jordan (New York: Pearson/Longman, 2005), act 3, scene 1, pp. 63–64.

4. William Butler Yeats, "Among School Children," *A Treasury of Great Poems*, ed. Louis Untermeyer (New York: Simon and Schuster, 1942), 1041.

5. Larry Rosenberg, *Living in the Light of Death: On the Art of Being Truly Alive* (Boston: Shambhala, 2000), 13.

6. Ibid., 14.

7. Ibid., 15.

8. Shakespeare, *Hamlet*, ed. Jordan, act 3, scene 1, pp. 63–64.

9. Untermeyer, *Treasury of Great Poems*, 1022.

10. A. E. Houseman, "To an Athlete Dying Young," *Treasury of Great Poems*, ed. Untermeyer, 1029.

11. John Donne, "For Whom the Bell Tolls," *The Complete Poetry and Selected Prose of John Donne*, ed. Charles M. Coffin (New York: Modern Library, 2001), 446.

12. Jeffrey Meyers, *Hemingway: A Biography* (New York: Harper & Row, 1985), 559–61.

13. Joyce Rupp, *Praying Our Goodbyes* (Notre Dame, IN: Ave Maria Press, 2009), 10.

14. The sculpture by Eamonn O'Doherty was completed in 1990 and is at Waterloo Place in Derry, Ireland. O'Doherty studied at the Graduate School of Design at Harvard University and at the University of Jordan in Nebraska.

15. Gerard Manley Hopkins, "Spring and Fall, to a Young Child," *Poems of Gerard Manley Hopkins*, ed. W. H. Gardner (New York / London: Oxford University Press, 1948), 94.

9

Family

Seeking the Fingerprint of God in Times of Illness

Beverly Anne Musgrave

In May of 1990 I was stressed beyond my limits, completing the writing of my PhD dissertation, tabulating the data, preparing for my oral defense in June, working fifty hours a week. Because of this mental and emotional overload, the truth of the statement "the body remembers" (Rothschild 2000) became for me a stark reality. Obviously I was running on empty, and I was brought to a screeching halt. My heart was racing over two hundred beats a minute. All at once, I found myself in the Coronary Care Unit (CCU) of a hospital.

For the purpose of this paper, I want to focus only on my first night in that CCU and what it meant to me. Anxious, weak, confused, and weepy, I was more concerned about the deadline for my doctoral defense than I was about my own health. After several hours of doctors, nurses, and specialists gathering round me, speaking in anxious terms, and beginning a series of tests and treatments, finally they all left my room. My friends, who were pacing the floor, also left because they were asked to leave. Now, all alone in the emptiness of silence, I face my self. The walls seem to close in on me, and my thoughts turn to the words of a great poet, W. B. Yeats:

Now that my ladder's gone
I must lie down where all ladders start,
In the foul rag-and-bone shop of the heart.

This seemingly protective environment of the CCU consisted of a small room with three cold glass walls. Many strange machines were ticking, clicking, beeping like hens in the barnyard. I could not make any sense of the mysterious lines and scratches that beamed over and over on the computer near my bed. I realize that I am like a prisoner, held captive by wires and tubes going in all directions. Like this, I try to pray.

At that moment my wonderful doctor came into the room, not with his usual welcoming smile but with a serious expression, reflecting something painful in his eyes. As he sits down on my bed, he expresses his concern for my problem. "If we can get you through the night," he says, "we will then work on a plan to get you better." Amazed, startled, and bewildered to hear this news with an "if" attached to it, in panic I ask him, "What is my problem?" That was when I was first introduced to my ventricular tachycardia. I ask for a layperson's definition and hear the ominous reply "it is sudden death syndrome." Then I ask him "are you telling me I could die at any time?" A kindly but dreaded response comes back to me. "Yes. But with proper medication and treatment, we will try to get your heart arrhythmia under control." Then, with compassion and genuine concern, he said he would see me through the process. He was true to his word.

Alone once again when he left me, I feel the chilling silence beating off the glass walls. I try once again to pray. Meeting God face-to-face tonight, I realize, is a real possibility. "I want to meet you, Lord, surely some time, but not so soon," I begged. And then I added quickly, "definitely, not now. I have work to complete." My anxiety rushes me headlong onto the seashore of my mind, collapsing me in the "rag-and-bone shop of my heart." I begin to examine my life and give thanks, by name, for the significant people who are a part of my life. Then, the waves of anxiety, like a heavy life-threatening tsunami, overwhelm my sense of safety and my very existence. Tethered to the bed and alone, I feel like an animal caught in a cage. All of this is so overwhelming that I cry. I cry from the depths of my soul, "God be with me!"

As I try to hold on to life by my fingernails, the night shift of the nursing staff comes in. When this happens and in the middle of my inner emotional tsunami, I see a beautiful and peace-bearing black nurse enter my room. After a brief greeting, she said, "Sleeping will help your heart. Do you think you can go to sleep?" I laughingly respond, "That is easy for you to say." With great empathy and a gentle voice, she responds, "You are in a serious condition. I understand. But a good sleep will help you get stronger."

Then this total stranger said something and did something that I believe changed my life. "I will take my chair and sit here in the doorway. I will be able to hear every change, and I will monitor your condition. I am with you." Desperately, I search her compassionate eyes. Finally, her eyes tell me I can believe her, and I fall fast asleep.

The next morning somewhere around 5 a.m., I awake. Through my eyelashes, I am able to see a faint vision that is forever etched in my mind. In the low dim lights of the CCU, I glimpse this warm, compassionate angel of mercy, sitting in a hard-back chair in the doorway of my life and death. This sight of a total stranger sitting with me through this dark night of my soul moves me to uncontrollable tears and profound gratitude. "It looks like we made it," I say in gratitude. "Indeed we did," she cheerfully responds.

Weeks later, after I was released from the tubes and wires and gratefully left the cold glass walls, I try to bring a gift to the beautiful stranger who sat with me through the night of my life and death, giving me faith and courage. In order to thank her, I returned to the hospital. At the nursing station, I gave the date and time of my first night in the CCU and offered a description of my gracious helper. After checking and rechecking their schedule, the nurse in charge informed me that there was no nurse in the nursing department that fit my description. My medical record showed that no one stayed with me through that night.

This startling realization brought to my mind the Greek god Hermes, the god of transitions, and I remembered that transitions always move through liminality. The English word *liminality* comes from the Latin *limen*, meaning "doorway" or "threshold." Entering a room or leaving it, one crosses a "limen" and into a borderline space. One is in liminality, if only for a half a second. The archetype that is represented by the Greek god Hermes reflects an experience that is a sensed presence of the unconscious. It happens whenever life throws us into a state of liminality (Stein 1983). This compassionate nurse sitting in my doorway that night offered to me a "holding environment." It was a fleeting moment of liminality that enabled a creative movement into the depths of the unknown psychological and spiritual territory of myself. This step into liminality created a major transition in my life.

The renowned British poet T. S. Eliot said: "The end of all exploring will be to arrive at the beginning and know the place for the first time." Illness is a dangerous experience of being taken into the threshold of life from which the end can be observed. This dangerous and paradoxical gift of my illness offered to me "a dangerous opportunity." The emotional tsunami of my life brought me back to the source of my life and to God's ever-caring-always-active presence in my life. And now, I know the place. I know the place for the first time.

Illness is often a detour, often a jarring moment in time that calls forth courage in the face of fear. It questions the meaning of life, and serious illness ushers in serious life tasks. Karl Rahner (1978) calls this task "the surrender of self trustfully and hopefully to the insoluble mystery we call God" (37). The paradoxical gift of illness is offered not only to the patient but to the family and loved ones of the patient as well. It is a "dangerous opportunity" for all. It can be for both the patient and the family a call to surrender to the insoluble mystery we call God.

This paper explores also what the paradoxical gift of illness can mean to the patient and to the family. To do so, it will turn to a defining and an exploring of some of the guiding principles that can assist the patient and family deal with an illness, namely, the meaning of family; the meaning of self; the self in relation to family; empathy and differentiation; anxiety; nonanxious presence; and lastly an exploration of a possible surrender to the insoluble mystery of God, as one moves through the unique personal journey of finding meaning in illness and liminality, a "dangerous opportunity."

The Family

When illness unexpectedly rings the doorbell, the family system is permanently jarred and the solidity of the family is often brought into question. Defining family in the midst of the complexities of modern life is a major dilemma. Defining a *normal* family is filled with complexities and exceptions, namely, single-parent families; lesbian and gay families; adoptive families; intermarriage; stepparents and stepchildren; interfaith marriages; and remarriage (Walsh 2003). As Epstein et al. (2003) state, attempting to arrive at a definition of a healthy or normal family seems to be, or indeed may actually be, a fool's errand. This was certainly my experience, when I tried to uncover a definition of family. In the McMaster Model of Family Functioning, the family is seen as an open system consisting of subsystems (individual, marital dyad) and relating to other larger systems (extended family, school, industry, religion) (Epstein and Bishop 1973). This definition, with the explicit and implicit rules and actions by members that monitor one another's behavior, informs my definition of family.

> Family is an open system. It is the "sacred and holding environment" of a life-long relational matrix. It is a relational system that sets up behaviors and patterns of communication, positive and negative, for its members

> that continue into their life-long interactions both inside and outside the system. Because the matrix of family life is present and operational in all personal interactions, it is to some extent always responsible for who I AM and for who I AM with others. Family is the foundational base for our intimacy journey. It sets in motion the ongoing narrative of our relational style from childhood to adulthood. Finally, family creates a developmental process that includes: trans-generational meaning, culture, religion, gender perspectives, values and beliefs. (Musgrave 2007, 179–80)

The holding environment of family life not only encompasses the parents and the siblings, but also includes, consciously or unconsciously, the multigenerational systems of beliefs, religion, values, and culture and the roles of gender in a particular family. In other words, this conscious or unconscious systemic core of family often rushes to center stage when loss, illness, and death knock on the family's door. At this moment in time, the many-colored threads that make up the family quilt can tighten or sometimes even unravel altogether. If family members have never worked together to find a common solution, have never taken the time to respectfully listen to one another, have never reflected on the unique differentiated relational style of individual members, then this crisis can be a breaking point. Or it can be an opportunity to grow.

The Self/the Self system

The family is a relational matrix; the relational matrix is made up of individuals. The family unit is central to our lives. It is in the family that we learn to be a self. For purposes of this paper, I offer my definition of the self: "Self is a process of extending oneself (a solid mature self) actively, listening and responding to the cognitive and affective world of another (empathy) while remaining a differentiated 'self-in-relation'" (Musgrave 2007,

178–79). Development of the story of the "real self," or the "self system," evolves over a lifetime. Most importantly, this experience of self is relational. The experience of self and the growth of the self are organized and lived in the context of relationship, relationship to self, to God, and to others. Harry Stack Sullivan (1940) states it this way:

> The individual is in continual interaction with other people. The individual's personality takes shape in an environment composed of other people. The personality or self is not something that resides "inside" the individual, but rather something that resides with others. Personality is the relatively enduring pattern of recurrent interpersonal situations which characterize a human life. (xi)

Focusing on individuals without considering the relationships that make up the interpersonal shaping of the self in the context of family is empty, especially when exploring the impact of illness. For a case in point, my uncle Lloyd was born with Down syndrome. He lived next door with my grandparents. On a daily basis, Lloyd visited our family and all five neighbors on the street, offering his gift of a warm smile and generous hugs after collecting the mail, his daily contribution to the community. On Sundays, he picked up the basket and at the appointed time proudly gathered the collection in our small country church. Everyone knew him, trusted him, and loved him. He lived a long wonderful life of sixty-five years, not the expected life for someone with Down syndrome.

When I look back at his long creative life, I am in total awe of my grandparents. They did not have a university education, nor did they have, in those days, the benefits of the recent medical and psychological knowledge on Down syndrome. But they did have a profound faith and boundless love and respect for the unique and special child God sent to them. When invited to dinner, it was clear that they would attend only if Lloyd was also welcome. He was always included in every family event; he was special and everyone was expected to respect him. Lloyd was given a loving "holding environment" and each one of us learned the meaning of acceptance of the other and appreciation of difference in the midst of the complexity of these family ties. The words of Desmond Tutu (1995) enrich the profound truth of this example.

> A fundamental truth about us is that we are made to live a delicate network of interdependence with one another, with God and with the rest of God's creation. We say in our African idiom, "A person is a person through other persons." A solitary human person is a contradiction in terms. We are made for complementarity. I have gifts that you do not; you have gifts that I do not. Voilà! So we need each other to become fully human. (xiv)

Differentiation

The emotional interrelational system comprises a complex web of family ties over generations, in which people simply cannot alter to whom they are related. We are made for complementarity. This generational web becomes the central focus when a member of the family becomes critically ill. Long before illness visits a family, it is imperative to develop a solid self. This self, which Bowen (1974) and others call the differentiated self, is an intrapsychic as well as an interpersonal concept. Intrapsychic differentiation is the ability to separate feeling from thinking. This ability to be a differentiated self means that one is an autonomous self with an autonomous identity (Friedman 1985).

David Schnarch (1997) takes Bowen's theory and clarifies differentiation in the following way. "Differentiation is your ability to maintain your sense of self when you are emotionally and/or physically close to others, especially as they become increasingly important to you" (56). Emotional fusion is the opposite of differentiation. Fusion is an invisible but tenacious connection. When someone is ill, it is important to allow the patient to continue to be a differentiated self. Sometimes in a desire to help, we fuse with the patient and in so doing take away the independence of the patient and leave the patient stranded with no way of doing for himself or herself and having no voice.

Differentiation is the key to mutuality. According to Shea (2005) the adult self is necessarily "a self-in-mutuality." Surrey (1991) notes that "the self gains vitality and enhancement in relationship and is not reduced or threatened by connection" (62). Said in another way, the adult, solid self is a differentiated self, able to relate to others in mutuality. The mutuality of differentiation demands an awareness of self in the context of the uniqueness of another; it involves awareness of the boundary between the self and other (Musgrave 2007, 181–83). The limen, the threshold, ushers us into the mystery that uncovers the mystery of God ever lurking within the mystery of human life itself.

A truly differentiated person is a "solid self," a "self-in-relation," open to the experiences of another, having the ability to be empathic. It is this mutuality of relating in the context of the uniqueness of another that is central to the family as illness envelops the system. As much as we may think we know a family member, we may not know the wishes and needs of this person in times of illness. This is where it is essential that we respect differences and allow the person who is ill to continue to be a differentiated self as long as it is possible. Illness should not take away that special aspect of the self, nor can we impose our beliefs and feelings on the person. This becomes more complicated in the family system, when several people believe that they know what is best even without consulting the patient—especially if the patient is still able to choose and decide for him- or herself.

So many systems are taken away from the patient in times of illness. The body fails and sometimes the medical system fails. For some people, it may seem as if the church too fails them when they need it the most. So it is essential that the family, having an unalterable and intimate relationship with the patient, sticks together and works as a relational unit for the good of the patient. The family members, in this relational matrix, each have a special relational style of communicating with one another. The ability to communicate in a spirit of mutual respect is necessary, if and when difficult decisions are to be made for the benefit of the patient. But making decisions at this critical time will often create anxiety.

Anxiety/Family Anxiety

Given the depth of the problem, given the possibility of major loss and even death, a family facing critical illness is a system in crisis. Sickness is systemic. Given the reality of a systemic effect, the challenge of maintaining a sense of self and a differentiated "self-in-relation," while tolerating the tension of the crisis, is pivotal. As a result of family tension, it is understandable that nerves get frayed and family members experience anxiety.

In his study of interpersonal process, Harry S. Sullivan (1953) focused on anxiety as the crucial factor determining the way an individual shapes his/her experience and his/her interaction with others. This is certainly the case when families are confronted with serious illness. As Sullivan noted, the fly in the ointment of nearly all human endeavors is anxiety. It affects thinking, communication, and processing information in an otherwise harmonious system of interpersonal communication (Mitchell and Black 1995, 68). The words of Martin Buber (1958) "all real living is meeting" aptly reflect and define the ideal of this kind of "harmonious system," which necessarily originates and endures in a family setting, because that is our primary place of meeting and of living. Nevertheless, the challenge of illness and the possibility of death call forth a special kind of meeting between the differentiated family members.

The first and possibly most difficult response to anxiety is empathy. For the purpose of this paper, I will use my own definition of empathy:

> It is the ability to tolerate the tension of being truly open to the experiences of another person, the ability to attempt actively to understand the subjective world of the other affectively and cognitively while at the same time remaining a differentiated self. (Musgrave 2003, 35)

When family members have very diverse points of view—from either their personal experience with the sick person or their unique position in the family (spouse, parent, sibling, or significant other)—which they feel gives them authority to speak for the person who is ill, it then becomes obvious that empathy, as defined above, is a major challenge. An ability to tolerate tension, to hear feelings, and to consider openly various points of view of others calls for a profound maturity. Often, earlier relational connections (or lack thereof) hurt, or unfinished business and guilt color the tenor of the family communications. Sometimes family members may not be aware of the depth of hidden pain and unfinished business that other family members bring to the table.

I recall meeting a woman in a hospital waiting room whose sister, to whom she had not spoken in twenty years, was dying. I asked if it would be helpful for me to go with her, when she visited her sister before she died. In preparing for the visit, she mentioned that she completely forgot the reason she and her sister had drifted apart. Now, of course, it made no sense for her to go on with her anger or for them to continue their estrangement. Their separation was especially sad and painful, since it was their last opportunity to ask forgiveness of each other and to spend time together with love and in peace.

Living with unexpressed hurt, anger, shame, or any other kind of negative relational feeling is an impediment to empathy and is, unfortunately, not uncommon when dealing with family illness. For that reason, it is valuable if at least one differentiated family member can offer what Friedman (1985) calls a "nonanxious presence." This offering of presence can facilitate the integrity and sometimes the peace of individual family members during the crisis of illness. The challenge is to be both nonanxious and present simultaneously. This is particularly difficult to do when a family loses its capacity to adapt to the stress of the moment.

Being both present and nonanxious, the family member contains her/his own anxiety and tries to develop clear-headed solutions. In other words, such a family member functions as a circuit breaker in the midst of the electrical storm of illness. When this occurs, anxiety is modified throughout the family system and the balance and boundaries of the family system can be clarified. This happens while empathically respecting the feelings and various points of view of each family member. Sullivan (1956) speaks to this in his desire to keep anxiety at a minimum, thus creating a space of security. This concern is stated, and very clearly, by Mitchell and Black (1995): "When anxiety is not a threat, the self-system fades into the background; needs for satisfaction emerge and operate as integrating tendencies drawing the individual into mutually satisfying interactions with others" (70). In the midst of the crisis of illness, loss, or death, it might be too much to expect that all family members will be drawn into the "mutually satisfying interaction." Especially in times of crisis and trauma, it is important to allow for individual differences and hopefully a "nonanxious presence" will offer the space and time for healing and for open communication. The words of the Roman Catholic Communion Rite, words we hear each time we attend Mass but possibly never really hear, can be a source of courage: "In your mercy keep us free from sin and protect us from all anxiety as we wait in joyful hope for the coming of our Savior, Jesus Christ." Hopefully, a nonanxious presence will be available and will offer the family space and time for healing and for open communication.

Seeking the Fingerprint of God

Life-death is a supreme mystery, representing the quintessential paradox from which no one escapes. Life and death are essential components that fill our days as surely as breathing and not breathing. Just as birth marks the joyous beginning of the first chapter in life, so death inevitably marks the last chapter and initiates the final movement in the dance of life back to God, from whence we have come. Gabriel Moran (2007) says "education begins no later than birth and ceases no earlier than death" (35). All living is an educational experience. His comment implies a major role in learning about the mystery of living and insinuates a question about the major role in learning about the mystery of illness and death in our education. What are we to make of the mystery of our human existence itself—in its beginning and in its ending? Our lives are always being shaped and reshaped from the first chapter of life until the closing curtain comes down. A significant aspect of this education often presents itself in the form of critical illness, a "dangerous opportunity." That is to say, illness and the "dangerous opportunity" that accompanies illness are part of our life-long education. Together they teach and inform purpose and meaning in the quintessential paradox of living and dying.

Elizabeth Dreyer (1994) states: "Our task as Christians is not to 'bring' Christ to the world but to be on the lookout and discover and uncover the Christ that is already present" (63). As reflected in the words of Isaiah, discovering Christ in illness, in loss, and in death is uncovering Christ already present in our lives.

> When you pass through the waters, I will be with you
> and through the rivers, they shall not overwhelm you;
> Because you are precious in my sight, and honored, and I love you,
> I give people in return for you, nations in exchange for your life.
> Do not fear, for I am with you. (Isa 43:2, 4–5)

That mystery is always a dimension in our lives, I truly believe. Mystery is pondered and accepted only within the dimensions of faith, which the apostle Paul called "evidence for things not seen." Encountering God in the mystery of daily life is a gift that is always present when we become open to that presence of God. "The sacred is the sacramental form of the secular. Grace underlies all of nature....The love of God is always present. Grace is everywhere" (Himes 2003, 18). This gift of grace, this gift of faith informs spirituality and enriches awareness of meaning and purpose in life. From the reality of that human awareness of who we are in relationship and what we discover of meaning and purpose in the experience of life, I have formulated my personal definition of spirituality.

> Spirituality is the core of the human condition, a "self-in-relation," daily consciously living all the graced experiences and events of ordinary life while actively seeking, in faith, the fingerprint of God in all of it.

In the words of spiritual teachers, a personal development of that awareness enables a sense of spiritual growth in understanding the mystery of human living and an acceptance of human dying. The plethora of sayings from religious leaders inspires theologians to provide a variety of descriptions of spiritual growth and the many different ways that it may become available to us in the journey of life. All seem to converge in openness to the mystery of our human living and dying.

Johannes Metz (1968, 23) accentuates the importance of that openness to mystery as an inevitable task in human life. As many do, he identifies God among us as an "invisible mystery," God who may become apparent to us in the very mysteriousness of our own being. "The mystery of who we are, our power, our strength are all derived from the well-spring of invisible mystery." Ewert Cousins (1985) expands that thought and captures a sense of the purpose and meaning of mystery when he states: "The spiritual core is the deepest center of the person. It is here that the person is open to the transcendent dimensions; it is here that the person experiences ultimate reality" (xiii).

Life in general is a journey, and as such it becomes a spiritual journey of discovery through which we become capable of penetrating mystery. Because illness, loss, and death are steps into liminality, they are necessarily pathways into mystery and also into spiritual growth. In his description of spirituality, Thomas Merton (1990) stresses the importance of interior growth and hints at the necessity of surrender to mystery as we encounter the imponderables of human life. "Our real journey of life is interior: It is a matter of growth, deepening and ever greater surrender to creative action of love and grace in our hearts" (118). Surrender to mystery is a gateway to faith, and the lived reality of faith is relationship. Relationship is a development across the life span and in the totality of lived experiences, not only toward God but in relationship with self and with others. John Shea (2005) notes that "adulthood not only makes an integral spirituality possible for us but it also makes an integral spirituality necessary for us" (40).

From a spiritual and religious point of view, the nature of spiritual growth is a deepening of insight into the mysteries of human living and dying. The great German theologian Dorothee Soelle (2001) uses the paradoxical expression the "Silent Cry" as a mystical name for God. She invites us to hear the often inaudible Silent Cry in ourselves, in others, and in the world. This Silent Cry is at the heart of living with loss, illness, and death. In a different approach, Karl Rahner (1978) reminds us that faith is also a matter of intellectual and emotional surrender. He calls this the task of "surrendering the self trustfully and hopefully to the insoluble mystery we call God" (37).

Spiritual leaders speak of "graced moments" when the "thin spaces" occur and the barriers between "the real and the unreal" collapse and become impalpable. Michael Himes (2003) states it this way: "The grace of God is here, always here, but what is missing all too often is someone to behold it. Those moments when we become beholders of grace are sacramental moments. All of us are learning to be such beholders. Grace is to be found everywhere" (15).

The gift of faith does come in the "graced moments" and the "thin spaces" of life and enables us to find meaning and become "sacramental beholders." When we accept the "insoluble mystery" of God in those moments and spaces, they can give us an understanding, however feeble, of who we are in our human existence and destiny. They are an invitation to enter into this unknown realm of mystery—of the "things not seen" and the "Silent Cry"—to discover that, in all our living and all our dying, we bear the fingerprints of God upon us.

References

Bowen, M. 1978. *Family Therapy in Clinical Practice*. New York: Jason Aronson.

———. 1974. "Toward the Differentiation of Self in One's Family of Origin." In *Georgetown Family Symposium*, vol. 1, edited by F. Andres and J. Lorio. Washington, DC: Department of Psychiatry, Georgetown University Medical Center.

Buber, M. 1958. *I and Thou*. 2nd ed. Translated by R. G. Smith. New York: Scribner.

Cousins, Ewert. 1985. " Preface to the Series." In *Christian Spirituality*, vol. 1, *Origin to the Twelfth Century*, edited by Bernard McGinn and John Meyendorff. New York: Crossroad.

Dreyer, Elizabeth A. 1994. *Earth Crammed with Heaven: A Spirituality of Everyday Life*. New York: Paulist Press.

Edwards, Denis. 1983. *Human Experience of God*. New York: Paulist Press.

Egan, Harvey D. 1998. *Karl Rahner, Mystic of Everyday Life*. New York: Crossroad.

Epstein, Nathan, Christine Ryan, Duane Bishop, Ivan Miller, and Gabor Keitner. 2003. "The McMaster Model: A View of Healthy Family Functioning." In *Normal Family Process*, 3rd ed., edited by Froma Walsh, 581–607. New York: Guilford.

Epstein, N. B., and D. S. Bishop. 1973. "State of the Art—1973." *Canadian Psychiatric Association Journal* 18:175–83.

Friedman, Edwin H. 1985. *Generation to Generation*. New York: Guilford.

Himes, Michael. 2003. *The Mystery of Faith*. Cincinnati, OH: St. Anthony Messenger Press.

Merton, Thomas. 1990. *The Modern Spirituality Series*. Springfield, IL: Templegate Press.

Metz, Johannes B. 1968. *Poverty of Spirit*. Paramus, NJ: Newman Press.

Mitchell, Stephen A., and Margaret J. Black. 1995. *Freud and Beyond*. New York: Basic Books.

Moran, Gabriel. 2007. *Fashion Me a People: The Educational Insights of Maria Harris*. New London, CT: Twenty-Third Publications.

Musgrave, Beverly A. 2007. "Intimate Relationships: Stabilizing and Solidifying Family Life." In *Restoring Family Life and Sustaining World Peace*, edited by Catherine Bernard and John J. Shea, 17–190. Chennai, India: SERFAC Pub.

———. 2003. "The Ontogenesis of Empathy: The Heart of Intimacy." In *In Search of Healing*, edited by Augustine Meier, 43–60. Ottawa: Society for Pastoral Research.

Musgrave, Beverly A., and John R. Bickle, eds. 2003. *Partners in Healing*. New York: Paulist Press.

Rahner, Karl. 1978. *Foundations of Christian Faith: An Introduction to the Idea of Christianity*. New York: Seabury Press.

———. 1992. *Theologian of the Graced Search for Meaning*, edited by Geffrey B. Kelly. Minneapolis: Fortress Press.

Rothschild, Babette. 2000. *The Psychophysiology of Trauma and Trauma Treatment*. New York: W. W. Norton.

Schnarch, David. 1997. *Passionate Marriage*. New York: Owl.

Shea, John J. 2005. *Finding God Again*. New York: Rowman & Littlefield.

Soelle, Dorothee. 2001. *The Silent Cry*. Minneapolis: Fortress Press.

Stein, Murray. 1983. *In Midlife*. Dallas: Spring Publications.

Sullivan, H. S. 1956. *Clinical Studies in Psychiatry*. New York: Norton.

———. 1953. *The Interpersonal Theory of Psychiatry*. New York: Norton.

———. 1940. *Conceptions of Modern Psychiatry*. New York: Norton.

Surrey, J. L. 1991."The Self-in-Relation: A Theory of Women's Development." In *Women's Growth in Connection: Writings from the Stone Center*, edited by J. V. Jordan, A. G. Kaplan, J. B. Miller, I. P. Stiver, and J. L. Surrey. New York: Guilford.

Tutu, D. 1995. *African Prayer Book*. New York: Doubleday.

Walsh, Froma. 2003. *Spiritual Resources in Family Therapy*. New York: Guilford.

10

"Recovering" from Maternal Bereavement

Can Psychotherapy Help?

Mary Ragan

One day a forty-two-year-old woman, Christine, came into therapy for a very specific reason: she couldn't forget. Sixteen years prior, her husband had killed their only two children and himself. The children, aged two and a half years and eight months, died strapped in the backseat as he drove his car into a body of water. Christine was hospitalized at the time of the deaths as a result of a beating he had given her several days earlier, a beating that resulted in the termination of her third pregnancy.

During the course of the next sixteen years, Christine made monumental efforts to forget: she never returned to the apartment that she shared with her husband and family; she moved to a new city; she never spoke aloud the names of her two children; when asked if she had any children she routinely responded no. Her efforts to forget meant that she often held two jobs, worked many hours of the day, and tried not to think too much. She avoided seeing babies whenever possible. Touching a baby was out of the question. The emotional control required to maintain such a delicate balance was achieved at a very high price. Christine was frantically busy: hiding her trauma and her grief, hiding her dead children, hiding her violent marriage, hiding her shame and her guilt. It should come as no surprise that therapy posed a profound threat to this compromise solution.

That she could maintain a certain emotional equilibrium, be successful in her job as a schoolteacher, and be productive and creative in her hobbies of sewing and quilting bespeaks the enormous resilience of her personality. These efforts to forget, however, were almost completely unsuccessful. She never forgot, not even a single detail. It was all lodged within her, never fully out of awareness. This might have gone on for another sixteen years had not two other events occurred within months of each other: the first was meeting a man with whom she would fall in love, and the second was experiencing the sudden death of one of the little girls in her classroom. It was the coincidence of these two events that brought her to the first session. Her purpose was clear: she needed to be able to forget better.

The topic of traumatic grief is deserving of intense scrutiny. Long before modern psychologists and psychiatrists began to study grief, novelists, poets, and playwrights described many of the features that would be recognized by contemporary researchers. Poetry is perhaps the ideal medium for expressing emotions of grief. Emily Dickinson, that intrepid chronicler of grief in all its forms, reminds us that mourners cannot simply try to fill the gap left by a loss. The only remedy, says the poet, is to "insert the thing that caused it." No substitutes will do.

Little has been written about what clinical interventions are most beneficial in psychotherapeutic work with a person suffering from traumatic grief. When loss is complicated by violence, domestic abuse, and a history of battering, the usual theories of loss and grief are simply insufficient. The interventions used here were six in number: establishing rapport with the client; facilitating the telling of the story in complete detail; providing psychoeducational information; managing trauma symptoms; managing grief symptoms; and identifying signs of recovery. Listing such techniques in numerical order may give rise to the mistaken impression that this work is ordered, neat, and almost entirely predictable. Nothing could be further from the truth.

Establishing Rapport

Rapport may be thought of as a sense of easy connection, simply being on the same wavelength with another person. It is of primary importance in the early phase of treatment when the "trauma story" is explored. The therapist listens in an empathic, nonjudgmental way and hopes to create what is called a safe "holding environment." When rapport is established, therapist and client tend to mirror each other's nonverbal behavior, breathing, posture, gestures, tone, and tempo of voice and movement. Essentially, the first year of treatment is devoted to developing the relationship and setting the stage for the expression of the transference. Basic trust and empathy are crucial to this process.

In the case described above, achieving this alliance or rapport could not happen quickly. Christine's presentation of herself was calm, measured, almost never accompanied by tears. She told her dramatic and horrific story without emotion. Early sessions were marked by reticence and a reluctance to give much detail. The initial interview revealed the fact that her husband had committed suicide, but it was not clear until very near the end of the first interview that her two children had also died with him. She had not, until that moment, acknowledged her children nor had she spoken their names aloud in over sixteen years. She was also, at that point, still referring to the event as an "accident." Only later did it emerge that she had been a victim of domestic violence and battering at the hands of her husband.

There are three techniques particularly useful in establishing rapport with a client who presents herself as Christine did. The first is willingness to wait for the details of the trauma, that is, to let the client set the pace. One of the most common mistakes made by therapists is to push clients to reveal traumatic material too soon. The therapist must be careful to honor the resistance of the client and to accept it as an important coping strategy developed over time. In fact, it is evidence of her strength.

In giving the client authority over setting the pace, the therapist communicates a respect for the client's self-healing processes and, at the same time, acknowledges the client's agency and competence. Trauma victims have usually experienced some loss of self-esteem as a result of their experience, and this is notably true with women who have been victims of domestic violence. In Christine's case, the pace of the sessions was sometimes optimal; sometimes a therapeutic impasse was reached; and sometimes the pace resulted in overwhelming anxiety for her.

A second technique used in establishing rapport is to pay close attention to the language, content, and affect of the first session, which often presents, in embryonic form, a blueprint of the therapeutic work to follow. Rapport with the client will rest, to some degree, on the therapist's *hearing* words at the deepest level and being willing to provide the reliability, predictability, and empathy needed by the client to confront very painful material. The therapist needs to understand that the client's difficulty in trusting is *not* about the therapist, presuming, of course, that the therapist has not demonstrated untrustworthiness. Rather, the client's feelings about the therapist are transferential, resulting from her early life experience and the aftermath of her traumatic experience.

The third technique useful in establishing rapport involves understanding the various factors present in the client's history that may indicate a high risk for clinical complications: family, culture, religious experience, and prior trauma. This assessment can, in itself, be destabilizing and needs to be conducted with great sensitivity to what the client can tolerate at any given time. Christine possessed every risk factor and more. This, of course, was not clear from the first session; it unfolded over time in an extremely tentative and gradual process. Any retraumatization of the client through premature or intrusive questioning, overidentification with the emotion, countertransferential avoidance of frightening material, or a failure to appreciate what is *not* said can upset the establishment of rapport and perhaps abort the therapy altogether.

It was because Christine was able to establish a relationship within which she could "do her work" that she was able to utilize her own self-healing capacities. This is not meant to imply that such work may not involve considerable depression. On the contrary, once the manic defense of "I don't need you and you can't really hurt me anyway" is given up, the underlying depression is often profound. The clinical work involves the client's relinquishing that which she holds most precious, the sense of self-sufficiency, in exchange for awareness of vulnerability and dependency. It is often enormously difficult for the client to grasp that such a move can be anything other than defeat. The experience of vulnerability and dependency is, however, a profound achievement that allows the client to experience the mourning required for true healing. In such a situation, depression is therapeutic not pathological.

Facilitating the Telling of the Story

The second intervention necessary for the resolution of traumatic grief is to facilitate the telling of the trauma story in detail. In Christine's case, this meant dealing first with the facts of the trauma, that is, what specifically happened to the children, to her husband, and to herself. This story must be told in all its specificity and terrifying detail. Asking questions that call for specific recollections is especially helpful in this regard: Where were you when you first heard about the deaths of the children? Who told you about their deaths? What exactly did they say? Were you alone? What was the first thing you thought? said? Who came to see you? What did they say? Did anyone touch you? hold you? What was the most helpful thing someone did? What was the thing someone said or did that you found most insensitive? For clients to answer these questions often triggers buried emotional response. Telling and retelling the story helps the client to gain mastery over the experience by reinterpreting it again and again until it makes sense in some way.

In gathering the "facts" of what exactly had happened to the children, it became clear that there was not an accident but rather a willful act on the part of her husband to kill himself and their children. Though the insurance company had ruled Daniel's death a suicide within months of the event and had paid survivor benefits for the children but not for him, it was a full five years more before Christine could fully believe this conclusion. She had waited sixteen years to begin therapy. It took her five years after the deaths of the children for her to believe that her husband had murdered their children. What else might she have to face? Eventually, the most deeply buried part of the story came to light: Daniel's physical and sexual abuse of her and her subsequent feelings of self-blame regarding the deaths of the children.

Self-blame is one of the most common reactions of women who are victims of domestic violence. The shame, horror, and self-hatred that a woman experiences at having her children die at the hands of a violent man who has repeatedly abused her are incalculable. Central to Christine's sense of shame and guilt was the feeling that she had failed to protect her children from Daniel. She alone knew his capacity for violence. Only she knew that after the birth of John, the second child, Daniel forbade her to breast feed him, to hold him, to comfort him. Only she knew that he was monitoring her behavior with the new infant to prevent any form of tenderness. Only she knew that he was apportioning infant formula to John in very small doses. Only she knew that Daniel's behavior had become so bizarre that she passively submitted to his strange demands rather than risk another beating for herself or further abusive behavior toward the baby.

Christine manifested behavior characteristic of women in abusive situations. She had learned that her responses made no difference in what happened to her. Reasoning with Daniel was futile; exposing the "secret" was dangerous. Compliance offered her a sense of minimal safety, while fighting him ensured additional beatings for herself and greater deprivation for the baby. Without a family network of support and living at a distance from any other friends or relatives, she felt quite certain that she would never be believed. After all, she was married to a respected member of the medical community, an ob-gyn specialist.

For battered women who stay in abusive relationships, "keeping the secret" is routine. In Christine's case, the silence surrounding her domestic abuse was complete. Even the infrequent visits to the hospital for treatment were shrouded in fabrication. When one ophthalmologist commented that the damage to Christine's eyes was consistent with the damage a prizefighter might have received, her response was to say nothing.

It is not uncommon for women who are abused to have been in abusive situations in the past. In fact, it is highly likely. The therapist needs to probe for any earlier instances. Usually no psychological predisposing traits are found. There is no evidence that the status a woman occupies, the role she performs, the behavior she engages in, her demographic profile or her personality characteristics influence her chances of intimate victimization. But before Christine ever revealed the facts about Daniel's abuse, her childhood history reflected some of those "susceptibility factors" that can render a woman more vulnerable to abuse.

She was adopted early in life by two people who had little ability to care for her. Her mother was emotionally distant and largely unavailable; her father was a chronic alcoholic who sexually abused her adoptive sister throughout childhood. While Christine was not the direct recipient of sexual abuse herself, the threat was always there. She needed to keep herself alert to danger and aware of her surroundings; there was no opportunity for relaxation and certainly no chance for play. There was little predictability in the home other than the almost certain knowledge that alcoholic drinking by the father would result in some form of disruption, conflict, or violence. Her form of coping with this situation was to escape from home as often as possible. When at home, dissociation was the defense she employed. This childhood pattern of leaving home and using dissociation became her basic way of coping after the deaths of her children as well.

In helping the client to tell her trauma story, the therapist cannot and should not maintain the "blank screen" of the psychoanalyst, that is, receiving all of the communications of the client with a kind of neutrality that betrays no emotion and offers little response. On the contrary, the therapist must validate the feelings of the client, sharing with her a sense of outrage and horror at the abuse. Silence in this context is a perversion of the therapeutic process and poses the very real possibility of retraumatizing the client in the name of analytic neutrality.

Eliciting the trauma story is stressful for the therapist as well as the client. Clients suffering from a traumatic syndrome often form a characteristic type of transference in the therapy relationship. In Christine's case, attempts to facilitate the conversation very often were met with absolutely no response from her. Always she was testing, demonstrating what survivors of trauma often assume, that is, that unless proven otherwise, the therapist cannot bear to hear the true story of the trauma.

Maintaining empathy when the treatment setting itself becomes a crucible is no simple matter. That the therapist will be cast in the multiple roles of victim, abuser, and supportive listener at various points in the therapy is essential to the therapist's understanding and to the maintenance of the therapeutic alliance. Without it, the countertransferential reactions of the therapist, for example, anger, discouragement, fear, feeling misunderstood or underappreciated, will contaminate the therapy and block the progress of the client.

The therapist's ability to help the client tell the trauma story in full detail addresses a number of the symptoms of traumatic grief. A central one is trying to avoid all reminders of the trauma. For Christine, this meant never speaking of the children, never telling anyone about what she had been through, never putting up pictures of the children anywhere in her house, never going through the boxes of their things left when the apartment was closed. Telling the trauma story invites reminders of every aspect of the event, but it also lessens the sense of numbness that has served as armor. Christine now began to feel in ways that previously had not been possible. As Judith Herman (1992) says, the paradox of speaking the unspeakable is at the core of trauma work.

Providing Psychoeducational Information

Clients can be helped enormously by being given a rationale for why they need to undergo processes of therapy. For some clients, reviewing feelings and voicing them are in direct opposition to what is consonant with their social, cultural, ethnic, generational, and/or religious conditioning. Trauma survivors often report that once catastrophe strikes, many people around them maintain an almost complete silence about the event. In Christine's case, this silence was exhibited most strongly by her parents. They removed all evidence of the children from their home and rarely spoke to Christine about them.

One powerful technique in addressing phobic avoidance of grief and the problems created by loss is explaining the importance of speaking. If a client has been raised in an atmosphere of emotional repression, translating internal emotional experience into an interpersonal dialogue is especially difficult. Further, if a person has reason to distrust the reliability and empathic concern of the listener, the difficulty is compounded.

Christine came from a family shrouded in silence. This silence was pervasive in her childhood and continued throughout her adult years. Once she began to talk, the reality of early childhood trauma related to alcoholism and sexual abuse became increasingly clear. The issue of her adoption at birth and the loss of the biological parents were important historical facts. In her adult life, her parents' divorce and remarriage, her father's imprisonment for vehicular homicide in an alcohol-related accident, her mother's inability to respond in any nurturing way regarding the deaths of the children—all these reinforced a pattern of abuse and neglect well established in Christine's early life.

The second area of education concerned domestic violence. Christine's shame about the abuse she experienced kept her from speaking or learning about it. Information about the effects of domestic abuse helped her realize why she became paralyzed in the face of Daniel's violence. She needed help to understand and monitor her thinking. Sometimes this meant testing idiosyncratic meanings ("I must be an incompetent person if I allowed such abuse to occur"), examining options and alternatives available to her, or labeling cognitive distortions resulting from her abusive history. The most serious cognitive distortion to be addressed in therapy was understanding where real responsibility for the abuse lay. Christine's tendency toward self-blame often obscured the fact of Daniel's ultimate responsibility for the deaths of the children.

The very symptoms of trauma need exploration. The person undergoing a traumatic experience receives an enormous amount of very complex information, including physical sensations like bodily pain and emotional reactions that include disgust, shame, anxiety, fear, and sexual excitement. The information can easily become so overwhelming that the average person's functional capacity for processing it fails.

Evidence of failure in processing includes flashbacks, intrusive imagery, and feelings of such intensity that the person fears losing his or her mind. Because of this fear, from the beginning the therapist needs to educate the traumatized person about the nature and course of these symptoms. The client can be advised not to try to block or arrest flashbacks from occurring. Instead, clients should be told to say to themselves: "I am having a flashback; it will pass." They can use these statements as a way of centering themselves and wait for the sensation to subside.

Avoidance is another symptom of trauma that the client is likely to exhibit. Attempts to lessen the pain through numbing of feelings, sometimes by using alcohol or other drugs, are usual. Having great difficulty talking about the event and withdrawing from others as a form of protection are also commonly seen. Educating clients about the normalcy of these reactions helps them to place their reactions in a context that is larger than individual health or illness, individual weakness or strength.

Finally, clients may also experience a range of arousal phenomena that are characteristic of the trauma response. An exaggerated startle response (that is, an overreaction to minimal threat) is neither pathological nor unusual, but rather evidence of the depth of trauma that the person has endured. Hypervigilance in all forms is part of the aftermath of trauma. Educating the client about these reactions and symptoms is an attempt to normalize what, in other circumstances, might be considered strange or aberrant behavior.

The client needs to understand grief and the various ways in which traditional "grief theory" fails. The idea that all or most bereaved persons respond similarly to trauma and loss at an emotional level is one of the key deficiencies in traditional models of grieving. Christine's progress in recovery was aided greatly by her understanding that traditional "grief theory" was insufficient and that her "delayed" grief had not served her well. She knew that she had to reclaim the identity of "mother" for herself and came to see that "forgetting the children" was not a viable goal of treatment. Remembering was her task, her form of grieving. It would bring unspeakable pain but would also be a way of reclaiming the children; it offered her the possibility of experiencing joy again.

Managing Trauma Symptoms

Parents of murdered children typically report recurrent and intrusive thoughts of their child's murder, recurrent dreams of the event, and sleep disturbance, which can begin a cycle of exhaustion and depression. The most common sleep disturbance is early morning awakening, followed by difficulty falling asleep at night, and sleeping more often than usual. Psychic numbing or emotional anesthesia are also common experiences for traumatized people, feelings that often result in a sense of detachment and estrangement from others.

Over the course of sixteen years, Christine had made little progress in dealing with the trauma and its related effects. Therefore, the earliest stage of the psychotherapeutic work dealt with recovering those "affect-laden" memories. Specifically, it meant that Christine had to confront the fact that Daniel was, in fact, *responsible* for the deaths of her children. It meant rereading the police report, reexposing herself to all the detail of that report. It meant reviewing again the report from her insurance company and the findings of her own private investigator submitted some five years after the event. It meant facing the fact that Daniel's remains, buried with the children in a cemetery hundreds of miles away, had to be moved. Finally, Christine faced facts that she had previously either avoided or never known: that her children were dead, that her husband had been a compulsive gambler since his college years, that her father-in-law had allowed it all to go on, and that she had allowed his abuse to go on. Experiencing the rage that this exposed, coupled with attempts to process so much new information, pushed Christine nearly to the breaking point.

During the first year of therapy when Christine began to confront reality, she reexperienced a traumatized state on a number of occasions. When a sense of protection fails, dissociation is often used as a defense against chaos. Once a friend of hers telephoned the therapist to say that Christine was saying inexplicable things about planning to join a convent. On another occasion, she left a restaurant in the middle of the meal, stood in the cold outside, without coat or car keys, "forgetting" where she was, whom she was with, or why she was there. At other times, she had the experience of driving somewhere only to forget where she was going or what the purpose of the trip was. All of these episodes are examples of the extent to which dissociative phenomena may operate when the intensity of the psychic trauma becomes unbearable. The client essentially "leaves" in whatever way possible.

Christine's use of dissociation became not only an impediment to the therapy but also a source of fear and anxiety for both therapist and client. For Christine's part, she began to wonder if perhaps she might not need a different therapist, a different therapeutic modality, a different approach altogether. On her side, the therapist asked herself: What is the proper diagnosis here? Has the evaluation for medication been thorough and comprehensive? Are these dissociative states evidence of a profound dissociative identity disorder rather than symptoms related to the impact of trauma? Clearly, the therapist's failure to recognize the early signs of decompensation and the extent of dissociation exacerbated Christine's emotional distress. Rather than getting better, she was getting worse.

The interventions at this point in the treatment were twofold. The first was to consult with a supervising psychiatrist and an interdisciplinary team regarding diagnosis and medication. Christine met with the psychiatrist for evaluation; the therapist met with both the medical doctor and the team. These consultations were essential for both client and therapist in that they provided further reinforcement of the safe "holding environment" by offering further advice, information, and education regarding trauma and its aftermath. The client understood that there was a larger network of support available to her; the therapist understood the same. The therapist was also reassured that the diagnosis of traumatic grief was, in fact, the proper one and that the symptomatology currently displayed was consistent with that diagnosis. One is reminded of Judith Herman's (1992) injunction that a caregiver must never do trauma work alone.

Engagement in this work poses some risk to the therapist's own psychological health. The therapist's adverse reactions, unless understood and contained, predictably lead to disruptions in the therapeutic alliance with patients and to conflict with professional colleagues. Therapists who work with traumatized people require an ongoing support system to deal with these intense reactions.

The second intervention involved a number of different strategies designed to reduce the intensity of arousal that Christine was experiencing. These included refocusing attention to the external reality, on the here and now. Relaxation techniques helped Christine to gain more control over her internal processes. Encouragement was given to increasing personal rest and reducing the demands in her external environment. The therapist addressed the extent to which harsh superego demands resulted in a perfectionist approach to her work and professional life. And finally, support was given to help Christine develop new structures around time, activities, and information. Since her method of coping in the past had involved working at least two jobs and engaging in countless other "free time" activities, helping her to reduce frantic activity without inviting a flood of traumatic memory was important to her sense of stability.

One of the perversions of therapy, and those who practice it, is that the emphasis in treatment can be so exclusively on the client's "problem" that the extraordinary resilience of the person is somehow lost. In Christine's case, she never lost her job, she never lost her friends, she never lost her mind. She never quit therapy, though she wanted to many times. She sought out group experiences for dealing with her loss though she hated speaking in groups. She weathered the emotional upheavals of treatment with remarkable courage and tenacity. Therapeutic interventions involved noting these strengths, underlining them, appreciating them.

Managing Grief Symptoms

Once trauma symptoms have been addressed to some extent, the person experiencing traumatic grief is now able to deal more specifically with the loss that has occurred and the accompanying grief. In Christine's case, she had to review carefully her lost relationships: with her daughter, with her son, with her husband. This review involved determining where she would "put" those relationships and how she would relate to them in the future.

She had Daniel's body removed from the cemetery, thus ending the relationship. Once he was finally separated from her children, she visited the new gravesite, and that action allowed her to feel the full extent of her rage and fury. It should not be assumed that this process was neat or linear; in fact, it was full of layers of guilt and self-recrimination.

Christine's relationship with her children was another matter. Rather than seeking an ending, her task now was to learn how to incorporate her children back into her life. This required doing the grief work that she had so long avoided. As a way of embracing this work, Christine made a number of decisions that were both courageous and necessary.

Christine's calendar year revolved around the date of the children's death. Once in therapy, she was able to embrace the experience of the anniversary reactions as an opportunity for further processing of the connections between the affect and the event. First, she visited the graves. Her children were buried far from her home; she had never returned to the gravesite since the day of the burial. She tried on one occasion several years earlier to visit the graves: she got only as far as the gate of the cemetery before a flood of feeling turned her away. This time she was able to enter the cemetery grounds and approach the gravesite. She told the children how much she missed them; she told them that she had never forgotten them, not even for a day; she asked their forgiveness for not having come sooner. She asked their forgiveness for not having protected them from their father. She struggled with the unnaturalness of children dying first and, like most survivors of a homicide, ruminated often about the "preventability" of the disaster. Christine wept for the children and for herself and expressed all of the emotion that had been locked inside her for so many years. This experience of catharsis did not happen all at once. She made this trip on three different occasions, each time being able to express more fully her love and grief.

The second decision the client made that was crucial to her recovery was having the children's remains brought to a cemetery located only minutes from her home. She was now an active participant in the burial of the children. She planned a memorial service; she chose readings and hymns; she invited important people to be present. She did, almost twenty years later, what was impossible for her to do at the time of the deaths: she said good-bye to her children in a way that honored them and freed her. Her choice to bury the children near her meant that she could go to them at any time; she could also choose to stay away. That was the freedom that had eluded her for so long. Conversations about the children, visits to the grave, conscious attention to the meaning of their lives all contributed to making the anniversary date less dreadful.

During this period, the therapy relationship served as the safe place to return to; it was the place where the story was told and retold. This reviewing and retelling and reliving is at the heart of the therapeutic process and at the heart of grief work. It is not necessary that the therapist be physically present at the gravesite or at the memorial service; the therapist must, however, have the capacity to be at the gravesite in imagination and empathy as the story unfolds.

The third decision that the client made that helped to facilitate the grief process was to open boxes filled with memorabilia of the children. They had been in her possession since the time her parents packed her belongings and closed her apartment, and she had never opened them. Once she had done that, she felt quite certain she could do anything.

Managing the grief symptoms that occur in the course of this therapeutic work addresses several of the criteria of traumatic grief: feelings of futility are reduced, the person has less difficulty facing the death and less difficulty imagining a full life, and the person deals with the feeling (and the fact) that a part of themselves has died.

Identifying Signs of Recovery

The question of what constitutes "recovery" is an especially critical issue for both therapist and client: When are they to know that the client's experience of traumatic grief no longer dictates the choices that she makes and the life that she leads?

We based Christine's "recovery" on several factors. She was now rarely subject to flashbacks or intrusive images. Because she was no longer overwhelmed with emotion or memories, she did not have to resort to dissociation as a way of coping. She was able to remember the past with feeling. When confronted with memories of the trauma, she would reexperience some of the emotions and bodily states that initially accompanied those events. Sad memories now elicited sadness rather than numbness.

The most dramatic evidence of Christine's recovery had to do with her renewed capacity for attachment and intimacy. This was evidenced by a choice she made four years after therapy began: she married again. Against all odds, she chose to make herself vulnerable once more to a man. In so doing, she displayed an optimism and hope in the future that her previous experience gave her no right to expect.

One final example of Christine's recovery lay in her ability to assign new meaning to the trauma. Christine did what trauma survivors before her have done: she sought ways to transform her experience in order that it might be of some use to others. In this way, utter disaster is saved from complete meaninglessness by intentional, other-centered action. To this end, she became a volunteer working with families of dying AIDS patients. Mostly they were parents; often they were mothers. She didn't tell her story; there was no need. She listened to theirs. Her experience of traumatic grief had hollowed out in her a space so large that she could not only contain their pain but respond to it as well. Having faced her own pain, she had no need to avoid theirs.

This single-case study of traumatic grief is one contribution to a growing field that deals with the intersection of trauma and bereavement. The process of therapy, sometimes as mysterious and miraculous as life itself, is not easily described or quantified. The depth and healing power of any important relationship, including the therapy relationship, are never easily explained. Theories about therapy and the stories clinicians tell about them do not proceed according to some grand narrative. Therapeutic conversations tend to be messy and circular, sometimes given to contradictions, often raising more questions than answers. These therapeutic conversations are also, at their best, profound experiences of connection that result in a sense of being known. The "interventions" used in sessions are most often improvisations, based on theory, shaped by experience, but inspired in the moment.

So, what is it that can be known about the healing of traumatic grief? This study deals with criteria that can be named and interventions that can, to a certain degree, be measured. It does that because that is the scientific method. What this study cannot do is deal with those intangible elements like courage and tenacity, empathy and trustworthiness. This study cannot quantify the role that hope played or how love made a difference. It cannot demonstrate that faith was a factor: faith in oneself, in the process, in the integrity of the work itself. Nonetheless, every client and therapist who journeys together in the service of recovery from traumatic grief knows that these intangibles are the bedrock from which the healing work is done.

Reference

Herman, Judith Lewis. 1992. *Trauma and Recovery: The Aftermath of Violence*. New York: Basic Books.

PART III

Healing Dimensions
The Experience of Loss, Illness, and Death

11

Spiritual Assessment in Ministry to the Sick

George Handzo

Introduction

Spiritual assessment is a relatively new concept in the realm of ministry to the sick, especially for those who are not professional counselors or chaplains. Used by counselors doing pastoral counseling or spiritual therapy, it has often been thought of as a skill that requires a great deal of training and experience to do.

To understand the subject of assessment, it is first essential to understand why we visit the sick at all. Certainly, it is a nice thing to do and something many of us as religious people feel required to do by our religious traditions. However, it is important to understand that our traditions command us to visit the sick because visiting when done well helps them cope with their suffering. Hopefully, it helps them feel better. It also, hopefully, helps them engage their faith and their religious practices to cope with their suffering.

While it is true that in-depth assessment as practiced by professional counselors does require a lot of training, all of us who visit the sick use some sort of assessment without even thinking about it. "How are you today?" and "Is this a good time to visit?" are assessment questions any of us might use. They are part of the way we bring ourselves into relationship with the person we are visiting. In ministry to the sick, we talk a lot about a ministry of presence. We talk about being with a person where the person is. If we are to be with a person where that person is, we need to find out where that place is. To do that, we need to ask questions.

The issue is not: Should we do assessment? Most of us already do it to a greater or lesser degree. The question is: What kind of assessment should we do and what questions are most effective?

Before we begin that process, it is important to be clear about the terms we will use. There is a lot of confusion about the relative meaning of the terms *religion* and *spirituality*. While there are a number of definitions of the two terms, many people in the field of pastoral care now accept the definitions offered by Koenig, McCollough, and Larson (2001, 18). They define religion as "an organized system of beliefs, practices, rituals, and symbols designated (a) to facilitate closeness to the sacred or transcendent (God, higher power, or ultimate truth/reality) and (b) to foster understanding of one's relationship and responsibility to others living in a community." They define spirituality as "the personal quest for understanding answers to ultimate questions about life, about meaning and about relationship to the sacred or transcendent, which may (or may not) lead to or arise from the development of religious rituals and the formation of community."

The major distinction between the concepts is that religion is an organized system of beliefs shared by a group of people. It is also practiced in community rather than alone. Spirituality, on the other hand, is an individual journey that may be practiced alone as well as within a community. In other words, according to these definitions, all of us would practice some form of spirituality, but only some of us would practice a religion.

The other important distinction is between screening and assessment. Screening is best thought of as a brief set of questions the goal of which is to discover quickly a particular need or condition. While it does not probe in depth, screening is geared to detect serious problems, if they exist. An assessment, on the other hand, probes an issue in depth to discover the full dimensions of any particular situation. Although we will discuss both screening and assessment, people visiting the sick will most often practice screening only. Even these few questions can lead to a significant discussion that will be helpful to the patient.

Why Is Spiritual Screening Important?

There are many today who would claim that people in the United States are becoming less and less religious. There is a belief that some, if not most, Americans are spiritual but not religious by the definitions above. However, this contention is not supported by the data available. In a 2003 Harris Poll, 90 percent of American adults said they believe in God and 84 percent said they believe in miracles. Galek, Flannelly, Weaver, and Vane (2005) found that 94 percent of people they surveyed describe God as loving, and 88 percent said they feel close to God. Finally, a 2002 survey by the highly respected National Opinion Research Center found that 98 percent of adult Americans pray at least once a week, 56 percent say they pray every day, and 85 percent say they read the Bible or Qur'an at least once a month.

So why is it that so many believe that people are less religious? Sivan, Fitchett, and Burton (1996) may have revealed the secret when they reported that only 42 percent of hospitalized patients they surveyed could identify a spiritual counselor to whom they could turn. This finding, combined with the others above, suggests that people are still quite religious in terms of their beliefs and practice. However, they are largely unaffiliated with a congregation or, at least, so loosely affiliated that they do not feel a tie to a spiritual leader that they can rely on for support.

To compound this problem, Koenig (1998) found, in a study of 337 hospital patients, that nearly 90 percent reported using religion to some degree to cope and more than 40 percent indicated that religion was the most important factor that kept them going.

Therefore, it seems clear that Americans are still highly religious in their beliefs and practice. They have a very positive view of God and God's place in their lives and rely heavily on their faith and religious practice during times of illness. Most significantly, while they are religious, many do not have a spiritual or religious leader to whom they can turn when they are sick, making ministry to the sick all the more important. What the data show is that there are many people who can benefit from your visits, because religion is important to them and there is no one else visiting them representing a religious community.

Besides the overtly religious needs, patients also seem to have needs that might be better qualified as spiritual. Galek, Flannelly, Vance, and Galek (2005) found in a survey that people named the following spiritual needs in order of importance:

Love and belonging
Meaning and purpose
Appreciation of nature and beauty
Spiritual/religious practices and guidance
Positivity, gratitude, and peace
Resolution with life and death

Spiritual Screening

The point of spiritual screening is, with a few questions, to determine if the person you are visiting has spiritual needs that are not being met. The questions also often serve, however, to open up conversation, help the patient understand that you are truly interested in what is going on with him or her, and begin a much longer conversation that makes patients feel respected and helps them cope with this suffering.

Many people who visit the sick in hospitals routinely ask patients whether they want to see a chaplain or a clergyperson of their faith. Many hospitals and chaplains believe, incorrectly, that this question is required by the agency that accredits hospitals.

This question and its answer are unnecessary, and can in fact set up a situation in which the patient thinks he or she may have blocked a chaplain or a clergyperson from visiting when this is not the case. Also, many patients feel obliged to agree to a chaplain's visit, even when they do not really want one, inconveniencing the patient and adding unnecessary work for the chaplain. A much better question is "Do you have any immediate religious or spiritual needs?" as a screening question for pastoral care referrals. This question allows the patient or family member to make any requests he or she wants, including prayer, receiving a sacrament, or having a visit from a chaplain.

When doing spiritual screening, it is important to keep in mind the distinction between spiritual and religious need on the one hand and the desire to see a chaplain on the other. Certainly, patients who want to be visited by a chaplain or a clergyperson of their faith, for whatever reason, should have that desire met. Nonetheless, it is always important to determine whether the patient simply wants to see a chaplain, needs to see a chaplain, or both. In today's hospitals, chaplaincy staffing is focused on those who are in spiritual distress, that is, those who are not coping with their illness as well as they might for some spiritual or religious reason. In a study of medical outpatients, 15 percent had "quite a bit" or "a great deal" of religious struggle (Fitchett et al. 2004). Religious struggle was significantly correlated with emotional distress. An important goal for lay visitors in most hospitals is to help identify those who may be in spiritual distress and direct chaplains to them.

There are a number of definitions of spiritual distress. A simple one espoused by Fitchett (1999) defines spiritual distress as a combination of high reliance on spiritual coping and low spiritual resources. High reliance on spiritual coping means that religious or spiritual resources such as prayer, reading scripture, or attending worship are an important part of how the patient deals with everyday life and copes with problems. Low spiritual resources means that, at this time, those ways of coping are not helping the patient. This situation could be caused simply by the patient not being able to attend worship regularly as done usually. Or it can be caused by the patient not being able to pray as the patient did before, because of feeling that God has abandoned him or her in the illness.

Another virtue of this formulation of spiritual distress is that it is very simple to use. One simply asks, "How important is religious or spiritual belief and practice to you in coping with your illness?" and "How well is your religious or spiritual belief and practice working in helping you cope now?" The first question determines how important religious belief and practice are to the patient's coping. The second question determines how well the coping mechanism is working now. A patient who answers that religious practice is important but it is not working now can be assumed to be in spiritual distress and should be referred to a chaplain. Combining this question with, "Do you have any immediate religious or spiritual needs?" constitutes a complete spiritual screening in most hospitals, in that it identifies those who should be referred for further care by a chaplain and satisfies the requirements of hospital regulatory bodies. It also quickly identifies patients with whom you might want to spend more time and differentiates them from those with whom you might want to have a short, pleasant visit and then move on.

Beyond this simple formulation, there are a number of other questions you can ask. Most people have coped with suffering or loss before in their lives and found ways to help themselves. Asking how they coped when they had a past loss or suffering can be very helpful. The question reminds them that they have strengths and resources they can call on. Asking about their faith community and encouraging them to call upon that faith community for assistance can be helpful. Many people are reticent to ask for help or even to let their faith community know that they are in need. One caution is that it is never appropriate for you to call a congregation on a patient's behalf, unless the patient specifically gives you permission. Even then, your call should be restricted to telling the congregation that the patient is in the hospital and would like a visit.

You are not permitted to tell the congregation anything about the patient's medical condition or even why the patient is in the hospital.

These simple questions may seem superficial. You will find, however, that even these can lead to a significant conversation about some issue that is bothering the patient deeply. Asking whether their belief and practice are helping patients or not can open up conversation about how they think and feel about prayer or their feelings about how their congregation is treating them. What may begin as an attempt by you simply to gather information can quickly lead to a visit that will be of great benefit to the patient.

Spiritual Assessment

Spiritual assessment goes beyond screening to what can often become a much deeper level of involvement with the patient or family member. Before you begin to deal with a patient on this level, it is essential to examine yourself to determine whether you are willing and ready to be involved with someone on such an intimate level. First, there is certainly nothing wrong with deciding that going beyond the level of screening is not something you feel comfortable doing. It is better to decide that you are not willing to engage patients on this level than to try to do it and communicate your discomfort to the patient. This caveat applies to all visiting of the sick. Your discomfort, which will be impossible to hide, may add to the patient's distress rather than provide comfort to the patient. If you are in doubt on this issue, have an honest conversation with the person who supervises your visiting. It also may be true that you are comfortable visiting certain kinds of patients and not others. For instance, many people are not comfortable visiting children in the hospital. Again, it is better to be honest with yourself and with others about this discomfort than to risk communicating to the patient that you really do not want to visit him or her.

Asking patients about deep spiritual issues and concerns requires courage on your part. Once you invite people to talk in depth about their anxieties and fears you need to be willing to go wherever that conversation takes you. You will never know what issues will come up. This can be true even when using the screening questions discussed above. You can never know when even a simple question will give the patient permission to share an important and intense part of a personal story. If you are anxious about where the conversation will go, it may be better not to enter this type of conversation at all. This kind of visiting means taking the risk of asking patients how they feel and what they are thinking and being ready to accept whatever they say, and then inviting them to continue with their story.

Many people who do this kind of visiting fear that they will harm the patient by getting the patient to talk about issues the patient might really not want to talk about. As long as the patient is in good mental health and you let the patient lead the conversation, this worry is generally misplaced. Patients are generally very good about refusing to answer questions or sidestepping issues they do not want to deal with. All you have to do is respect that refusal and not push them because you think they should talk about a certain subject. The patient needs to feel in total control of what is discussed and what is avoided. If you are ever in doubt about whether a patient wants to continue on a certain subject, it is always permissible to ask.

There are two basic approaches to assessment. One is to ask a predetermined set of questions that will cover all of the issues and areas of concern. This approach is suitable for a therapist and a client who are beginning a long-term counseling relationship. In pastoral visiting of the sick, assessment and providing assistance merge. Assessment, in this setting, is essentially inviting patients to tell whatever part of their personal story they feel open to sharing at that moment. In asking the questions and being open to the responses, you help patients verbalize some emotions and examine some things that may be bothering them. Think of yourself as a mirror. You do not give answers to questions, but by helping patients see themselves the way they are, you help them find comfort and relief for themselves. Also, by accepting whatever patients say and feel, you give them the message that there is nothing wrong with their thoughts and feelings.

Assessment is, at base, a process where you as a caregiver accompany the patient on the patient's journey. Your questions come from your concern and compassion. You are encouraging the patient to talk about what seems to be going on with the patient at that moment. How you exactly do that is largely a matter of your own style. The conversation can begin with a simple statement about how the patient is feeling. It can begin with an observation from you about something that you notice upon entering the room. It may look like the patient is in pain. The patient may look anxious. You may see cards or flowers and ask who sent them. You may use the screening questions above. Where you begin is generally not as important as your willingness to make the comments or ask the follow-up questions, which indicate to the patient that you are willing to continue the conversation at whatever level the patient finds helpful. The basic strategy is to keep inviting patients to tell you as much of their story as they want to tell.

Learning this skill takes a lot of practice, and it is best to practice with the help of a supervisor and a group of other learners. Most professional chaplains learn through a process called "action-reflection-action." Simply, this means that you visit patients and then reflect on those visits with others, being very open about where you felt the conversation did not go forward the way you thought it should have. You then take new learning with you to future visits. To be successful in this learning process, you need to be open about what you did not do well and be willing to hear from others where parts of who you are become barriers to deeper relationships. This process of learning is one that should never end. However, to the extent that you can accompany a person who is suffering in this way, you will give that person a great gift. You will give the gift of a nonjudgmental relationship, a gift that can help patients share their sufferings and thus share their burdens.

Bibliography

Fitchett, G. 1999. "Screening for Spiritual Risk." *Chaplaincy Today* 15, no. 1: 2–12.

Fitchett, G., P. E. Murphy, J. Kim, J. L. Gibbon, J. R. Cameron, and J. A. Davis. 2004. "Religious Struggle: Prevalence, Correlates, and Mental Health Risks in Diabetic, Congestive Heart Failure, and Oncology Patients." *International Journal of Psychiatry in Medicine* 34, no. 2: 179–96.

Galek, K., K. J. Flannelly, A. Vance, and R. M. Galek. 2005. "Assessing a Patient's Spiritual Needs." *Holistic Nursing Practice* 19, no. 2: 62–69.

Galek, K., K. J. Flannelly, A. J. Weaver, and A. Vane. 2005. "How Americans See God." *Spirituality & Health* 8, no. 3: 27.

Harris Poll. 2003. *The Religious and Other Beliefs of Americans 2003*, The Harris Poll #11, February 26, 2003. www.harrisinteractive.com/harris_poll/index.asp?PID=359.

Koenig, H. G. 1998. "Religious Attitudes and Practices of Hospitalized Medically Ill Older Adults." *International Journal of Geriatric Psychiatry* 13, no. 4: 213–24.

Koenig, H. G., M. E. McCollough, and D. B. Larson. 2001. *Handbook of Religion and Health*. Oxford: Oxford University Press.

National Opinion Research Center. 2002. *General Social Survey 2002*. Chicago: University of Chicago.

Sivan, A., G. Fitchett, and L. Burton. 1996. "Hospitalized Psychiatric and Medical Patients and the Clergy." *Journal of Religion and Health* 36, no. 3: 455–67.

12

Professional Partnerships in Grief and Loss

Yvette M. Sealy and Janna C. Heyman

Ester and Benjamin were married for fifty-four years. In the last two years, Benjamin's health was compromised by emphysema and diabetes. Initially he had trouble getting around, but as his condition progressed, he had difficulty even getting up to dress. Ester helped to take care of Benjamin's needs, but after a difficult respiratory episode one night, he needed to be hospitalized. He was able to return home, but his illness left him in a weakened state. Benjamin passed away in his sleep a few weeks later. Ester found herself alone at age seventy-six, not sure how to fill her time, not used to paying the bills, and feeling empty and confused.

Sophie was twenty-nine when she became pregnant. She and her husband Steve had been trying to conceive a baby for the past year. They were looking forward to beginning a family, now that their lives were settled enough to welcome in a baby. They went to see the doctor together regularly and were looking forward to the birth. They announced the news to their family and friends, who happily rejoiced along with the couple. During the third month, when everything seemed to be progressing normally, Sophie had a miscarriage. The doctor was unclear as to why the pregnancy terminated spontaneously but told Sophie and Steve that it happens to many couples and they could try to conceive again in a few months. People tried to comfort Sophie, telling her not to worry, but Sophie's heart was broken.

Joseph, shortly after his fifty-seventh birthday, noticed that his vision was blurry and distorted. He shrugged it off to getting older and thought to himself "I guess I'll need glasses soon." Joseph continued to work as a contractor, and often after work he would head over to his friends to watch sports. Joseph was always known as the "go-to guy," because he could always fix things. However, the gradual deterioration of his vision forced Joseph to see his doctor. He was diagnosed with age-related macular degeneration (AMD), a retinal disease that causes progressive loss of vision. Joseph's life changed dramatically. Within a year, he could no longer see well enough to continue his job, and he had difficulty getting around without assistance. Now he found it hard to ask for help. He also found himself too embarrassed to go out and be with the guys.

These snapshots provide an example of how loss has impacted the lives of three different individuals. Grief and loss can occur because a loved one has died or because of a loss of cognitive or of physical functioning. Some individuals describe their grief as a broken heart, while others speak of not knowing what to do. Emotional responses may include shock, disbelief, sleeplessness, loss of appetite, uncontrollable crying, and feelings of loneliness. In general, the grief process has been described as "more like a roller coaster—with overlapping responses and wide individual variability—rather than orderly stages" (Hooyman and Kiyak 2005, 507).

During such a time, it is important to remember that the grieving process is complex. Each individual will experience grief and adjust at his or her own pace. Holmes and colleagues (Holmes and Masuda 1974; Holmes and Rahe 1967; Masuda and Holmes 1978) conducted a series of comparative studies about physiological and psychological stress. They found that the death of a spouse is perceived as equally stressful by partners both young and old, while younger adults view the death of a close friend as more stressful than older adults. Some older adults may have difficulty dealing with loss, depending on the amount of loss in a given time and limitations of social supports. On the other hand, the research of McLeod (1996) has also recognized the resiliency of older adults in dealing with grief, because of their maturity and their previous coping experiences.

Another interrelated part of an individual's response to loss may be determined by cultural norms. Professionals need to be sensitive to individuals' cultural beliefs and value systems, including religion and spirituality. Spiritual beliefs are closely connected to an individual's cultural background. Some cultures are more likely to consult with a spiritual leader or advisor than others, while others may use their religious, spiritual, and cultural mandates about how mourning is to be handled. Many professional organizations underscore the importance of addressing diversity in their respective codes of ethics and professional standards. These standards thus recommend practice without discrimination in areas such as age, class, culture, disability, ethnicity, race, and religion (American Association of Pastoral Counseling 1994; American Psychological Association 2002; National Association of Social Workers 1999). Professionals need to understand cultural differences by "recognizing, affirming, and valuing their beliefs and values in a manner that protects and preserves each client's dignity" (Hodge 2006, 321).

While there is no agreed upon definition of spirituality and religion, religion is viewed as a more formal organization and spirituality is often referred to as a search for meaning and connectedness. Religion has been defined as "an organized, structured set of beliefs and practices shared by a community related to spirituality" (Furman et al. 2004, 772). Canda (1989) refers to spirituality as the "basic human drive for meaning, purpose, and moral relatedness among people, with the universe, and with the ground of our being" (573). Some research has found that religion and spirituality can help individuals cope with loss. In a study of middle-aged and older adults, Brennan (2004) found that spirituality predicted adaptation to vision loss. Professionals should be able to build on this resource to help those individuals for whom spirituality and religion play an important role in dealing with loss.

Some individuals may need professional support to help them

through the grieving process. It is essential to explore the individual's feelings of grief and loss in the context of his or her biological, psychological, social, and spiritual functioning. This assessment is a way to gather information and get an understanding of individuals and their lives in order to form the basis for action decisions (Hepworth, Rooney, and Larsen 2002). This comprehensive assessment enables the practitioner in partnership with the individuals to suggest specific interventions that address the complex needs of individuals and their families, while bringing about some relief from their distressing circumstances. With the increased recognition of the role of spirituality and religion in the lives of individuals, the Joint Commission for the Accreditation of Healthcare Organizations (JCAHO) now requires that a spiritual assessment be gathered on all patients admitted to acute care hospitals or long-term care settings and those receiving home health services (Clark, Drain, and Malone 2003; Joint Commission 2004). Hodge (2006) in his discussion of the JCAHO assessment explains that the "spiritual assessment can be thought of as the process of gathering, analyzing, and synthesizing spiritual and religious information into a specific framework that provides the basis for, and gives direction to, subsequent practice decisions" (318).

The case examples illustrated in the beginning of this chapter show how experiencing grief and loss is in no way restricted to experiencing a death. Ester, Sophie, and Joseph each experienced considerable losses in role, status, security, stability, and physical functioning. Furthermore, the unwavering reliance on spirituality for some and questioning of it for others can also be explored during the assessment process. Practitioners should begin any assessment by inquiring about the nature of a client's physical health status. Since physical health conditions have been found to be associated with emotional distress and mental illness, a health examination is essential to developing an appropriate treatment plan. A psychological evaluation is the next component of the assessment process. This assessment will give practitioners information on the client's mental status (e.g., mood, affect, appearance, orientation, memory, thought processes, judgment, and suicidal ideation) and overall emotional outlook. When having experienced an event, such as those described earlier, or in any circumstance where grief and loss are the predominate feeling states, clients may naturally describe having a sad, depressed, uneasy, or anxious mood. According to the Diagnostic and Statistical Manual of Mental Disorders, 4th edition (DSM-IV), each of these moods can lead to the individual having: difficulty concentrating, disturbed sleeping patterns, unintentional changes in weight, loss of energy, low self-esteem, irritability, muscle tension, and/or a decreased interest in doing the things that he or she once enjoyed (American Psychiatric Association 2000). During the social assessment, the practitioner can explore whether there is a richness or a paucity of resources in the individual's environment and, if so, whether the individual has equitable access to those resources. The practitioner has the opportunity to explore the interface between the individual's level of functioning and issues related to areas such as employment, education, poverty, and housing. The spiritual assessment inquires about the individual's spiritual or religious beliefs. Individuals should be consulted on the nature of these beliefs and practices and the role that these beliefs have in their lives. Through the spiritual assessment, the practitioner can determine if the individual's spiritual or religious beliefs are a positive resource used for coping. If this is affirmed, then the practitioner can seek to utilize and strengthen this resource (e.g., making a referral to clergy, discussing how beliefs have helped during difficult times in the past, linking the individual with a faith community) in the action plan.

Case 1—Ester

Although no physical problems were specifically mentioned for Ester, the death of her husband and natural bereavement may trigger an episode of depression or anxiety, which may manifest in a physiological complication or exacerbate a preexisting medical condition. After fifty-four years of marriage, Benjamin's death has left Ester feeling alone. Since she spent the last two years being her husband's primary caretaker, she became isolated from the couple's few remaining social supports. Through conducting the psychological assessment, the practitioner discovered that Ester perceived herself as not having a sense of purpose since Benjamin's death. It also became evident that Ester had lost weight recently and was not sleeping at night. Her anxiety about maintaining her household without consultation with or direction from Benjamin emotionally paralyzed her to the point that she stopped attending to all aspects of financial management, including paying the bills timely. This lapse in judgment further reinforced Ester's depression and anxiety. Ester reported being comfortable financially, since she was receiving income from Social Security and a pension. She reminisced over having a good life. We may not have realized, without conducting an assessment, that Ester was a spiritual individual who has the support of her rabbi and temple congregation. In fact, Ester often turned to prayer as a way of gathering strength to cope with her loss. After the social worker completed an assessment and worked with Ester, they decided that she could benefit from individual counseling, attending a community support group for women who had lost their spouses, as well as continuing to attend weekly services and other activities at her local synagogue.

Case 2—Sophie

In working with Sophie and Steve, we know that Sophie experienced a miscarriage in the first trimester of her pregnancy. Although much remains unknown about why miscarriages occur, most women who experience a miscarriage typically go on to deliver healthy babies in the future. A physical examination will provide definitive information on Sophie's health status and uncover any medical complications that need to be addressed before a subsequent pregnancy is considered or attempted. Whenever Sophie expressed any feelings of sadness over the miscarriage, Steve would offset her feelings with statements like "keep the faith" or "you have to believe." When Sophie met with the practitioner for a consultation, she disclosed that she felt an "emptying" of her soul immediately after the miscarriage. This emptying was accompanied by strong feelings of guilt. The recurring thought of "I must have done something wrong to lose my baby" echoed in Sophie's mind and contributed to her feelings of inadequacy. She was always taught that "God would make a way," and now she questioned why she had been abandoned by her God. She vacillated between feeling guilty over the possibility that perhaps her own behaviors contributed to the miscarriage and feeling guilty over the crisis that she was experiencing in doubting her faith. According to the DSM-IV, feelings of worthlessness and excessive or inappropriate guilt are symptoms of a major depressive episode (American Psychiatric Association 2000). The psychological assessment revealed that Sophie did not have a prior history of depression, yet she currently reported experiencing five of the nine diagnostic criteria necessary for a diagnosis of major depression. Sophie began individual counseling that included a few couple's therapy sessions. She and Steve also spoke with their minister, who helped them to see that the loss of their baby was not a punishment by God. The couple grew in their faith as the combination of counseling and spiritual guidance gave them the strength to face their loss together.

Case 3—Joseph

An updated physical examination and ongoing medical attention were necessary for Joseph whose age-related macular degeneration had a significant impact on his level of functioning. The regular evaluations and information obtained from Joseph's physician and occupational therapist can be a guide in developing a treatment plan that includes recreational or other activities appropriately tailored to his level of functioning. Joseph's initial reaction to his diagnosis was one of anxious resolve. With each passing month Joseph's negative self-talk replaced his normally easygoing personality. In the past, when Joseph experienced tough times, he turned to his faith for comfort and support. Joseph shared with the practitioner that this challenge was different than any other he had experienced before. He was distressed that no matter how much he prayed and sought spiritual guidance, he could not rid himself of "this anxious feeling." Prayer was normally a comfort to him, but struggling to read his daily devotionals had the opposite effect, since he had trouble seeing to read. He even described being so tense that on one occasion he began to hyperventilate, sweat, and became lightheaded and nauseated. He described fearing that he would not be able to take care of himself and live independently. Due to these symptoms, when Joseph went to his local emergency department, he was diagnosed as having had a panic attack. For Joseph, who was diagnosed with this disease, a referral was made to a large city program that helped individuals with vision loss. Joseph received a specialized eye examination and optical devices were prescribed to help him maximize his remaining vision. In addition, Joseph also received rehabilitation support to help him learn about how to get around his home and his community.

These case examples demonstrate how the comprehensive assessment was used to develop a plan of action that includes setting goals (e.g., reduce symptoms of depression, improve occupational function, increase socialization) and coming up with practical ways of achieving said goals (e.g., attending counseling sessions, joining a social group, enrolling in a rehabilitation program). This plan of action, also known as a *treatment plan* or *care plan* depending on the setting, is the road map toward relieving the distressing sadness or anxiety typically associated with grief and loss. When developing this plan of action, both the individual and practitioner determine what resources (e.g., financial, housing, employment, recreational, and social supports) are needed to achieve the agreed upon goals. In addition, it is important to determine which professionals with specific training and expertise will participate in the plan of action. As such, professionals are encouraged to develop networks with other practitioners to meet the individual's needs in the most comprehensive, efficient, and timely manner.

Professional Partnerships

Social workers, pastoral counselors, psychologists, physicians, nurses, and other professionals work toward helping individuals during difficult times. When reviewing these cases, it became apparent that Ester, Sophie, and Joseph benefited from the individual spiritual leader. These professional partnerships were instrumental in helping the clients highlighted in this chapter cope with their loss. In some instances, it was the social worker or the psychologist who recommended that the clients speak with their spiritual leaders, and in other instances it was the pastoral counselor who recognized that the individual needed formal psychological assistance. This is an example of professionals understanding the strengths and limitations of their professional training on a case-by-case basis. Making referrals to other professionals who possess the required expertise (e.g., knowledge of mental illness or knowledge of spiritual/religious doctrine) ensures that the individual gets the help needed. Coordination and discussion of the needs of the individual are vital to successful intervention.

A multidisciplinary approach increases knowledge and understanding and opens avenues for pursuing a range of resources that can help the individual. It is not always possible that a single professional, agency, or program can meet the needs of those individuals who have experienced a loss. Since grieving is complex, involving professionals from different disciplines may help meet the diverse needs of our clients. Communication between professionals can help clients, as well as strengthen professionals' skills and competencies.

Yet, how do we as professionals collaborate with others more effectively to help individuals who are grieving after a loss? Recognizing Each other's Specialized Professional Expertise and Coordinating care Together (RESPECT) can be the solution.

Recognizing each other's knowledge and expertise as a contribution to a client's care plan is an important step toward creating a dialogue between professionals from different disciplines. Professionals can learn about the work of other professionals by attending multidisciplinary conferences—internationally, nationally, regionally, or locally—to hear about different projects, research, and endeavors in other fields. Attending conferences can be one way of sharing professionals' expertise, as well as exploring a range of approaches that can make a difference in individuals' lives. Another way we can expand our knowledge is to read peer-reviewed articles, books, and proceedings. This strategy may sharpen our own skills and/or present alternative ways of looking at the situation.

An educational approach that has been valuable in enhancing training for physicians, nurses, social workers, pastoral counselors, and other professionals is using case studies to help understand the different types of situations practitioners may encounter. Often the cases are complex, including ethical issues and individual and family problems surrounding the case. Professionals in agencies may prepare cases for discussion among staff members or in collaboration with another agency or organization. Case studies can help professionals use their knowledge and critical thinking skills to address the range of problems that are raised about the case. Grief and loss case studies can be developed to help professionals, as well as students, understand the range of loss experiences by different individuals. Case studies can be used to understand how different factors (e.g., age, culture, ethnicity, and class) play a role in how individuals cope with grief and loss. The use of case studies can provide professionals with an approach that facilitates in-depth discussion, addresses specific situations, and provides professionals with strategies to deal with complex cases (Clark 2002; Lynn 1999; Scales et al. 2002).

Portraying the stories of Ester, Sophie, and Joseph in the assessment process is one way of illustrating how important it is for professionals to work together to coordinate a plan of care that helps each client. Continuous dialogue between professionals is essential.

Networking, sharing expertise at professional conferences, and working together are ways to encourage better communication. Finally, we need to talk with one another and RESPECT the skills that each professional offers. The lives of Ester, Sophie, and Joseph were explored through assessment, but by professionals working together and by understanding their spiritual strengths to help them cope with their loss, their lives were enhanced.

Works Cited

American Association of Pastoral Counseling. 1994. *Code of Ethics*. Http://www.aapa.org/ethics.cfm. Accessed January 30, 2007.

American Psychiatric Association. 2000. *Diagnostic and Statistical Manual of Mental Disorders*. Rev. 4th ed. Washington, DC: American Psychiatric Association.

American Psychological Association. 2002. *American Psychological Association Ethics Code*. Http://www.apa.org/ethics/code202.pdf. Accessed January 30, 2007.

Brennan, M. 2004. "Spirituality and Religiousness Predict Adaptation to Vision Loss in Middle-Age and Older Adults." *International Journal for the Psychology of Religion* 14, no. 3:193–214.

Canda, E. 1989. "Religion and Social Work: It's Not That Simple." *Social Casework* 70, no. 9:572–74.

Clark, P. G. 2002. "Values and Voices in Teaching Gerontology and Geriatrics: Case Studies as Stories." *The Gerontologist* 42, no. 3:297–303.

Clark, P. A., M. Drain, and M. P. Malone. 2003. "Addressing Patients' Emotional and Spiritual Needs." *Joint Commission Journal on Quality and Safety* 29, no. 12: 659–70.

Council on Social Work Education. 2001. *Educational Policy and Accreditation Standards*. Alexandria, VA: Council on Social Work Education.

Furman, L. D., P. W. Benson, C. Grimwood, and E. Canda. 2004. "Religion and Spirituality in Social Work Education and Direct

Practice at the Millennium: A Survey of UK Social Workers." *British Journal of Social Work* 34:767–92.

Hepworth, D. H., R. H. Rooney, and J. A. Larsen. 2002. *Direct Social Work Practice*. 6th ed. Pacific Grove, CA: Brooks/Cole.

Hodge, D. R. 2006. "A Template for Spiritual Assessment: A Review of the JCAHO Requirement and Guidelines for Implementation." *Social Work* 51, no. 4:317–26.

Holmes, T. H., and M. Masuda. 1974. "Life Change and Illness Susceptibility." In *Stressful Life Events: Their Nature and Effects*, edited by B. S. Dohrenwend and B. P. Dohrenwend. New York: Wiley.

Holmes, T. H., and R. Rahe. 1967. "The Social Readjustment Rating Scale." *Journal of Psychosomatic Research* 11:213–18.

Hooyman, N. R., and H. A. Kiyak. 2005. *Social Gerontology: A Multidisciplinary Approach*. Boston: Pearson.

Joint Commission. 2004. *Spiritual Assessment*. Http://www.jointcommission.org/AccreditationPrograms/Hospital/Standards/FAQs. Accessed December 30, 2007.

Joint Commission Resources. 2003. *Comprehensive Accreditation Manual for Hospitals: The Official Handbook*. Oakbrook Terrace, IL: Joint Commission on Accreditation of Healthcare Organizations.

Lynn, L. E., Jr. 1999. *Teaching and Learning with Cases and How? The Research Base for Teaching with Cases*. Mahwah, NJ: Lawrence Erlbaum.

Masuda, M., and T. H. Holmes. 1978. "Life Events: Perceptions and Frequencies." *Psychosomatic Medicine* 40, no. 3:236–61.

McLeod, J. D. 1996. "Life Events." In *Encyclopedia of Gerontology*, edited by J. E. Birren. San Diego: Academic Press.

National Association of Social Workers. 1999. *NASW Code of Ethics*. Washington, DC: National Association of Social Workers.

Scales, T. L., T. A. Wolfer, D. A. Sherwood, D. R. Garland, B. Hugen, and S. W. Pittman. 2002. *Spirituality and Religion in Social Work Practice: Decision Cases with Teaching Notes*. Alexandria, VA: Council on Social Work Education.

13

Healing In the Christian Tradition

A Reflection on a Course for Nurses

Marylin Kravatz

"Healing in the Christian Tradition" is a course I have taught for nurses. The idea for the course originated when I met with the chairwoman of the theology/philosophy department of a college, where I taught as an adjunct professor. The college, founded in the Catholic tradition, offered to all students the opportunity to study courses in theology and philosophy.

At first, I was taken aback when the chairwoman asked me if I would entertain teaching a course specifically for nursing students. These particular students already practiced as nurses and were returning to college to complete undergraduate studies. She knew that I had been trained and had practiced as a nurse some years before, and she thought my experience might be beneficial to them. As I thought about it, I began to like the idea. After all, I knew their language and I could relate to their experiences.

After perusing the litany of the theology/philosophy courses offered, I told my colleague that whatever course I did teach, I would want to make it relevant to the nursing profession and to the experience of the students. From within, I felt I was being drawn to teach a course that was related to healing. The chairwoman immediately surfed through a filing cabinet of syllabi and told me that such a course entitled "Healing in the Christian Tradition" was offered at one time for any interested student. In concurrence with my inner voice, I decided on this course, and, with the copy of an "old" syllabus in hand, I walked out of the office of the department chair with thoughts of reshaping the course specifically for nurses.

Time would tell if such a course would be beneficial for nurses. The original course description stated: "This course will explore the biblical roots of healing, suffering, and death, the theology of the cross and resurrection, liturgy, and health care as sources of reflection, theological and philosophical approaches to the meaning of human suffering, and attitudes toward suffering and death in American culture." I immediately added to the description that the course would be directed specifically for nurses, and I devised course objectives that would enhance it in an exclusive way for the nurse as a person and as a professional.

Nurses certainly experience suffering, death, and healing in their work. Perhaps they might gain new theological and philosophical insights about such experiences as well as to the meaning of these terms as the course processed and progressed. I began to think this might be a good experience both for the students and for me as the teacher.

I wanted the students to have an opportunity to grow both personally and professionally and hoped that an engaging, well-rounded course of study might help them to develop the resources and confidence they would need as they experienced the healing, suffering, and death of their patients. The course objectives, which would serve as our map in attaining these goals, evolved as:

1. To provide for nurses an understanding of healing, suffering, and dying as presented in the Hebrew and Christian scriptures, various texts and articles, and videos that enrich the topics;
2. To explore the Catholic Church's message to health care providers and its teachings on the sacraments of healing;

3. To review the history of nursing and to identify the shifting paradigm of nursing as it relates to healing, suffering, and dying in contemporary times;
4. To offer nurses the opportunity to evaluate their personal human, spiritual, and cultural attitudes in regard to healing, suffering, and death and to realize these attitudes in other persons;
5. To recognize the practical and ministerial roles of the nurse in the healing, suffering, and dying experiences of those they care for.

The reshaping of the course was finalized with the required and recommended texts, evaluation and general information, and specific requirements. I looked forward to the discussions and to exposing the students to the writings of published authors in fields related to this course. I also anticipated the thoughts and shared experiences of the students from which, no doubt, we all would learn. The beginning of our journey called for the study of the evolution of the nursing profession from its roots to its contemporary state, so that the students might understand and relate to the status quo as they saw and experienced it.

The Contemporary Landscape of Nursing

The first question I asked the students was, "What motivated you to become a nurse?" The responses varied, but there was a common thread—each had the desire to care for another human being, and working in the nursing profession was a way for them to fulfill this desire. Each student had taken the steps to prepare for this profession of caring for the sick and infirm of our society, and now each was continuing the education in order to enhance that work, both qualitatively and professionally.

Intensive care units, emergency rooms, operating and recovery rooms, adolescent psychiatric units, oncology departments, and pediatric and gerontology units are examples of the specific care areas in which the students worked. The profession of nursing indeed is concerned with caring for others, and the students were vocal about this. At the same time, they also were situating nursing within hospital systems that functioned as "big businesses," where staff shortages, unreasonably demanding patients and their families, and the lack of time prevented them from building relationships. This included patients from varied cultural and ethnic backgrounds and those who lacked financial and medical resources. It was evident that the realities of disappointing systems were impeding the ideal of why they entered the profession.

In their work *Called to Care: A Christian Worldview for Nursing*, Judith Allen Shelly and Arlene B. Miller (2006) suggest that the changes experienced in the field of nursing today stem from a paradigm shift in our culture. Nurses once were motivated by the spirit of service and compassion, but that motivation has changed to a professionalism that demands power, status, and appropriate compensation (14–16).

Shelly and Miller echo the sentiments of the students, regarding the tension brought on by this shift in the paradigm:

> Why are we in nursing? Is it only to earn a decent wage? Are we hoping to gain power and prestige or academic status? While nurses have traditionally entered nursing to serve God and care for the sick, those motivations seem to be rapidly changing. Too many nurses line up at the time clock to punch out while patient call lights flash. Others retreat to academia to avoid the unpleasant tasks of staff nursing. (2006, 23–24)

I soon realized that one of my roles was to help the students explore the possibilities of being true to their ideals, in spite of the situations that seemed to obstruct the quality of care they wanted to provide for their patients. Exposing the students to Christian theological and spiritual thought would offer them an opportunity to recapture their ideals and to enrich their experience. A study of the history of the nursing profession could help the students to better understand its contemporary status.

A Brief History of the Nursing Profession

Caring for the sick was in evidence in ancient biblical times. The Hebrew Scriptures provide a number of instances wherein the need for attending to the sick is significant. The prophet Ezekiel uses a parable with a shepherd theme in order to admonish the leaders of Israel for not strengthening the weak, healing the sick, or binding up the injured (Ezek 34:4). Midwives are mentioned in the books of Genesis (38:28) and Exodus (1:15–21). People are known to petition God for healing in the Hebrew Bible (Num 12:13; 2 Kgs 20:5–8).

Later on, the Gospels of the Christian Scriptures offer many examples of Jesus' caring for and healing the sick and the suffering. Actually, Shelly and Miller claim nursing developed out of a Christian worldview that is based on the teachings and example of Jesus Christ and the Gospels (2006, 18). In addition, Matthew 25:31–46 offers a teaching that not only reflects Jesus' own concern for preparing oneself to enter the kingdom of God but also presents a practical religion of deeds of loving-kindness and love of neighbor. Jesus instructs his followers to feed the hungry, to give drink to those who thirst, to welcome the stranger, to clothe the naked, to care for the ill, and to visit the imprisoned. Some biblical translations use the term *comfort*, translated from the Greek *episkeptomai*, meaning "to look after" and "nurse" for this particular passage (Viviano 1990, 669).

In the early Christian church, deacons and deaconesses were appointed to care for the poor, the sick, and the marginalized members of society. Eventually, Catholic monasteries served as hospitals and nursing orders of nuns and other religious orders continued to care for the sick and needy. Such care was founded on Christian service, charity, and caring for the body to reach the soul.

Beginning in the Renaissance period and continuing through the eighteenth century, Catholic religious orders were disbanded or suppressed in Protestant countries and hospitals began to deteriorate. As a result, nursing ceased to be a public role, as it moved out of the church and into the home. Except for a few nursing orders of nuns, the field of nursing was disorganized and corrupt by the nineteenth century.

Reform came through the work of such persons as Elizabeth Seton (1774–1821), Catherine McAuley (1778–1841), Elizabeth Fry (1780–1845), and other members of the Christian churches who provided care for the poor and sick.

The early 1900s introduced much needed formal training for those who cared for the sick. Florence Nightingale (1820–1910) single-handedly reformed nursing by bringing it back to its Christian roots and by setting high educational and practice standards. However, an unexpected conflict among her followers developed. Some understood nursing as a calling from God, while others viewed nursing as a secular profession. That is to say, the role of the deaconess was understood as a biblical office that exercised charity and cared for the body to reach the soul for the purpose of eternal salvation. The nurse, on the other hand, was viewed as having a worldly vocation, concerned with the present welfare of the patient and with financial compensation. These philosophies of service and professionalism existed side by side, causing tension in the field.

In recent decades, the training of nurses has entered the world of higher education, although a conflict between service and professionalism seems to still exist. By exposing these philosophies in class and examining their impact on the development of the field of nursing, the students could now label the conflict they were experiencing. With that objective accomplished, it was time to introduce the theme of the course: healing. The meaning of the term, its process, and the students' role in the healing of those they cared for needed to be examined and explored.

Marylin Kravatz

To Cure or to Heal?

I asked the students to offer a meaning for the term *healing*. Their responses indicated a focus on the scientific dimension of the physical components of the person. In other words, they answered in terms of *cure*. A discrepancy exists, in my opinion, between the meanings of the terms *healing* and *cure*, and it is one that calls for clarification.

The term *cure* is rooted in the Latin *curare* meaning, "to take care of." The term developed to mean "a medical course of treatment for a body ailment." This meaning was in sync with what the students thought to be the meaning for *to heal*.

The term *healing*, on the other hand, is rooted in the Old English *hāl* meaning "to make sound or whole." Wholeness connotes an integral sense of having all the components. The human person is not only physical in being but emotional, spiritual, and social as well. When asked about the spiritual and psychosocial dimensions of the person, the students recognized the existence of these dimensions and their responsibility to be aware of them, but they admitted their own inadequacies and were comfortable to leave such topics, other than the physical, to the hospital chaplain and/or social worker.

Shelly and Miller acknowledge that, while medicine has traditionally focused on the scientific dimension of the human body, the uniqueness of nursing, being both an art and a science, emphasizes caring for the whole person as being embodied (2006, 16). I believe the students would agree with this acknowledgment, but it was obvious that some might be uncomfortable with the spiritual and psychosocial dimensions. While I welcomed their honesty, I also felt the need to invite the students to a deeper understanding of the term *healing*, to their role in the healing process of those they cared for, and to explore their own personal sense of wholeness. I hoped for them to make both a professional and a personal connection to the meaning of healing.

Jacqueline Perez (2003), a physician, seems to concur with Shelly and Miller. She states, "Healing is a process by which one is made healthy, whole, or sound of body and mind. Medicine is the art and science of restoring or preserving health through the healing process" (101). The students would comply with this definition. But Perez offers additional thought to a meaning of healing.

Acknowledging that modern medicine is firmly rooted in scientific method and practice, Perez claims there is a need for medical personnel to pay attention also to the spiritual needs of their patients, as such a gesture is significant in the healing process. She clarifies:

> I have learned through my own experience in caring for patients there is a spiritual dimension in the doctor-patient encounter. And I have only begun to formulate several concepts that I believe, when incorporated in an encounter, can help actualize that "divine-human bond," fill the "spiritual emptiness," alleviate some of the feelings of fear and uncertainty, and create a spiritual dimension in which true healing can occur. (110)

Three factors are necessary to actualize the divine-human bond that promotes healing. These, according to Perez, are communication, connection, and communion.

Communication requires the following three aspects: listening, speaking, and silence. Listening is the ability to focus totally and completely on what is being said. It allows the listener to not only hear but to understand. Communication through speaking is the act of talking openly and honestly from the heart. Silence is absolutely necessary if true listening and honest speaking are to take place. It allows the listener to understand truly what is being said, and it allows the speaker the ability to formulate what they wish to say as well as discern what is truly in her or his heart (110–11).

Important in the healing process is the ability for two or more people to connect. This coming together is created through the creativity of space, safety, and sacredness. First, physical, mental, and emotional space are necessary for the creation of a sense of openness that would provide a source of nourishment and support for the encountering parties. Mental space allows for complete attention and presence to what is occurring in the encounter. Emotional space is the opening of one's heart to the other person. Second, the creation of a safe place is necessary if people are to feel a sense of security and trust that will enable them to expose their thoughts and feelings. Security and trust are promoted when confidentiality, empathy, and compassion are exuded in the process. Third, intentionality, hope, and gratitude are the necessary ingredients for sacredness. Perez explains:

> Being intentional means having specific reasons for doing something and knowing what exactly it is that one is doing and why. Hope is an essential ingredient in the healing process. It provides energy to those who are suffering and is the seed of comfort in the healing process. Gratitude is a state of humility in which, aware of one's own limitations and lack of control, one is accepting of all that has and will occur. It too is a seed in the healing process, a seed from which peace is born. (111)

"Communion," according to Perez, "is a state of grace in which the Divine enters and healing occurs" (111). Communion transpires, when communication and connection have taken place. Communion invokes a feeling of lightness and peacefulness for all parties of the encounter, as all come together and exist in one presence. This moment of grace is an experience of God's free and forgiving self-communication. Such an experience enables humans to share in the trinitarian relationship of love with Father, Son, and Holy Spirit (Hilkert 1995, 577).

Perez also makes a plea to the health care professions to put the care back into health care. She calls for the bridging of the gap between the art and science of medicine and to reawaken the interest in humanity that is foundational to the calling of health care providers and healers. Taking care of the physical, mental, and spiritual needs of the patients that are encountered will help to bring them back to health and wholeness (2003, 112).

Perhaps the absence of a holistic ethic of care was what the students sensed they were missing in their encounters with their patients. They not only sensed it, they named it as being the work of the psych/social workers and chaplains. Could this have been part of the ideal that lured them to respond to the call of the nursing profession but was misplaced, as they were overcome with other demands of the job and the belief that holistic care was solely the responsibility of other professionals? Could nurses understand themselves, along with other professionals, to be instruments of communication, connection, and communion tending to the spiritual and emotional as well as to the physical needs of their patients?

While Perez offers some specifics concerning the process of healing, I needed to make a connection with healing in the Christian tradition, since this was the object of the course. This connection would include a study of Jesus Christ and healing, the sacraments of healing offered in the Catholic tradition, and Christian views of the role of the nurse in the healing process.

Healing in the Christian Tradition

At the center of Christianity is Jesus Christ. The name *Jesus* or *Yeshua* in Aramaic means "Yahweh is Salvation." *Christ* means "anointed one." Salvation was central to his mission and to his ministry. The Gospel of Luke 4:16–23 iterates Jesus' self-awareness of his mission: "The spirit of the Lord is upon me, because he has anointed me to bring glad tidings to the poor. He has sent me to proclaim liberty to captives and recovery to the blind, to let the oppressed go free, and to proclaim a year acceptable to the Lord.…Today this scripture passage is fulfilled in your hearing." Healing, liberation, and salvation were the hallmarks of the mission of Jesus Christ. The central theme of Jesus' teaching was about the kingdom of God, a new life in God. This kingdom pertains not only to a deeper life with God after physical death but also to a life where we are saved from personal sin, ignorance, weakness of will, disoriented emotions, physical illness, and death.

Francis MacNutt (1999) advocates that Jesus came to do two basic things: (1) to give us a new life, a loving relationship of union with his Father and with himself, through the Holy Spirit; and (2) to heal and free (save) us from all those sick elements in our lives that need to be transformed, so that the new life may freely enter in. For MacNutt, healing is "simply the practical application of the basic Christian message of salvation, a belief that Jesus means to liberate us from personal sin and from emotional and physical illness" (40).

The Gospels reveal a variety of healing episodes in the ministry of Jesus. These healing acts of Jesus include healing of the spiritual, emotional, and physical aspects of the human person. *The New Jerome Biblical Commentary* (1990) attests that these acts not only affirmed Jesus' mission; they were the vehicles for his mission (Brown, Fitzmyer, and Murphy 1990, 1372). The theme of faith also plays an important role in Jesus' healing ministry. Jesus initiates the healing only after he or the disciples have challenged the person's faith (Perkins 1988, 66).

Many of these healing episodes begin with Jesus being moved with compassion and/or pity at the sight of a person's suffering (e.g., Matt 9:36; 14:14; Mark 1:41; 5:19; Luke 7:13). The healing encounters of Jesus with a suffering person can appear to comply with Perez's call for a process of communication, connection, and communion. This format appears in the healing stories of Jesus. One example is the healing of the woman with a hemorrhage from Luke 8:43–48. A woman was afflicted with hemorrhages for twelve years. She spent her whole livelihood on doctors and was unable to be cured by anyone. When she saw Jesus, she came up from the crowds behind him and touched the tassel on his cloak (connection). Immediately her bleeding stopped. Jesus realizes and verbalizes that someone touched him, because he felt the power go out of him (communication and connection). Trembling, the woman comes forward and explains to all the people why she touched Jesus (communication). She adds that she was healed immediately. Jesus then says to her, "Daughter, your faith has saved you; go in peace" (communication and communion).

Also in the Gospel of Luke (9:1–2; 10:1, 8–9) Jesus gives the same healing power to his disciples in order that they might preach his message of good news. Contemporary disciples continue to minister to others and to proclaim the good news through their caring. The community of the Catholic Church also continues to carry out the mission of Jesus' caring for those who are suffering or ill in the celebration of two sacraments of healing: the Sacrament of Penance and Reconciliation and the Sacrament of the Anointing of the Sick.

The *Catechism of the Catholic Church* defines sacraments as "efficacious signs of grace, instituted by Christ and entrusted to the Church, by which divine life is dispensed in us. The visible rites by which the sacraments are celebrated signify and make present the graces proper to each sacrament" (CCC §1131). These two of the seven sacraments, the Sacrament of Penance and Reconciliation and the Sacrament of the Anointing of the Sick, intend to provide specific healing effects: (1) The Sacrament of Penance and Reconciliation sacramentally makes present Jesus' call to the penitent to a conversion from sin to the love of God, who reconciles, granting pardon and peace for the sake of inner healing. (2) The Sacrament of the Anointing of the Sick is given to strengthen those who are ill with the gifts of peace, courage, and a renewed faith and trust in God, in order that they might overcome the challenges of illness or the frailty of old age; the sacrament is meant to lead the sick person to the healing of the soul and of the body.

While prayer has a role in the healing process, so does medicine. God also works through doctors, nurses, psychiatrists, and counselors to facilitate the process of healing. Prayer and medicine together should be cooperative partners in healing. MacNutt explains:

> There are some Christians who set up an artificial opposition between prayer and medicine—as if God's

> way of healing is through prayer while the medical profession is a secular means of healing, somehow unworthy of Christians who have real faith. Consequently, they encourage people to pray and not to see their doctor. But God works through the doctor to heal as well as through prayer for healing—the doctor, the counselor, and the nurse are all ministers of healing. All these different professions, with their different competencies, go to make up God's healing team. Any time we disparage any person who helps bring about the healing of the whole person we are destroying the kind of cooperative healing ministry that the Christian community might have and are setting up false divisions between divine and human healing methods. (1999, 131)

Physical healing on the part of Jesus was intimately connected with the proclamation of the gospel, and its ultimate purpose was to restore people to a vital relationship with God and the community. For Shelly and Miller, nursing is a vocation, a calling from God, and it cannot work toward the goal of health without including the clear proclamation of the gospel as well as providing physical care with a servant attitude (2006, 24). This is their hope for the profession, and it is expressed in their definition of nursing with a Christian viewpoint as "a ministry of compassionate care for the whole person, in response to God's grace toward a sinful world, which aims to foster optimum health (shalom) and bring comfort in suffering and death for anyone in need" (17–18).

The *Charter for Health Care Workers*, promulgated by the Pontifical Council for Pastoral Assistance, concurs with Shelly and Miller's aforementioned considerations and includes a missionary dimension to the profession of the health care worker. While a variety of health care workers participate in the diagnosis, treatment, and recovery to health, the charter proclaims that scientific and professional expertise is not enough—the personal empathy toward each patient is required (CHCW §2).

To view the health care worker as an instrument of God's outpouring of love for the suffering person is to acknowledge that ministry and mission play a role in health care. For the Christian, showing an act of love of God in ministry is an actual continuation of the healing love of Christ. The occupation of the health care worker provides a locale where profession, vocation, and mission meet, and in the Christian vision of life and health, they are mutually integrated. Seen in this light, health care assumes a new and more exalted meaning as "service to life" and "healing ministry." The health care worker is a minister of and a collaborator with God, who restores health to the sick body while serving a person's spirit. The psycho-physical unity of the person is to be recognized through the love, attention, understanding, sharing, kindness, patience, and dialogue offered by the health care worker (CHCW §4).

With the presentation on healing in the Christian tradition completed, it was time for me to help the students internalize the teaching with their experience. Since much of their work is concerned with suffering and dying persons, their role in the healing process needed to be addressed within the context of suffering and death and dying.

The Nurse: Minister to the Suffering and Dying

1. Suffering

For the class on suffering, the students were assigned to read three articles on the suffering experiences of the authors and to write a comparative paper. Some of the requirements of the assignment were to have them express their human and spiritual reactions to the articles, to articulate how they determined their professional role in each scenario, and to share what they may have learned from these true stories. This assignment evoked the following questions:

1. What is suffering?
2. What are some forms of suffering?
3. Why do you think suffering exists?
4. Does everyone suffer?
5. What is God's relationship to human suffering?

The discussion prompted by these questions was thought provoking and lively. The comments included variations of the following ideas about suffering:

1. It is a punishment from God.
2. It is a test to discipline the human spirit.
3. It is good for us for some reason.
4. Some people seem to "get" more suffering than others.
5. Since God is in control of everything, then God causes us to suffer for whatever reason (including those already mentioned).

It became clear that there existed a need to explore and possibly to explain why suffering exists and the role that God may have in suffering.

The first resource I presented was the Book of Job, classified as one of the Wisdom books found in the Hebrew Scriptures. The legendary story of Job is a composite about a man whom God tested and found faithful. The story is a rich and profound exploration of human innocence and suffering that includes the struggle of divine power versus the human search for meaning. The author of Job created a story that places the fundamental human question about suffering within Israel's belief in Yahweh. The ultimate lesson learned is that, from the midst of doubt and questioning, comes trust (Boadt 1984, 482).

Another resource I deemed necessary for this class was Harold S. Kushner's (1981) work *When Bad Things Happen to Good People*. Not only does Kushner give further insight into the

Job story but he also offers a perspective that God does not do things to us that cause us to suffer. Kushner explains:

> If God is a God of justice and not of power, then He can still be on our side when bad things happen to us. He can know that we are good and honest people who deserve better. Our misfortunes are none of His doing, and so we can turn to Him for help. Our question will not be Job's question "God, why are You doing this to me?" but rather "God, see what is happening to me. Can you help me?" We will turn to God, not to be judged or forgiven, not to be rewarded or punished, but to be strengthened and comforted. (50–51)

A discussion followed on the existence of good and evil and the concept that suffering is the consequence of sin in the world. Included in the conversation were the thoughts of Augustine, Thomas Aquinas, Alfred North Whitehead, and feminist theologians Elizabeth Johnson, Sally McFague, Anne Carr, and Dorothee Soelle. The feminist viewpoint particularly was similar to Kushner's thoughts. This position finds unacceptable the idea of a God who permits great suffering while remaining unaffected. Instead, feminine theologians see divine power not as domineering or controlling but as a liberating power of caring connectedness. God's compassionate love is present in the world in order to transform it from within. This does not solve the mystery of suffering or explain it away but offers hope to draw on, as we continue to struggle against evil (Fischer and Hart 1995, 121–23).

2. *Death and Dying*

"Death," states Elisabeth Kübler-Ross, "is still a fearful, frightening happening, and the fear of death is a universal fear even if we think we have mastered it on many levels" (1969, 19). With this statement in mind, I began the class on death and dying with an invitation to the students to converse with one another about the following questions:

1. What are your attitudes about death and dying?
2. What do you think of your own mortality, and how does that make you feel?
3. How do you see your role with the dying person and the person's family?
4. What do you think is the general attitude toward death in the United States?

This time the conversation was more sedate. Most admitted a fear of death on some level, but most concluded that the approach of the culture toward death played a significant role in one's personal attitude.

In order once again to help the students internalize the teachings of the class, they were given a group assignment to act out creatively or role-play the five stages of dying proposed by Kübler-Ross. By identifying with the denial, anger, bargaining, depression, and acceptance that many of their patients experience, the hope for the assignment was to help the students be more empathetic to the dying patients they care for. This little exercise triggered surprisingly for some students the need to revisit some unhealed hurts concerning death issues that they were harboring. Being in the safe environment and through the compassion of their classmates, the students were able to express their emotions freely.

Germane to the topic of the class was to present Christian attitudes toward death and dying. The students needed to be aware that even Christians fear death, as did Jesus himself. Each of the Synoptic Gospels gives an account of the distress and agony Jesus experienced over his impending crucifixion and death, as he prayed in the Garden of Gethsemane. He asks that this cup be taken away from him, if that is God's will. It is written in the Gospel of Luke 22:44 that Jesus was in such agony that his sweat became like drops of blood.

Christian thought presents its own paradoxes concerning death, and personal conflicts may vacillate between the human experience and the Christian message. There may be terror but hope at the prospect of seeing God, and/or a fear that God's judgment may overshadow the promise of eternal life in Christ. Yet the Christian tradition offers that the relationship with God that started on earth will continue after death, and the teaching on the Communion of Saints proclaims that all the faithful, both living and dead, share the common life of the body of Christ.

The students learned that through the Paschal Mystery, that is, the suffering, death, rising, and ascension of Jesus Christ, humanity finds the hope of passing from life to death to new life again. Christian tradition tells us that all the faithful will share a glorious, heavenly life with God. Chapter 15 in the first letter of Paul to the Corinthians proclaims that like Christ, the dead will be resurrected and God will transform the whole person to that which is appropriate to the new life of the kingdom of God.

In the Gospels, suffering and death remain great mysteries of life. Yet Jesus is concerned with how we are to respond. In Jesus, God enters into our circumstances through his empathy, compassion, and companionship. He does this by (1) forgiving sins and calling people to conversion; (2) healing those with physical, emotional, and spiritual conflicts; (3) conquering suffering and death by his resurrection; and (4) asking his disciples to continue to struggle against sin and evil in the world (Fischer and Hart 1995, 124).

Within a Christian framework, the nurse is called to minister to the suffering and the dying, bringing comfort, hope, and healing. In the Christian tradition, Sr. Rosemary Donley offers three distinct approaches to suffering:

1. Compassionate accompaniment—through the presence and care of the nurse, the patient is helped to sustain the burden of suffering and may experience the presence of God, even though the situation may not be alleviated.
2. The search for meaning of personal and communal suffering—when suffering is endowed with the glorious

role of bringing a person closer to God, the person experiences relief, even when the suffering itself remains.

3. Providing excellent physical care—providing pain control, a pleasant environment, and additional comfort measures help a dying patient to relax and be able to relate to loved ones; the intention of this action is to remove the suffering itself.

Each of these approaches respects the person as reflecting the image of God. They are necessary, even if a cure is not possible. These approaches offer hope in the face of suffering and death (Shelly and Miller 2006, 213–14). Donley's approaches enrich the approaches of Perez (i.e., communication, connection, and communion) and vice versa.

Conclusion

Soon after beginning the course, I suggested to the students that we pray together each week. They were accepting of this, and I arranged each prayer service to relate to the topic of the class. Prayer enabled the students to experience spiritual reflection on the topic, while it provided a transitional experience from their day at work to the class.

In addition to the assignments already mentioned, the students completed reflection papers each week on particular case studies, provided a presentation on persons noted for healing who would act as role models, welcoming the students to the idea that they too could be active participants in the healing of their patients, and a final research paper concerned with current issues faced by health professionals. For the last requirement, they could choose a topic that interested them. Some topics they researched included abortion, caring for a dying spouse, nursing and the issue of poverty, sexual abuse, the death of a child, and nursing the mentally or physically challenged person. Not only did these topics interest them but, for some, these were personal experiences. In addition to providing adequate research and resources, this assignment, for some of the students, was cathartic. They, too, were experiencing healing.

The students began to be in touch with their own woundedness, and that would make them better ministers. How? The minister is called to be the wounded healer, the one who must look after her or his own wounds and at the same time be prepared to heal the wounds of others. Personal woundedness sharpens one's ability to be more compassionate, caring, understanding, hospitable, and forgiving (Nouwen 1972, 82–89).

Others felt "called" to a different type of nursing, such as working with persons who suffer from poverty. Some stated that they now had a more spiritual perspective within their own nursing vocation. Some, suffering with their own illness or grief, realized, like Job, that God was not responsible for their suffering but would be a companion on the journey.

Eventually the students and I would complete our time together. It was an honor and privilege for me to have been in their presence and to experience their growth and, for some, their transformation. They seemed to have a new enthusiasm. While they were still very much aware that the realities causing their frustrations still existed, they seemed to be confident in realizing their priorities. Wherever they were on their own spiritual and faith journeys, they had learned a way to be instruments of healing and hope for the suffering and dying persons entrusted to their care.

Bibliography

Boadt, Lawrence. 1984. *Reading the Old Testament*. Mahwah, NJ: Paulist Press.

Brown, Raymond E., Joseph A. Fitzmyer, and Roland E. Murphy, eds. 1990. "Miracles." In *The New Jerome Biblical Commentary*. Englewood Cliffs, NJ: Prentice Hall.

Fischer, Kathleen, and Thomas Hart. 1995. *Christian Foundations: An Introduction to Faith in Our Time*. Mahwah, NJ: Paulist Press.

Hilkert, Mary C. 1995. "Grace." In *The HarperCollins Encyclopedia of Catholicism*, edited by Richard P. McBrien. San Francisco: HarperCollins.

Kübler-Ross, Elisabeth. 1969. *On Death and Dying*. New York: Scribner.

Kushner, Harold S. 1981. *When Bad Things Happen to Good People*. New York: Anchor Books.

MacNutt, Francis. 1999. *Healing*. Notre Dame: Ave Maria Press.

New American Bible, The Catholic Bible, Personal Study Edition. 1995. New York: Oxford University Press.

Nouwen, Henri J. M. 1972. *The Wounded Healer*. New York: Doubleday.

Perez, Jacqueline C. 2003. "A Healing Presence: Meeting with Patients." In *Partners in Healing*, edited by Beverly Anne Musgrave and John R. Bickle. Mahwah, NJ: Paulist Press.

Perkins, Pheme. 1988. *Reading the New Testament*. 2nd ed. Mahwah, NJ: Paulist Press.

Pontifical Council for Pastoral Assistance. 1995. *Charter for Health Care Workers*. Boston: Pauline Books.

Shelly, Judith Allen, and Arlene B. Miller. 2006. *Called to Care: A Christian Worldview for Nursing*. 2nd ed. Downers Grove, IL: InterVarsity Press.

United States Conference of Catholic Bishops. 1997. *Catechism of the Catholic Church*. 2nd ed. Washington, DC: Libreria Editrice Vaticana.

Viviano, Benedict T., OP. 1990. "The Gospel according to Matthew." In *The New Jerome Biblical Commentary*, edited by Raymond E. Brown, Joseph A. Fitzmyer, Roland E. Murphy. Englewood Cliffs, NJ: Prentice Hall.

Webster's Third New International Dictionary. 1986. Springfield, MA: Merriam-Webster Inc.

14

Holy Living–Holy Dying

Paul A. Metzler

One of the special privileges of pastoral ministry is to be a companion to a parishioner facing dying. When the process of dying is openly anticipated, it offers the pastoral minister the opportunity to be present to the fears and hopes that characterize the journey to death, to tender patience, to offer understanding, and to represent the sustaining love of the faith community. In these circumstances, coping with dying can become *living with dying*, distinguished by a humble acceptance of the fact of death. Living with dying means appreciating life, even as it grows shorter, and living each day with gratitude and faithful confidence that joy, growth, and love can thrive, even in the face of death. Thus, life itself is sanctified on the journey to death. Holy living and holy dying are joined.

This perspective was profoundly expressed centuries ago in the writings of Jeremy Taylor, a Church of England priest who wrote two books of spiritual direction, *The Rule and Exercises of Holy Living* (1650) and *The Rule and Exercises of Holy Dying* (1651). They soon became bound as a single *Holy Living—Holy Dying* volume and were enormously popular. Multiple editions were published during the seventeenth century and beyond to meet the deep demand for spiritual support in both living and in dying.

As other great spiritual writers of his day, such as Francis de Sales in *Introduction to the Devout Life* (1609) Taylor sought to help faithful people live more fully into the Christian life. *Holy Living* and *Holy Dying* were originally written for his spiritual directee, Lady Carbery, though she died unexpectedly even as Taylor was writing his *Holy Dying* text for her. He chose to complete it in order to present it to her widower, the Earl of Carbery, on the first anniversary of her death in October 1651. Taylor's own wife, Phoebe, also died before Taylor had finished writing, and he buried her, as he had done his five sons.

Thus, Taylor was no stranger to death and loss, yet his poetic and elegant writing in the midst of such personal loss brought his readers into the mystery of life and death from the Christian perspective. Though portions of his spiritual writing may seem antiquated to us, I think his faithful rendering of the sacred truths of the Christian witness continues to support believers in our own day, particularly we who would minister to the dying and the bereaved. When, from time to time, I have read portions of *Holy Living—Holy Dying* again, I have felt joined to those who over the centuries have been spiritual partners to the dying and the grieving.

Prayerful Preparation

A prayer composed from the devotional sections of *Holy Living—Holy Dying* continues to be used in the authorized Book of Common Prayer of the Episcopal Church (1979) in this country. This *Collect*, or short unified prayer, has been variously placed either in the Pastoral Offices for Visitation to the Sick or in the Rite for the Burial of the Dead in revisions of the prayer book. As an Episcopal priest, I find this Collect to be a form of spiritual direction by itself, guiding me and those with whom I pray it to a deeper understanding about the frailty of life and also about a profound confidence in the abiding presence of God's love and mercy.

> O God, whose days are without end, and whose mercies cannot be numbered: Make us, we pray, deeply aware of

> the shortness and uncertainty of human life; and let your Holy Spirit lead us in holiness and righteousness all our days; that when we shall have served you in our generation, we may be gathered to our ancestors, having the testimony of a good conscience; in the communion of the Catholic Church, in the confidence of a certain faith, in the comfort of a religious and holy hope, in favor with you, our God, and in perfect charity with the world. All this we ask through Jesus Christ our Lord. Amen.[1]

In this graceful prayer, Taylor's poetic phrases capture important aspects of ministry to the sick and dying: the witness of a good conscience, the communion of the church, the comfort of confident faith, and the perfecting of charity with the world. I will return to these four themes as a framework to guide active ministry to the dying, but I also commend this prayer to you or similar ones from your own faith tradition. As pastoral ministers, we must begin always with prayer, trusting that ultimately what we do to support those facing dying, death, and bereavement is joined to God's purpose. I believe we can be companions of hope in the midst of situations of loss only to the degree that we are grounded in the faith of the community we represent. Personal prayer, reflective reading of scripture, and study of the grief literature are fundamental to our capacity to fulfill this ministry faithfully.

Personal Loss Awareness

I believe pastoral ministers must be aware of their own life experience with loss and grief. Intentional examination of our history with death or other losses helps us to identify the underlying feeling we bring to our ministry to the dying and can help us gain insight into our attitudes and ideas.

For example, my first awareness of a death took place when I was ten years old. My cousin, Dickie, age nineteen, died within two weeks of being diagnosed with leukemia. There were few treatments for childhood leukemia then, so the disease rapidly took his life. His death felt as sudden to me as a car accident death. His mother, Aunt Anna, was also my godmother, but I was not allowed to see her or to attend Dickie's funeral. My mother thought it best to shield me from the sight of Aunt Anna's raw grief, as she threw herself upon the open casket or as she frequently collapsed, screaming, to the floor. I learned about these things, as ten-year-olds often do, by eavesdropping on whispered conversations. I was stunned by the fact that someone just a few years older than I was could die but also quite alarmed by the fact that grief was truly overwhelming.

It has been important for me as a priest, psychotherapist, and hospice grief counselor to examine this alarming introduction to grief early in my life. Through examining this earliest loss experience, I have been able to overcome the idea impressed upon my ten-year-old mind that death is too terrible to be near or grief is too frightening to be seen. I had to grow in confidence that I could relate to the feelings of grieving persons and not be preoccupied with fear that emotions will get out of control. Without these insights from reflection on my personal loss awareness, I would be less able to be emotionally present and effective in ministry to the dying and bereaved.

It is also important to examine our past experiences with all types of loss to see if we have *carried grief*, a term Alan Wolfelt (2007) uses to describe unresolved grief that is carried forward because the loss was never properly mourned. A noted grief expert, Wolfelt offers a personal *Loss Inventory* that pastoral ministers may find useful. In order to help survey our losses over our lifetime as well as to recognize those that may continue to be painfully unresolved, he categorizes the many possible losses in life. Here is an adapted version of the Wolfelt *Loss Inventory*:[2]

Loss of People You Love
Separation (physical and/or emotional)
Rejection
Hostility/grudges

Illness (such as Alzheimer's, debilitating conditions)
Divorce
Abandonment/betrayal
Death
Empty nest

Loss of Pets

Loss of Aspects of Self
Self-esteem (often through physical, sexual, or emotional abuse)
Health, physical, or mental ability (due to aging or acute illness)
Job (downsizing, firing, failed business, retirement)
Control (addiction, victimization)
Innocence (abuse, exposure to immoral behavior)
Sexual identity/ability/desire
Security (such as through financial problems, war)
Expectations about how our lives should/would be)
Reputation
Beliefs (religious, spiritual, belief in others we trusted)
Dreams (hopes for the future)

Loss of Physical Objects
Home (fire or natural disaster, move or transition)
Linking objects (special items such as photos, jewelry)
Money (financial conditions, larceny)
Belongings (through theft, fire, etc.)
Nature/place (through a move, changing land use)

Loss through Developmental Transitions
Toddler to childhood
Childhood to adolescence
Adolescence to adulthood
Leaving home

Marriage
Having/not having children
Mid-life
Take care of parents
Retirement
Old age

Losses Not Noted Above
(Write in your own)

Wolfelt suggests that you first check off all the losses that you have ever experienced. Then return to each of them to recall more fully the loss and to identify if significant emotions and thoughts continue to surround the event. In this way, it is possible to identify losses that have not been fully mourned. Since carried grief is unfinished grief, it can block our ability to be fully attentive to the grief of others because it absorbs our emotional attention. However, it is possible in the present to revisit experiences of loss that were not adequately grieved at the time and to complete the grieving process more fully.

As others have noted, it takes "courage and resilience"[3] to be a partner in healing, so a useful thing to do is to have several partners each complete the inventory and then share your mutual recollections. Since many types of loss besides death are included, your survey will be a thorough consideration of your life experiences. As you share these memories in a larger circle, you will be linked with others who share this ministry, while you gain mutual insights into your individual experiences with loss. If you discover carried grief within yourself, the sharing with others will help you move toward greater resolution of that grief in the present time.

Nonanxious Presence

Our personal review of loss also helps us to recall which persons were available to understand and emotionally to support us through experiences of grief. The Psalmist says: "The Lord is near to the brokenhearted and will save those whose spirits are crushed." (Ps 34:18). We can learn much about how to be authentic pastoral ministers by recalling who was able to mediate God's nearful presence to us when our spirits were crushed.

In training classes, when I ask pastoral caregivers or hospice volunteers "Who was helpful in times of loss?" and "How did that person show effective care?" the most common response is "She listened a lot" or "He was very calm, even though I was distraught." If I ask further, "Can you recall what your helper said that was the most useful?" I usually learn that nothing stands out about what the helper said. Instead, what is vividly recalled is how the helper paid careful attention, listened patiently, and expressed genuine regard, respect, and empathy simply by being fully present.

This is often referred to as the capacity to be a *nonanxious presence* in the midst of a crisis. Rabbi Edwin Friedman (1985), an eminent family system therapist, defined nonanxious presence as the ability to be emotionally understanding of others but also personally secure enough to be nonreactive to those in distress. It involves the capacity to maintain an inner calm without absorbing or spreading anxiety, while also being deeply attentive and empathically engaged with another person in distress.

From our Christian perspective, this is similar to the theological concept of being incarnationally present to another person as we seek to represent the abiding and healing presence of God in Jesus Christ in all of life's experiences. When we have prepared our own heart and mind through prayer and study, when we have grown in self-awareness and can be nonanxious, even in the presence of death, we will bring the fruit of these preparations to our ministry with the dying. We trust that our presence will communicate the promise of God's never failing love and care, especially to those who are living with dying.

Jeremy Taylor's Approach to Holy Dying

For Taylor, there is a stark realism about death that appreciates both its universality and its inevitability. Death is neither to be feared nor longed for but simply to be prepared for by living in such holiness each day as we can that, when death comes, we are ready for it. Taylor recognizes God's grace in death, since it is "that harbour whither God hath designed every one, that he may find rest from the troubles of this world."[4] He expresses the classic Christian conviction that a holy life, led in piety, repentance, and faithfulness in Jesus Christ leads to assurance of a holy death and a heavenly rest.

Thus, the guiding concerns for Taylor, as expressed in the Collect quoted above, are that death can be approached with the testimony of a good conscience, in the communion of the church, with the comfort of confident faith, and in charity with the world. These themes offer guidance to the pastoral minister serving as a partner in healing to a parishioner facing dying.

Good Conscience

There are many theological, moral, and psychological dimensions to experiencing a good conscience, when death is approaching. The pastoral minister is wise to approach this dimension of dying with reserve and respect for the complexity of matters of conscience in each life. Yet, to avoid this subject may ignore a dying person's deeper spiritual need to engage in an examination of conscience. An examination of conscience provides an opportunity for profound remembrance and deep reflection that can lead to emotional resolution, interpersonal reconciliation, and spiritual peace.

The church has always supported those facing death with the invitation to sacramental confession and absolution, whereby forgiveness of sins is proclaimed and reconciliation can be effected. In addition, however, I think good pastoral practice includes extended conversations with a dying person about his or her life story. Since sacramental confession and reconciliation are priestly acts, the longer conversations of life review may fall more naturally to those offering a pastoral ministry of presence and listening over the course of many visits.

These longer conversations of *life review* are an important part of preparation for dying. Gerontologist Robert Butler (1963) helped to popularize the concept by recognizing that life review is not reserved to the elderly, but is a process naturally undertaken by anyone faced with the realization of approaching death. It is also not idle storytelling just for enjoyment, though it can include that. Life review is purposeful remembering in order to gain perspective about the meaning of one's life. A life review process can be formal, seeking to assess all periods of one's life, or a general conversation about what satisfactions or disappointments have given shape to a particular life story.

I have found that life review can be encouraged by gently asking questions: As you think of your life, what stands out? Did you experience grace and holiness? What are you most pleased about? Do you have regrets? What are you grateful for? What would you have done differently? Are there unsettled conflicts? Are there things you still wish you could accomplish? Are you at peace?

Questions such as these invite a time of reflection that may bring a genuine sense of completion and gratitude that a life has been well lived. On the other hand, such review may surface long-buried guilt or regret about attitudes, behavior, or broken relationships. Sacramental and other rituals of reconciliation may be needed to address guilt or shame for sorrowful actions and choices. Even when a conscience is burdened with the failures of life, the pastoral minister can affirm both the grace and brokenness that characterize most of our lives.

In Communion of the Church

Partners in healing can also encourage appropriate opportunities for connection to the community of faith, including the Holy Eucharist, scriptures, prayers of commendation, and other appointed rituals.[5] Through these actions, it becomes evident that a pastoral minister, whether ordained or lay, is a representative of the larger community of faith standing with and behind his or her minister.

There are many ways that a parish can reach out to the dying. I once was an associate priest to a parish that would gather the lay eucharistic ministers at the altar as the Sunday Holy Eucharist was ending to proclaim that we "send you forth in the name of this congregation bearing these gifts," as they prepared to take Holy Communion to the sick and dying. If it was the last liturgy of the day, it was also the practice for the Altar Society to divide the floral arrangements into smaller bouquets, so that these could be brought to the home as another symbol of the parish holding the parishioner in prayer. Technology today makes it possible for parishes to offer audio recordings or even live Web casts of worship services to help extend community to those unable to be present. These are tangible ways to express the communion of the church in its widest meaning.

While partners in healing typically function within the Christian community, it is important to not presume that a relationship to the faith community is active or positive. There are many Christians in our time who have drifted away from the communion of the church or grown cynical in their faith. In these circumstances, the pastoral minister must continue to be a nonanxious presence, receiving and understanding the inner struggles of an individual who is dealing with ultimate questions about the meaning and purpose of life in the face of death. It is certainly appropriate to hope that a person estranged from the church or from God may be able to overcome misgivings and experience a renewed sense of communion at the end of life. However, it is also important that the pastoral minister be confident that God's love and grace are not restricted by our human attitudes and reactions.

Comfort of Confident Faith

According to a major online news and commentary Web site focused on spirituality and religion, many Americans identify themselves as "spiritual but not religious" (www.beliefnet.org). While this phrase has varied contextual meanings, it identifies a growing distinction in our society between those who espouse spiritual values but have no affiliation to a religious organization and those whose spirituality is closely linked with a traditional faith community.

In the time of Taylor, however, the words *spiritual* and *religious* were essentially interchangeable. When he prayed for the "confidence of a certain faith" and the "comfort of a religious and holy hope," Taylor meant a seamless experience of Christian religious affiliation and spiritual practice. He might be surprised by the diversity in which a pastoral minister today seeks to support a terminally ill person spiritually. Unlike Taylor, we can no longer presume common religious understandings, experiences, and practices.

Professor Robert Fuller (2001) has observed that many contemporary factors have undercut loyalty to traditional religious organizations, including greater respect for science compared to theology, a crisis of faith due to modern biblical scholarship, and growing cultural relativism. His research suggests that many persons still authentically express the sacred in life, but have less connection to organized religion and are more focused on sacredness in this world rather than holiness in an afterlife.[6]

Thus, the pastoral minister may find ministry to the dying or bereaved more complex in a spiritually diverse world. The comfort and confidence stemming from the singular faith that Jeremy Taylor envisioned cannot be presumed. It requires of us a greater openness to varied spiritual practices, letting the person who is dying teach us about what comforts that person and gives meaning to his or her world. Even within the context of a faith congregation, the pastoral minister will encounter a significant number of people who are deeply spiritual but who do not share their religious understandings.

Charity with the World

Dying in charity with the world can be expressed in a variety of ways, but certainly having one's affairs in order and personal relationships at peace are important components of charity with the world. By encouraging a dying person to address any unfinished business, whether legal or personal, the pastoral minister will contribute to a more peaceful and holy dying. This can include things such as being certain that an advance directive for health care decisions has been completed or a will has been written to guide distribution of worldly goods. Unfinished business also includes relationship issues, such as unexpressed sentiments that a dying person needs to communicate. It is important for pastoral ministers to become familiar with the many resources available to help complete unfinished business during ministry to the dying.

An advance directive is a legal document, sometimes called a living will, filed with the medical provider and family members. It details a person's wishes concerning medical treatment at the end of life, such as when life-support measures should be discontinued if a person is in a persistent vegetative state from which there is no hope for a recovery. An advance directive usually also includes the appointment of a health care proxy, who is authorized to make medical decisions on behalf of someone unable to make or communicate his or her own decisions. Unfortunately, many people do not take advantage of these legal instruments for assuring that their wishes for end-of-life care will be known or followed.

Since advance health care planning is so often neglected, it is appropriate for a pastoral minister to raise the topic, especially when a life-threatening illness has been diagnosed. The National Hospice and Palliative Care Organization's *Caring Connections* Web page (www.caringinfo.org) provides guidelines for how to start a conversation about end-of-life choices and has links to download the specific advance directive and health care proxy forms for each state in the United States.

A will, sometimes more formally called a last will and testament, provides guidance for how the property and other material resources of a person are to be dispersed after death. Many people put off writing a will, assuming it is only needed in old age. However, since an unexpected death can happen at any time, everyone of legal age should have a will. Those offering ministry to the dying can sensitively ask if a will has been properly prepared according to the laws of the state where the person is legally resident.

Faith communities are regularly in a position to educate and encourage members to have these end-of-life documents prepared well before there is any apparent need for them. Premarital counseling sessions as well as baptismal preparation classes are good openings for clergy or other pastoral ministers to discuss the importance these documents have for the well-being of individuals and families.

In recent years, the idea of writing a *spiritual will* has grown in popularity (Colletti and Colletti 2007) and is an important development for ministry to the dying. A spiritual will reclaims the idea of passing on the beliefs and lessons of life that the dying person wants to share with family and friends. There are many ways a spiritual will can be created. Some use the simplicity of a letter written to "my family and friends." Sometimes a spiritual will is expressed in individual letters or essays composed for specific persons, such as a spouse, sibling, or child. I know of a dying parent who left "legacy letters" for his young daughter to be given to her at certain milestone periods of her life, such as when she turned thirteen, when she began high school, and also when she graduated. In these letters, he tried to imagine her future life and express his love for her as she continued to grow and mature. Audio and video recordings also provide meaningful ways for a spiritual will to be communicated.

Dying in charity will also be restricted if there is unfinished business because of conflicted relationships between a dying person and loved ones. The pastoral minister can be watchful for conflicts in relationships in order to support conversations of reconciliation between a dying person and those with whom unfinished business lingers.

Dr. Ira Byock, a hospice physician, has made a strong case for the possibilities of growth that can occur even during the final months of life. He encourages his hospice patients to focus on "the five things of relationship completion"[7]: I forgive you; Forgive me; Thank you; I love you; and Goodbye. While this may seem a simple script to remember, these topics delve deeply into relationship concerns, opening hearts to the possibility of healing and reconciliation.

If the pastoral minister can encourage and facilitate conversations that touch these topics with directness and honesty, the final days of living can indeed be sanctified and made holy. When charity in the form of forgiveness and gratitude between loved ones is experienced, especially during life's last days, dying itself is transformed from a mere physical event to a sacred occasion.

Conclusion

Henri Nouwen, a twentieth-century spiritual writer, has followed in the tradition of Jeremy Taylor by writing a book that also offers guidance about how to approach our own dying and the dying of others. He, too, seems to recognize that living with dying is possible, that the fact of death does not need to be avoided at all costs but can be directly woven into the fabric of life. In fact, he wonders, "is it possible to befriend our dying gradually and live open to it, trusting that we have nothing to fear...to prepare for our death with the same attentiveness that our parents had in preparing for our birth?"[8]

As a partner in healing, I hope that you will find yourself increasingly able to befriend dying and death without fear, but with faithful confidence. As you do, you will be able to support the holy living and the holy dying of others.

Notes

1. *Book of Common Prayer* (New York: Church Hymnal Corporation, 1979), 504.

2. Alan Wolfelt, *Living in the Shadow of the Ghosts of Grief* (Ft. Collins, CO: Companion Press, 2007), 81–82.

3. Beverly A. Musgrave and John R. Bickle, eds., *Partners in Healing* (Mahwah, NJ: Paulist Press, 2003), ix.

4. Jeremy Taylor, *The Rule and Exercises of Holy Dying*, new edition (London: Rivingtons, 1889), 92.

5. Elaine Ramshaw, *Ritual and Pastoral Care* (Philadelphia: Fortress Press, 1987).

6. Robert C. Fuller, *Spiritual, But Not Religious: Understanding Unchurched America* (New York: Oxford Press, 2001).

7. Ira Byock, *Dying Well: Peace and Possibilities at the End of Life* (New York: Riverhead Books, 1997), 140.

8. Henri Nouwen, *Our Greatest Gift* (New York: HarperCollins, 1994), xiii.

References

BeliefNet. *Spiritual, But Not Religious.* www.beliefnet.com. Accessed September 21, 2007.

Book of Common Prayer. New York: Church Hymnal Corporation, 1979.

Butler, Robert N. "The Life Review: An Interpretation of Reminiscence in the Aged." *Psychiatry* 26 (1963): 65–76.

Byock, Ira. *Dying Well: Peace and Possibilities at the End of Life.* New York: Riverhead Books, 1997.

Carroll, Thomas K. *Jeremy Taylor: Selected Works.* Mahwah, NJ: Paulist Press, 1990.

Colletti, Louis, and Joseph Colletti. *Leaving a Spiritual Legacy: Writing a Spiritual Will.* n.p.: Self-published, The Woodledge Group, 2007.

de Sales, Francis. *Introduction to the Devout Life.* (New Edition, 1885) Dublin: M. H. Gill and Son.

Friedman, Edwin H. *Generation to Generation: Family Process in Church and Synagogue.* New York: Guilford, 1985.

Fuller, Robert C. *Spiritual, But Not Religious: Understanding Unchurched America.* New York: Oxford Press, 2001.

Musgrave, Beverly A., and John R. Bickle. *Partners in Healing.* Mahwah, NJ: Paulist Press, 2003.

Nouwen, Henri. *Our Greatest Gift.* New York: HarperCollins, 1994.

Ramshaw, Elaine. *Ritual and Pastoral Care*. Philadelphia: Fortress Press, 1987.

Taylor, Jeremy. *The Rule and Exercises of Holy Living*. 1650. New impression, London: Longmans, Green and Co., 1899.

Taylor, Jeremy. *The Rule and Exercises of Holy Dying*. 1651. New edition, London: Rivingtons, 1889.

Wolfelt, Alan. *Living in the Shadow of the Ghosts of Grief*. Ft. Collins, CO: Companion Press, 2007.

15

Prayerful Preparation
Introducing Partners in Healing to the Faith Community

Eleanor Ramos

Introduction

It is hard work to walk the sacred path with those in need of healing. Partners in Healing do well to remember that their formation is an ongoing process and they need the nurturing guidance of their supervisor and the support of their fellow partners along the way. Their preparation extends well beyond the initial training period.

During my years as coordinator of Ministry to Seniors for the Archdiocese of New York, we trained hundreds of parish volunteers, who ministered to even greater numbers of homebound elderly and ill persons. We continually revised and evolved our training programs, which received national recognition. At one point, we even collaborated with Partners in Healing to bring our volunteer visitors to the next level in their ministry.

One of the challenges we faced was convincing potential volunteers that training was essential. Whether they were too busy or felt that visiting the sick was a simple good deed, it was a struggle to gather them together for the workshops. A few of us decided to become parish volunteers ourselves in order to learn firsthand the challenges facing the volunteers, the idea being that this would enable us to better prepare them for service.

Surprisingly, my experience as a parish visitor was not at all what I expected. At the time, I felt I was well prepared. After all, I was in charge of developing the volunteer training programs and had trained many of the volunteers in this same parish. I was also taking courses in pastoral counseling and belonged to a bio-spiritual focusing group. And yet, there were days when I wondered, What am I doing here? or found myself searching desperately for the "right" thing to say. Then, I would remember to pray, which is at the core of this ministry.

The benefits of volunteering in the parish were many. My own spirit was nourished by the faith of the remarkable woman I visited. I realized that the Partners in Healing need to walk with another on the journey in a unique way—from a place of awareness, awareness of their own issues, feelings, imperfections, limitations, and "brokenness," and awareness of how those issues affect the relationship. This realization reinforced what I think of as a mutual vulnerability that creates a sense of intimacy. The intimacy nurtures the relationship and builds trust. Anthony de Mello, SJ, believes that "we see people and things not as they are, but as we are" (1992, 88). Therefore, it is essential that Partners in Healing work on their own spiritual journey in conjunction with their ministry.

Basic Training for Partners in Healing

Perhaps the most significant outcome of my volunteering was the ability to confront resistance to training in the faith community. I could now speak out of my own experiences about the necessity of prayerful preparation.

Jesus prepared for his ministry in the desert for forty days. And during his ministry he often took time alone in prayer and contemplation to renew his spirit. After curing many sick people and driving out demons, Jesus rose early before dawn and "went out to a deserted place, and there he prayed" (Mark 1:35). When

I am feeling particularly stressed out and overwhelmed, it is always comforting for me to remember that even Jesus needed a "break." According to Henri Nouwen, it is not a person's expertise, authority, or credentials that matter as much as "claiming his own loneliness as a source of human understanding" that enables a minister of healing to be of any service (1979, 85).

These truths underlie the practical skills that are required in order to be compassionate and effective Partners in Healing. As such, they are an essential part of the basic training and of the first session especially, which lays the foundation for the eight-part Partners in Healing Training Workshop and gives participants an overview of the program and the training sessions. During this first session, I present Wicks and Rodgerson's concepts of overcoming resistance and intentional caring (1998, chs. 2 and 4) and discuss the unique qualities and gifts of Partners in Healing and help potential partners understand their calling and address any concerns regarding this ministry.

The introductory session also provides an opportunity to welcome and to get to know the trainees, as they participate in the discussion and reveal their motives for working with the sick. The process of group formation begins. This session helps them understand the program's focus, what the training encompasses, and what is expected of them as Partners in Healing. It builds their confidence, because it is reassuring to have a structure, a contact person, a support network, and practical skills training in this work. To be a Partner in Healing is:

1. to walk on "sacred ground";
2. to be present in a caring way;
3. to listen in a caring way;
4. to see an opportunity for growth.

Walking on "Sacred Ground"

Before each visit, remember to pray. "Let me say what you want her to hear; let me be your ears to listen to him." Partners are a shadow of Christ's loving presence, Christ for one another. Beginning each training session with scripture and prayer emphasizes the unique spiritual character of this ministry for potential partners and provides them with different reflection and meditation techniques to use later.

Listening and Being Present in a Caring Way

Partners in Healing have the responsibility to develop the skills of empathy, listening, probing, and challenging that help one to become an effective instrument. One does this by caring to listen, which, to paraphrase Wicks and Rodgerson, includes "conveying an atmosphere of trust," seeing things from another's perspective, "recognizing...nonverbal signals, being aware of one's own reactions to the conversation and always keeping the focus on the one being visited" (1998, 18).

Instead of giving advice or trying to solve the person's problems, partners empower those they visit to identify their strengths and resources and to do their own problem solving. Participants in the training workshop learn how to do this by reflecting on their own feelings, strengths, experiences, and resources.

To help participants in this process, I use practical exercises and personal anecdotes to illustrate my own version of Wicks and Rodgerson's concepts: exploring feelings, focusing on assets, clarifying issues, and identifying alternatives (for a more in-depth treatment of these concepts, see *Companions in Hope* [Wicks and Rodgerson 1998, ch. 4]).

Exploring Feelings

Before each visit, partners need to take time to be present to themselves and become aware of any feelings, issues, or "baggage" that might affect their ministry. Using a simple exercise will help training workshop participants to practice exploring feelings.

Close your eyes and take several deep cleansing breaths.
Empty your mind of all the noise and cares of the day.
Set these thoughts aside; you can come back to them later.
Right now you want to take time to be present to your self.
How are you feeling right now?
How do you feel about this new ministry you are about to
undertake?
Do you feel anxious, scared, overwhelmed?
Be with these feelings in a caring way.
Do not judge them. Do not try to fix them.
Just see what they want to tell you.

After this exercise, take several minutes to share. It is an excellent means to get doubts and misunderstandings about Partners in Healing out in the open. It also gives potential partners an example of how to prepare for each visit. By learning how to be aware of their own feelings, trainees learn to be sensitive to the feelings of those they will visit.

Focusing on Assets

Since one of the purposes of the introductory session is to bolster confidence, it is helpful to have participants become aware of the strengths they bring to this ministry. This can be accomplished by having them write down their assets or gifts on a piece of paper. Or if they wish, they can write down a time in their lives when they faced a particularly difficult challenge and overcame it. After several minutes of recalling and writing, the group is invited to share once again.

This exercise helps the participants work with a tool that may later help those they visit to identify their own strengths and assets during times of trial and illness. I call it a "cheerleading" exercise, which partners can also use when they get a bit discouraged. Recalling past successes (how I quit smoking or how I got my master's degree while raising a family) inspires hope and reminds participants of all the qualities they possess that will see them through difficult periods in their lives.

Clarifying Issues and Identifying Alternatives

A concrete example from the trainer's own experience helps to explain how partners can help those they visit come to grips with troubling feelings, issues, and past hurts that need to be healed.

During my volunteer service, the woman I visited spent some time in a nursing home. One Sunday she appeared slightly confused, disheveled, and very frail. She still recognized me and greeted me with a warm smile. I escorted her to Mass in the nursing home auditorium. That morning I was feeling very agitated and unhappy myself but I couldn't figure out why. Maybe it was the old "too much to do and it will never be done the way I want it to be" refrain. There's not enough time. Even the gospel that day was about time: "You do not know when the time will come." "Be alert!"(Mark 13:33–37).

Was it that "I'm not the way I should be" that was bothering me so much? Was that why it was so hard for me to visit the sick in hospitals and nursing homes? So many people "not the way they should be." They were crying out to me and I didn't understand them, I didn't know what to do. Despite all my knowledge, experience, and studying, these were the dark thoughts going through my head. This was how I was feeling, my issues. But I tried to be with my partner and even tried to listen to the other patients. It was so difficult.

After Mass I took her upstairs to the dining area. We chatted. She seemed peaceful. I got ready to leave. I was doubting my ability to be empathetic in any way. "Why am I here, Lord, anyway?"

All at once she began talking about someone named D. Her face looked so painful. "You know D." she said to me, thinking I was someone else. When I replied "No I don't know her," she got angry, but I didn't take it personally. I let her talk. "Tell me about D., maybe I'll remember." And she told me a story about a friend, a close friend who had died of cancer. "I miss her so much," my partner said. This friend had confided that she had cancer and made my partner promise not to tell anyone, including the friend's family members. "That must have been so hard for you, to have this secret, to keep your word." Yes. She went on with the story, angry, hurt, so sad. Finally, she told me that she had to tell the friend's husband about the cancer. "I had to tell him, I had to break my word." She cried. I never saw her cry like that before. "It was hard for you to break your promise but you had to tell him. What happened then?" She told me about telling her friend what she had done. The friend died shortly after that.

I asked her "Why do you think D. told you this hard secret and not her husband? Could it be because you are so strong?" Then she smiled and began talking about how the doctors say she is so strong. We talked about how she had survived so much in her own life. She brightened. We discussed her therapy and her goal of walking again. When I left, I'm not sure if she knew me or still thought I was a friend of hers from the past. She wanted to be with the other patients and was calling them by names from her past.

I think that this was an issue in need of healing for my partner. She had been given a terrible secret from a beloved friend and had to carry the anguish of her friend's cancer alone, without sharing it. Then she had to break her promise when confronted by her friend's husband, and this was even more distressing. She was feeling anger, grief, guilt, and loneliness for her friend. And even though her mental state was confused, her "body knowing" of these feelings was very alert.

I hoped I had been God's instrument for my partner that day. At least I had let her talk about her pain. At least I listened and used some skills I had learned. Maybe I was not as hopeless as I felt when I walked into the nursing home that morning. So again, mutual healing had taken place for both visitor and the one visited.

Sharing personal experiences like the one above prompts the participants to remember and share similar experiences with the group. It also reinforces the principles of Partners in Healing: be present, listen, do not judge, do not fix.

Overcoming Resistance

It is natural to feel some trepidation when beginning a new ministry. What if I say the wrong thing? Or don't know what to say? What if the sick person needs help I cannot provide? It is beneficial to get these misgivings out in the open from the very first session.

In chapter two of *Companions in Hope*, Wicks and Rodgerson identify certain blocks to caring listening: anxiety, the "Savior

Complex," periods of silence, and dealing with strong emotions (1998). I have applied my own interpretations to these "blocks." By using anecdotes and group sharing, the participants are helped to become aware of doubts or fears that might affect their ability to be caring listeners.

Anxiety

One way I convey this concept is to confess my own anxiety. I always get stage fright when doing a presentation, no matter how well prepared I am. Then I ask: "How many are new to this ministry? Are you anxious about visiting the sick?" Once again, the potential partners are reminded that being with their feelings before each visit will help them be with those they visit. Their anxiety and fear will help them to understand the fears of those they visit, help them to "walk in their shoes," help them to empathize. The sharing that takes place will reinforce these concepts, which will be treated in more depth during future workshop sessions.

The Savior Complex

Partners for the sick are not there to fix or solve problems, a very difficult idea to get across to the helpers who are drawn to this ministry. They need to discover that they are human beings, not "human doings." An anecdote from a colleague helps.

> Once I received a phone call from a woman who was struggling with the decision whether to place her husband in a nursing home. I had no real advice for her, so I listened and reflected her thoughts back to her. I hadn't really "helped" at all, yet she was so grateful, which surprised me.

It is often difficult to listen, hard to keep from jumping in with well-intentioned suggestions, and frustrating to resist saving the person. What it is really about for Partners in Healing is letting go of the outcome of their visit and just being there for those they visit, which is truly freeing.

Silence

Dealing with silence is very difficult for twenty-first-century beings. Think of what many people do as soon as they enter their quiet house—turn on the TV, the radio, the computer, or whatever it takes to end the deafening silence. Yet in the silences that occur during visits, tremendous healing can and often does take place. Resist the urge to fill an awkward silence with comments or even to change the subject. Gently encourage the person by repeating her last thoughts and then wait, prayerfully. See what happens.

Dealing with Strong Emotions

Again, the exercise of exploring their own feelings and learning from them will help partners when those they visit express difficult feelings that may stir up emotions. Encourage the potential partners to share times that they were confronted with anger, despair, doubt, or other scary outbursts. This provides an opportunity for guidance from the trainer and group interaction. It demonstrates that they are not alone in this ministry and builds their confidence as they face their fears about becoming Partners in Healing.

Qualities of Partners in Healing

The trainer begins with a brainstorming session. Ask the potential partners what qualities are important in this ministry and write the responses on a dry-erase board or pad. The following qualities, as adapted from the *Called to Caring Training Manual* (Croke 2003), are especially important for Partners in Healing, who will be deeply involved in personal exchange and sharing with those they visit:

Compassionate caring
A personal response to illness and loss
Selflessness—the ability to focus on the welfare of another
Empathy or the ability to "be with" others
Openness to different people and situations (being nonjudgmental)
Comfort with the expression of feelings
Spirituality—a sense of God's presence in their ministry
Commitment to ministry/reliability
Patience
A sense of humor

Throughout the training workshop, Partners in Healing will develop:

Skills and confidence in working with those who are ill or bereaved
A deeper understanding of the special needs of those in need of healing, including cultural considerations
Listening skills
An understanding of empathy
Consideration of the medical and ethical concerns of caregiving
Insight into the opportunities one often discovers when faced with a life crisis

The above outline can also be adapted as a handout. It provides an overview of the Partners in Healing Training Workshop and reinforces the importance of attending future training sessions, where the skills so necessary in this ministry will be further developed.

Unique Gifts of Partners in Healing

Partners in Healing offer unique gifts to those who are ill or bereaved. The following outline is adapted from the *Called to Caring Training Manual.*

Ministry
Partners in Healing:
Bring a caring presence
Care to listen
Respect and accept the person as s/he is
Act out their faith in service to others
Have a deep spiritual sense of their service

Empowerment
Partners in Healing:
Focus on a partnered approach of pastoral ministry
Empower people to face and live with illness or grief

Confidentiality
Partners in Healing:
Provide a safe environment for sharing
Act as a confidante in personal matters

Link to Community
Partners in Healing:
Keep the person connected to their faith community
Provide information on community services if needed

Discussing these gifts helps to sum up the essence of the introductory session and provides a review. It is also an opportunity to reinforce the importance of confidentiality, which will be emphasized throughout the training sessions. In a faith community, building trust is essential and everything must be kept in the strictest confidence. Never repeat to anyone what a person confides during a visit. The exception is when a partner learns that the person being visited may be in some danger, either as a result of self-neglect or from others. In this case, the partner consults the supervisor of the program in the faith community.

Remind the potential partners that they are not social workers but may be important "eyes and ears" for those they visit, especially if the person they visit is isolated from the community. For example, during my tenure as coordinator of Ministry to Seniors, parish volunteers had alerted their supervisors to the following potentially life-threatening situations: a homebound man who was not eating and a woman who threatened suicide. These cases were then referred to the appropriate professionals. As the training workshop continues, partners will also learn about resources in their community to share with those they visit, if the need arises.

The Call to Be a Partner in Healing

Partners in Healing, who answer the call to minister to the sick and those in need of healing, are very special. Reasons for undertaking this ministry are as varied as the individuals themselves and may include:

Personal experience of suffering—physical or mental
The suffering of a loved one—a family member or close friend
Gratitude for the many blessings received in their lives

Confirming the Call

Being a Partner in Healing is a wonderful calling. However, not everyone is suited to this ministry. It is important for potential partners to reflect on their call. It can be helpful to ask the following questions:

Is ministry to the sick or dying what I am called to do at this time in my life?
Do I feel comfortable in the company of people who are sick, dying or disabled?
What do I expect from this ministry? What do I hope to get out of this ministry? What do I hope to give in this ministry?

What is my personal experience of illness, suffering and death? Where is God in that experience?

It is important to pray over the call to become a Partner in Healing and be open to what God is saying to us.

Practical Considerations

In reflecting on the call to Partners in Healing, the candidates can now consider the amount of time they can give, the level of commitment they can make to the program, and the kind of presence they would like to provide. They may consider:

Do I enjoy listening? Am I comfortable with the expression of feelings?
How much time can I dedicate to Partners in Healing?
How long a commitment can I make? (Be realistic!)

The commitment to minister to the sick and dying as a Partner in Healing is not for everyone. Some of those attending this first session may discover that this is not the way for them to serve. Or it may not be the right time for them. The above reflection helps potential partners to discern whether this ministry is for them. It can be done as a meditation, a prayerful way to end the introductory session, and a prayerful way to prepare for a sacred ministry.

References

Croke, C. 2003. *Called to Caring Training Manual*. New York: Catholic Charities of the Archdiocese of New York.
De Mello, A., SJ. 1992. *Awareness*. New York: Image Books.
Nouwen, H. J. M. 1979. *The Wounded Healer: Ministry in Contemporary Society*. New York: Doubleday.
Wicks, R. J., and T. E. Rodgerson. 1998. *Companions in Hope: The Art of Christian Caring*. Mahwah, NJ: Paulist Press.

Part IV

Personal Dimensions and Memories of Life, Loss, and Death

16

Caring for Caregivers
Sharing the Care

Margaret Kornfeld

"*Margaret, take care of yourself!*"

I knew my friend meant well, but I found her advice annoying—in fact, it made me mad. She had just added another pressure. Take care of myself?! I knew I needed a haircut—I hadn't had one in months. I'd not even had the time to do that. My husband, Larry, had been home for six weeks, suffering terrible back pain—he could only crawl upstairs. Somehow, I had been able to take care of him and still work.

It was now 11 p.m. I had just returned from the hospital, where in the morning he was to have serious spinal surgery. I was exhausted. I'd worked all day and hadn't had supper. I thanked the baby-sitter, and then I heard my sweet five-year-old, Sarah, call, "Mamma, is that you?" We'd both missed each other. I wished I was taking better care of her.

A few weeks later my friend Gretchen called, saying, "Larry comes home tomorrow, anything you need to do? I have a baby-sitter for the kids. We could even have coffee." In fact, I needed to go to a medical-supply store. I never would have thought to ask for her help, but it came to me and I said "yes!" On that ride, I let my hair down. I told Gretchen how it really was with me. Our friendship was bonded.

There's that word "hair" again. I now know that it would have been good not only for me but also for Larry if I'd taken time for myself and had it cut—it really was quite wild! I would have liked myself more when I looked in the mirror, and Larry would not have been reminded that I didn't have time for myself. I knew Larry was worried. He knew the stress I was under and insisted that I take cabs home—not the subway. I did it but worried about the money. Even his worry felt like pressure. Larry was grateful but felt guilty. He hated being so dependent on me. I was resentful, but I didn't know it.

This was 1973. At that time we did not have much information about caregiving. It's now known that those receiving care do much better when they are aware that their caregivers are able to care for themselves *and* are also being cared for. Worry impedes healing. Had I known this back then, I would have had the haircut *for* Larry. I had more work to do on myself to be able to do it *for myself*. Fourteen years later, I had a chance to address my caretaker self in an AIDS support group.

Caretakers: More Blessed by Giving than Receiving

I come from a western Colorado family that values caregivers—although we then called them "caretakers." Family caretakers were our heroines and heroes. We had caretaking stories about Great-grandmother Mitchell, who pulled up stakes from her prosperous Iowa farm to go with her new baby to barely settled western Colorado, because Great-grandfather had severe asthma and the dry air—and rest—would help him. And stories about my grandmother Olson, who saved my mother's life through her nursing skills and even studied home nursing to do it better. And stories about my grandfather Zipse. When my father was little, his foot was caught in a wheat-threshing machine on their Kansas farm. His foot was nearly severed, but Grandpa Zipse had learned that a famous Scots surgeon was coming to the Mayo Clinic. He took my father there and, like those coming to Jesus, said, "take care of my son." My grandfather was a man of faith. The surgeon operated, and my father could walk, with a limp.

When I was a senior in high school and it was evident that my grandpa, who had cancer, needed hands-on care, my aunt, my father's youngest sibling, came from California to take care of him. She took a leave of absence from her fulfilling professional career and stayed until after he died. Later, when Grandma needed care, my aunt returned and did not go back to California. I never knew whether she was asked to come or if she just knew she was needed. My aunt did not *need* to be needed—there's nothing "co-dependent" about her—but in our family "we take care of one another."

There's no question that my aunt cared for my grandparents out of love, but the strength of family roles can pull people away from their own path. Being a family caretaker can create a "road not taken." Western family caretakers learned to expect themselves to "do it alone." Even though the rest of the family was also involved in Grandpa's care, when my aunt returned, she moved into my grandparents' home and assumed *personal responsibility*. She has since told me that returning seemed necessary, because everyone else had families. She was unmarried and had no children. She has accepted this role as the path God planned for her.

I don't believe that our family thought of my aunt as someone who needed to be "cared for." She came to take care of Grandpa. She was strong, focused, and competent. She had the ability to take care of herself. She never seemed needy. She was selfless without being whiny. She was a western woman! The family was grateful when she arrived, and to the nieces and nephews it just seemed "natural." We had no idea of the gift she was giving.

I was "chosen" to be a family caretaker. It's not unusual for the eldest daughter to be given that role. Not only am I older than my sister, but I was the first grandchild on both sides of the family. Unmarried daughters—and sometimes sons—are also expected to assume this role.

Families don't explicitly say, "you're being given the mantle." They teach you to be helpful, and good, and to "take care of your little sister." Then you are taught to think of others first. Then you graduate to bigger tasks such as making sure—when your mother is very sick—that "you keep your sister 'good' so Mother won't be upset." You absorb family anxiety. You also learn from the example of others. I learned from my grandmother Olson—and from all those hero and heroine stories. As a child there were rewards along the way—being "good" gets you liked. It's only later that "good, helpful, unselfish girls" learn the downside.

I had already internalized my role as caretaker by the time my aunt returned. But she was a reinforcing example. She embodied the caretaker; she "took care." She understood her role: taking care was her duty, responsibility, family obligation—her life's path. The role was unconsciously *chosen* for her and had become part of her identity—and she had the gift of caring.

"Thinking of others first" is a basic unwritten rule for caretakers. At first, "taking care" does not feel like a loss of self—it *is being* one's self. However, many who have taken care of loved ones have lost themselves. They've not had time for personal interests, friends, leisure, fun, self-care, or soul work. They've become lonely and isolated. And since they feel guilty when they cannot do it *all* themselves, they can't ask for help. They feel burdened and resentful. (Resentment is unexpressed anger.) They were taught "it is more blessed to give than to receive." They might feel important in the family, but they do not always feel blessed.

Feeling "No Choice": A Danger to Caregivers

We now use the nomenclature *caregiver* instead of *caretaker*. *Giver* seems more generous and voluntary; one can *choose* to take care. But many in my generation (I'm seventy-one), and even those who are younger, are still *caretakers*. Among the 44.5 million unpaid caregivers in the United States who take care of adults, and the six million caregivers who provide care for children with mental or developmental disabilities (and this does not even count the parents who take care of sick children—often with protracted illnesses), there are millions of us who feel we "have no choice."[1]

Believing that one "has no choice" has serious implications for the caregiver. In fact, it can kill. According to the 2004 national survey *Caregiving in the U.S.* by the National Alliance for Caregiving and AARP, the feeling of "having no choice" was the most accurate predictor for caregivers of adults who experience the most stress, are most at risk for *serious* physical and emotional illness, and have the greatest financial burdens because of giving care.[2]

Medical professionals now have a category for this condition: *caregiver syndrome*. It comprises a host of mental and physical symptoms that are rooted in stress, exhaustion, and self-neglect. Researchers Janice Kiecolt-Glaser and her husband, immunologist Ronald Glaser, have found that caregivers are more likely to get infectious diseases and are slower to heal from wounds. Other findings show that caregivers have greater elevated blood levels of a chemical linked to chronic inflammation, which puts them at increased risk for heart disease, arthritis, diabetes, cancer, and other diseases. In addition, they are more prone to anxiety and depression.[3]

Of those surveyed, 39 percent of the estimated forty-four million American caregivers (from ages eighteen to sixty-five and over) feel that they "had no choice" but to take on their responsibility (that's 17,160,000 people!). Those feeling they have no choice are typically women (42 percent), while fewer men (34 percent) feel they have no choice. (Contrary to the stereotype that women do all the caregiving, four out of ten caregivers are men, although most carry less heavy burdens than women.)[4] Those who feel they have no choice are older (17 percent are fifty to sixty-four and 22 percent are sixty-five and over) and are themselves already in poor health (51 percent), perform the heaviest burdens of care (60 percent), and live with the care recipient (45 percent). Interestingly enough, coresiding caregivers are less likely to feel they did not have a choice than caregivers who live less than an hour away. Perhaps some of these who coreside are caring for their spouse or partner. Although they find it difficult, they still *choose* to give care to their life partner. The survey found that 22 percent of the sixty-five and over caregivers (5,720,000 people) are caring for a spouse. The average age of the care recipient is seventy-five.[5]

The issue of the experience of "choice" is a vital concern to those who care for caregivers. It is noted that 61 percent of caregivers feel they *do* have a choice. Who are they? Conversely, how much of the sense of "not having a choice" is influenced by internalized caretaker roles? Why do some, who have the same level of caregiving burden, feel that they *do* have a choice? Do those who feel they have no choice have more unmet needs that could be tended to by those who care for caregivers? How can those caring for caregivers who reject their care give to those who have been taught that it is more "blessed to give than to receive"? Is it possible to intervene in the lives of these more than seventeen million caretakers, before they are killed by diseases of caregiver syndrome, or is it too late?

Demographics, and the reality that federal and state budgets are cutting funds for caring for the sick, disabled, and elderly, will produce a huge increase in the number of caregivers who will be undersupported. In the next few years, people over sixty-five are expected to increase at a rate of 2.3 percent, but the number of family members available to care for them will only increase at a rate of 0.8 percent.[6]

Caregivers *are* America's long-term care system. If the health of those with no choice continues to decline, not only will the country have an epidemic of critically ill older caregivers, but this will create crisis for their elderly care recipients. Women (mainly) in this category are fifty to sixty-five and over. Many have cared for spouses for over ten years. They have the heaviest burden of care, less income, and receive the least financial assistance. One half live in their own homes.[7] Owning one's home is no help. Until recently, elderly people could own their own homes and still be eligible for home care assistance. Now, owning one's own home is a detriment. The value of the home is counted as an asset, which makes them appear more wealthy on paper than they in fact are. Now, even people with lower-middle incomes can be "too rich" for entitlements.[8]

Care*takers* keep on *taking care* and many feel vindicated. Their ancestors with farm values are right—"if we don't take care of ourselves, by ourselves, keeping our troubles to ourselves, who will?" The weight of America's health care system cannot stand for long on the frail shoulders of caregivers.

From Caretaker to Caregiver through an AIDS Support Group

Although I went to New York City to seminary, became a pastoral counselor, married Larry, birthed Sarah, and never returned to Colorado, I remained a western caretaker. After his spinal surgery, Larry had several hospitalizations for pneumonia that I dealt with in the usual individualistic caretaker way—keeping home, practice, and mothering afloat. The thought of self-care was not on the radar screen.

In 1987, I was blessed by the beginning of a paradigm shift: I gradually moved from care *taker* to care *giver*. In this shift, I finally understood that caretakers have definitively learned that they must assume *personal responsibility* for the care of another. Although they probably receive some assistance from others, the burden is theirs. To be a caretaker is their role in the family; it is the image of self.

Caregivers, on the other hand, have learned, or are learning, to share responsibility, delegate tasks, discover resources, and ask for help. Often, they have discerned that they already are part of a *network of care* that supports their personal situation. While they may have inherited the role, they have learned to become "captain" of a family care team—not the sole player.

I was given this blessing in the church of which I am a member, Judson Memorial Church, in the heart of New York City's Greenwich Village. In the mid 1980s, Judson was devastated by the HIV-AIDS epidemic. It was our new leprosy. Many of our members and our extended congregation of neighbors, artists, and activists were sick, and some were dying. Many in the congregation were becoming caregivers and activists. In response, the church organized a task force to study the pastoral and spiritual needs of people with HIV-AIDS and their companions. As we explored these needs, the task force said, "Hey, that's us!" We were all deeply connected to people with AIDS (in fact, one of our task-force members did not yet know that he had HIV; he died a few years later).

We recognized that we must stay together. We needed to support one another and to develop spiritual resources to help us care for *ourselves* and for *one another* and to reach out to those with HIV-AIDS. Our mission had changed. We were no longer gathering data about the spiritual needs of others. We were experiencing our *own* needs. All of us were already supporting friends who were ill, and we were beginning to run on empty.

Being part of the group was my first step away from the rugged individualist caretaker mode. As a child, I had learned not to complain. Previously, if I talked to people about my caretaking overload, I felt as if I were complaining. The group helped me understand that this was not complaining: I was sharing, so that I could receive support. Gradually, when asked to make a hospital visit, I was able to say, "Sorry, I'm not able to go to the hospital tomorrow afternoon. I'll call my backup." I had *never* been able to say no to a request for a sick friend. However, it took me much, much longer to ask for help *for me*—and it's still not easy. That habit dies hard.

I'll be ever grateful to the group for helping me confront the two caretaking rubrics: "think of others first" and "it's more blessed to give." Even though I knew the airlines' think-of-yourself rule (put on your oxygen mask first and then put one on your child), that was for me still a form of caretaking. I could think of myself first *in order* to take care of Sarah.

Although I knew intellectually the wisdom to self-care (and even taught it to students), it was for me new to begin to practice thinking of myself and acting on behalf of my well-being and happiness before helping others. Group members did not make me mad by saying, "Margaret, take care of yourself." They helped me do it. Group members also gave words of appreciation and thoughtful gifts to one another; gratitude was often in the air, and I learned to receive it. I was blessed by *both* receiving *and* giving. It was not either/or. And we had fun. Our members were the wittiest folks I've known.

But most importantly, I learned to be part of a care*giving* team. Although I had major responsibility, it was not *my* group—it was *ours*! It was not *my* job to take care, to keep people alive. It was my privilege to be *with* those who lived until they died and then entered into profound rest. I, too, was learning to let go.

The 2004 *Caregiving in the U.S.* survey found that caretaking is a family affair, and 83 percent of caregivers are relatives caring for relatives. The group we formed was in the 17 percent category of those who care for people outside their families.[9] We were not blood relatives but an extended family of friends who cared for one another. We met in my pastoral psychotherapist's office for the next six years. Eight of us remained the core members, but over the years there were more than one hundred members who participated in the group, until their needs were met: Some were ill. Some were dying. Some were friends and family who came to support and learn to care for their friends. Some were family members who came to understand or to reconcile with their gay sons. Some came to mourn either members of the group (seven died) or other friends who had died. Some came to celebrate the life of a friend. Some came to deal with survivor's guilt and reclaim their own lives. Some were burned-out caregivers, who came for rest and renewal. Some were professionals, clergy, pastoral counselors, social workers, or psychiatrists who worked with people with HIV-

AIDS and were relieved to be with others who shared that experience. We all needed to be spiritually fed. As one member said, "the group is a life raft—always here when it is needed."

Care Supported by Prayer

Prayer and meditation were central to our group. Every Thursday night, we began our meetings by catching up with one another, sharing our specific concerns, and asking for what we wanted from the group that night. After we had connected with one another, we entered into a spiritual meditation growing out of Quaker practice. Before moving into centering silence, we named those whom we wished to "hold in the Light." We were then led in a relaxation and breathing exercise that helped our bodies relax and our minds become clear. We were learning how to rest. Sometimes someone brought a reading to "plant" into the silence, or we remembered that important Scripture from the Hebrew Bible: "choose life so you might live." Then the silence deepened, often for as much as a half hour. We moved into very deep places in ourselves, into our souls. Out of the silence, members then shared messages that had come to them, some in images, some in thoughts. We closed by holding hands, naming, praying, and holding in the Light those who needed healing, those in our care and those who gave care, those with HIV-AIDS who had no care, and those who had died. We then gave one another the kiss of peace. Often, there were hugs and tears.

We then had something to eat and often settled down to make plans for the care of a friend, or to hear about the latest ACT UP event (political agitprop) or the next rally for better health care. Worship, meditation, connectedness, caregiving, change making, laughing, and grieving were all part of a whole.

As time went by, we became aware that the group was a community that had healing power, because it was rooted in spiritual practice that supported our persistent caregiving. Because we began each meeting in silent meditation, each of us could tap into our own religious tradition. But we all felt held by the Spirit, and that connection created a healing community; caregivers and recipients were one. We knew that, at that time, there was no cure for AIDS, but we were experiencing healing. Some of us were healed of fears and anxiety, some of the effects of homophobia, shame, and injury to self-esteem, some of loneliness and alienation, and some of family hurts. We were learning to let go, to rest, and to *be* at rest. We were learning to breathe, to live, and to become ready for death. We prayed.

When asked by the researchers for the *Caregiving in the U.S.* survey about how they coped with stress, 73 percent of the caregivers said they prayed. African American (84 percent) and Hispanic (79 percent) caregivers are significantly more likely to cope through praying than white (71 percent) or Asian (50 percent) caregivers. Women are more likely to pray than men (80 percent vs. 61 percent). Those in fair or poor health prayed more than those with excellent health (82 percent vs. 70 percent), and those with higher levels of burden prayed more than those with lower levels of burden (85 percent vs. 66 percent).[10]

The survey did not ask respondents whether or not they prayed alone or if they also prayed with their faith community. Nor did it ask about support services for caregivers within their faith community. I can only hope that those who prayed used the power of both prayer and a loving community to help them deal with their stress. Although the researchers did not ask about community, they did find that 61 percent relieved their stress by talking with or seeking advice from friends or relatives. Only 27 percent talked to a professional or spiritual counselor.[11]

Today's caregivers have found that their first solution to coping with stress is *spiritual*. Their second solution is *relational*, and 61 percent said they talked with friends and relatives, unloading their burdens and asking for advice. Predictably, more women (67 percent) used this method than did men. But 51 percent of the male caregivers also confided in friends and relatives.[12]

These were also the solutions to the stress of caregiving that the Judson group found decades ago: we prayed together, asked for advice, received information, and unloaded our burdens—in community.

The Needs of Today's Younger Caregivers

Today, there is a cadre of caregivers who parallel the age and experience of members of the Judson group. The 2004 *Caregiving in the U.S.* survey has found that over 26 percent of the nation's caregivers are between eighteen to thirty-four years old and that they care for someone between the ages of eighteen and forty-nine (42 percent). The average age of care recipients is thirty-three. Their most common problems are mental illness or depression, although 5 percent are mentally retarded. Many of the caregivers are friends, not family (25 percent), to recipients who are single (45 percent) or divorced (16 percent), and one in four lives alone. Of these younger caregivers, 15 percent are caring for a sibling and 27 percent are caring for an adult child.[13]

This group has many unmet needs. Of all groups, they have the lowest educational level and most are primary caretakers with the least financial support. When they need information and support, they search the Internet and talk with friends. Often, these caregivers are single people caring for single people who have demanding issues: mental illness and depression. These are caregivers who truly cannot do it alone, but many try. They need support from groups for the mentally ill and their caregivers.[14]

It has also been reported that there are caregivers even younger. Some 1.4 million children, ages eight to eighteen, provide care for an adult relative, and 72 percent are caring for a parent or grandparent. Fortunately, most are not the sole caregiver. These youngest caregivers have been off our radar screen, because they are usually overlooked and certainly don't speak up. They must be identified and cared for by care teams that can surround them and their families with loving attention.[15] It is not a surprise that our invisible, youngest caregivers are vulnerable and our oldest are most at risk for caregiver syndrome. This mirrors the brokenness of our nation's health care system.

The typical family caregiver is a woman who is forty-six years old, has had some college education, is married, employed, and has another twenty-hour-a-week job, caring for her mother (or another relative), who lives less than an hour away. She might supplement her care by paying for her mother's housekeeper or health aide. This care lasts an average of 4.3 years.[16]

Meeting the Unmet Needs of Caregivers

If I had been interviewed in 1973 by the researchers of *Caregiving in the U.S.*, I would have told them that my unmet needs were: (1) finding time for myself, (2) balancing my work and family responsibilities, and (3) managing my emotional and physical stress. These same unmet needs are at the top of the list of today's caregivers (another unmet need—keeping the person cared for safe at home—was ranked number 2 by those who care for persons with Alzheimer's or dementia).[17]

Giving caregivers the gift of time, even in small quantities, is precious. Remembering my friend Gretchen, I know that four hours of time that might seem small to others was big for me. She broke through my caretaker mind-set by asking what I needed to do and being available to help me do it. This gave me time to do things and also time for friendship. Often, small gifts of time can make a great difference to a caregiver who is craving time for herself.

If a caregiver is to have more time, someone else will have to do what she's been doing, or not doing. If several friends could each give only four hours a week, a caregiver could catch her breath. If friends stayed with her care recipient, performed a routine caregiving task, or even helped with some of her own grocery shopping, housework, and unfinished tasks the caregiver would have time to do something for herself. Sometimes, the caregiver is so overwhelmed with the big picture that she cannot see specific tasks and cannot ask for help. But if a friend came and said, "I can help you with that paperwork," she would be overjoyed, and she would have more time.

When helping the helper, it is wise to identify and offer to do "small" things, because you can keep on doing them. Often, caregivers make this easy by asking for specific help. My friend Ann is the "captain" of her family care team of cousins who all pitch in to care for their elderly aunts and uncles. She has a talent for noticing their needs and then finding small ways to make a difference by asking others to help. She notices that an uncle seems down, so she calls her cousin and says, "If you're going to the ball game, could you take Ernie?" Or when their aunt seems more confused about her finances, she asks a cousin to stop in to see what he thinks should be done. And cousins call her if they've been taking care of a relative who is becoming more than they can handle. This family needs many hands to do lots of small things, lest one or two members burn out.

When caregivers don't ask for help, it must be offered. Help may be needed, but first somebody needs to notice. A common caregiving scenario is the "sandwich generation" caregiver—we'll call her Mary—whose mother is becoming more and more demanding and less and less satisfied by her daughter's attempts to meet her needs. Mary may be too worn down to reach out, but if others become aware, there are many small things that can help. Grandchildren can call or visit. Grandsons, particularly, know how to "jolly" grandmothers. Another might offer to visit her mother while Mary goes to a yoga class. Other family members might have a conference call to make a plan for Mary to get a break. Or a friend could suggest to Mary that her mother needs a medical consultation to evaluate her behavioral change and could offer to accompany Mary to the appointment. This would touch Mary directly. She's been worried that her mother might be showing early symptoms of Alzheimer's or dementia.

Several months earlier, Mary's mother's needs were less insatiable. While her mother napped, Mary had some time for herself.

She meditated, made phone calls, and caught up on some of her own office work. Now her mother is restless, and Mary no longer has a quiet space to meditate, pray, and keep track of herself. When Mary meditated regularly, she was centered. She was able to balance the care she gave her mother with her own busy life as mother of two teenagers, wife, household manager, professional executive secretary, and friend. She also was able to fit in walks and went to church, where she got community support. Without some time to meditate and have just a little space for herself, her life is out of kilter. She neglects herself. Mary becomes more vulnerable to her mother's personality change. She has begun to reflect her mother's insatiability by making unreasonable demands on herself, spending more time trying to make it work. She is exhausted. If Mary could ask someone to give her a small gift of time so that she could meditate again, a major shift could occur in her life.

With the gift of time, caregivers are more able to balance the care they give to another with their own responsibilities to family, home life, and jobs. Because of this balance, which is always shifting, caregivers will experience less emotional conflict and their lives can be more stable. Because they have not lost track of themselves, they will be able to pay attention to their own health, be less exhausted, and even have some fun. Very often, friends not only give the gift of time, but they are part of the action by going on walks, making doctors' appointments for both of them, scheduling a massage. Time and relationships go together.

Care Teams: A Kind Way of Caregiving

The desire to care for one another is built into our DNA. Generations ago grandparents and elderly relatives moved into their children's homes, and entire families were involved in their care. This happened cross-culturally. The family and their neighbors were an unofficial care team. Elders were honored as part of the family, and they played their part. As their bodies wore out, they were tended to. Homeopathic medicines helped, but they often died quickly, because of the lack of modern medicine. For those with no families, religious and community groups built homes for the elderly to provide care.

Today, the situation has changed. People are living longer and, although they have health issues, many are active. Recently friends, two couples in their nineties, have buried their sixty-year-old children, who died of cancer. My friends regularly play golf, walk, and ride stationary bikes–and even dance. Their adult grandchildren have visits (vacations!) with them. Several friends in their eighties are moving closer to their adult children but are not living with them. Many are moving to the independent side of assisted-living residences. On the other hand, other friends are living on social security with small pensions and Medicare. They are barely squeaking by. Some of them have family nearby, but because of our mobile society, others do not. And they are very frightened that adequate health care will not be available when they need it.

Not only are we living longer because we're healthy enough, but our lives are being prolonged by medical science. Some procedures—like hip and knee operations—can give new mobility and vitality. Other procedures can prolong life in vegetative states. These changes have affected the rhythm of caregiving. Sometimes caregiving can be intense but fairly short in duration, as when a family member has a one-day procedure for gall bladder or eye surgery. But other amazing procedures requiring only an overnight stay, such as hip replacements, require much more home care. And other conditions—Alzheimer's, dementia, strokes and their aftermath, Parkinson's, cancer, with its remissions and reappearances, and care for the elderly—can require caregiving in the home for months and even years. Others requiring this long-term care are in special treatment centers, hospitals, or hospice centers. Even though they are no longer at home, caregivers come to feed them meals, tend to other needs, and visit daily. This is care for the long haul that requires many hands.

Care teams, which have always been invisibly present through the acts of loving-kindness for the sick and their families, are becoming more recognized, organized, and supported, particularly by the information on the Internet. When caregiving moves beyond the work of the primary caregiver, organization and coordination are necessary. Lotsa Helping Hands (www.lotsahelpinghands.com) provides a free-of-charge caregiving coordination Web service, allowing a patient and a family's community circle to assist more easily with the daily meals, rides, shopping, baby-sitting, medical management, bill paying, and errands that become a burden during times of medical crisis or caregiver exhaustion. When someone asks "What can I do?" the name of a new member is added to a database, and the new member can immediately see the various tasks that require volunteer assistance and can then sign up by clicking on the task. Confirmation e-mails are automatically sent to the family and coordinators, as well as e-mail reminders one week and one day prior to the commitment. The needs of the primary caregiver can also be added to the list—"Mom needs to go to the doctor, beauty shop, church retreat, yoga, and we need more funny DVDs." This tool is particularly useful when caregiving is required for years. Over time, many caregivers and those who care for the caregivers will change, but the need goes on, particularly for the care of the primary caregiver. New helpers can sign on and pick up tasks. Care continues.

While many caregivers do not use the Internet, the service it provides is instructive. Organization and coordination of care volunteers make caregiving, particularly over time, more possible. This coordination is usually more than the primary caregiver can take on. She or he has personal tasks, and they also need care. However, a friend with organizing skills can be the captain of a care team that performs these multiple tasks.

Share the Care (www.sharethecare.org) is a model and handbook that shows how to create a "caregiving family," when the primary caregiver is unable to carry the load alone. The group supports not only the person in need but the whole family as well as those with no family nearby. By clicking onto the National Family Caregivers Association's Web site (www.thefamilycaregiver.org), one can find in-depth information and resources that support the common needs and concerns of all caregivers about caregiving and care of caregivers. The National Caregivers Library (www.caregiverslibrary.org) is an extensive online library, consisting of hundreds of useful articles, forms, checklists, and links to topic-specific external resources. The National Alliance for Caregiving (www.caregiving.org) is a coalition of national organizations that focuses on the issues of family caregiving. It is a national resource that does research, policy analysis, and advocacy.

The challenge is to find ways of getting these resources to those who need them most but do not use the Internet, caregivers sixty-five years of age or older. They might not use it, but their children and certainly their grandkids do. A grandchild could create an intergenerational link by searching the Web and getting information about caregiving to his or her grandparent-caregiver. For instance, the grandson could create a listserv of family, extended family, and friends, and attach to an e-mail the information he discovers. And the listserv members could add additional attachments to this network of information and also sign up for caregiving tasks. In the process, he has created a *virtual* caregiving team.

Faith Communities— The Heart of Caregiving

> "Let us remember in prayer Lettie, who has returned home after her recent radiation series, and her husband, Bill, and daughter, Karen, who have been faithfully caring for her."

It was just a small thing, but the congregation noticed. The priest always prayed for the sick, but this was the first time he prayed—by name—for their caregivers. As he continued this practice week after week, the congregation's consciousness was raised and an intentional ministry to caregivers was begun.

We have seen that caregivers choose prayer as their first way of coping with the stress of caregiving. They are cared for by their spiritual practices, and their spiritual homes are the natural places for them to come for sustenance. However, it is often their care recipient who is publicly named for prayer. This does not mean that caregivers are overlooked. Many faith groups have rituals of healing and prayer, where they are blessed and strengthened. However, the priest, in that small act of naming caregivers, was signally identifying their special need.

Of all social institutions, faith communities have the deepest awareness, involvement, and influence with families caring for their loved ones. They have already been praying, visiting, and performing countless acts of kindness. Because these families are in their midst, they can also become powerful educators by intentionally creating opportunities for the extended family of relatives and congregants to learn caregiving and listening skills, to become a part of care teams, and to become aware of special needs of the primary caregiver and find ways to care for him or her. They can begin by taking the first simple step of making a bulletin board for information about caregiving resources.

Because members of a faith community already trust one another, even a care*taker* who feels she has no choice but to do it alone can be encouraged to let others help. She can be influenced by her friends, in spite of resistance, to join a group for caregivers of Alzheimer's patients, for instance, particularly if her friend goes with her. Or she might be encouraged to become a "buddy" of another caregiver in the congregation, who is also struggling. As buddies, they can share support and information. These new connections can break the cycle of their isolation and self-neglect and can bring hope. Because of trust, a sensitive clergyperson or friend who has been paying attention to the moods of the congregation's caregivers might be able to detect anxiety and depression and open the way to referral for professional help.

Sending a small signal in a prayer can touch caregivers' souls. When their community is a safe place, there will be those to whom they can "tell it like it is," their frustrations and anger, exhaustion, sadness, and loss, particularly when their loved one no longer knows them.

Because they can be real in their community, burdens can be lifted, and isolation melts. Caregivers need the healing they find in communities that share the care. Faith communities are challenged to be as faithfully committed to caregivers as caregivers are to their loved ones over the long haul.

Notes

1. National Alliance for Caregiving and AARP, *Caregiving in the U.S.* [national survey], 2004, 62.
2. Ibid., 60.
3. Sjeree Crute, "Caring for the Care Giver," *The Magazine—AARP*, November–December 2007, 66.
4. *Caregiving in the U.S.*, 8.
5. Ibid., 60–61.
6. Katherine Mack, Lee Thompson, with Robert Friedland, *Data Profiles, Family Caregivers of Older Persons: Adult Children* (Washington, DC: Georgetown University, Center on an Aging Society, 2001), 2.
7. *Caregiving in the U.S.*, 43.
8. Gail Sheehy, "How Can We Help Our Nation's Caregivers?" *Parade Magazine*, September 6, 2007, 7.
9. *Caregiving in the U.S.*, 34.
10. Ibid., 68.
11. Ibid.
12. Ibid., 69.
13. Ibid., 9.
14. Ibid.
15. National Alliance for Caregiving and the United Hospital Fund, *Young Caregivers in the U.S.* [national survey], 2005.
16. *Caregiving in the U.S.*, 20.
17. Ibid., 73.

17

My Brother's Keeper
Reflections on Child-Sibling Grief

Sarah Rieth

The purpose of this chapter is to reflect on the experience I had in 1957 as a five-year-old when my baby brother died and to use this experience to make recommendations to pastoral caregivers who are ministering to child-siblings following the death of a child. Where I comment on the responses of my family I have strived to speak my truth in love.

A Baby Is Welcomed into the Family

I am the eldest of five and the only female among my parents' children. My second brother was born when I was five years old, just before I finished kindergarten. I remember being excited as Mommy's tummy grew and as our family prepared for the arrival of baby Jimmy. After Jimmy was born, I played the role of the big sister, caregiver, and Mommy's helper much more than I had been able to when my first brother, Billy, was born when I was thirteen months old. Jimmy was "my baby," and he was and is a part of myself.[1] It was important to me that Jimmy have a mobile over his crib so that he could be engaged, delighted, and soothed when he was alone. My father took me to the store so that I could help choose a mobile for Jimmy. I loved to play with him and watch the mobile catch his sweet gaze.

Up to that time I had attended Presbyterian church school regularly. A fond memory is of sitting with my classmates on the floor and learning to sing "Jesus Loves Me."[2] I felt safe and loved in the womb of my church school class. I was happy that I belonged to Jesus and I wanted to know and be known by Jesus because he loves me. It all felt trustworthy. Spiritual formation had begun.

When Jimmy was two months old he had his checkup and DTP shot with his pediatrician.[3] At the same time, my maternal grandmother, who lived four hundred miles away in another state, had taken ill with another "near-death spell" and called for my mother to come and see her. This was before the interstate had been built, so the emergency car trip was long and arduous.

My parents traveled with two young children and an infant fussy from having had a shot earlier that day. The next afternoon at my grandparents' house, the day Jimmy was two months old, my mother asked me to go upstairs and check on him in his bassinet. I obeyed her request. I do not remember what I saw, but I do know that I saw that something was wrong. I came downstairs and told Mother that there was something wrong with Jimmy. My exhausted mother did not respond to what I told her and stayed downstairs for a while. She had already fed, patted, and changed the baby, and thought that she had done everything possible to care for him up to that point. When she did go upstairs she found my brother dead in his crib.

My grandfather rushed my parents and Jimmy to the hospital. Jimmy's death was attributed to Sudden Infant Death Syndrome (SIDS, often referred to as "crib death").[4] While they were at the hospital, Billy and I were with our grandmother. She accused me of killing my brother since I was the last to see him alive.[5] I repressed this memory until my training therapy in my late twenties. I did not tell my parents of the accusation until then. They assured me that I had not killed my brother and were distressed that I had experienced that trauma. This repression was what I came to believe was a sign of God's mercy, as it enabled me to move on in my life without actively engaging the trauma until I was in a situation in which I could handle the memory and have people in my life who could help me process the trauma and my grief.

Emotional and Spiritual Confusion

In 1957, the culture was such that one did not speak of death openly. Widespread cultural awareness and empowerment to speak openly of bereavement and other issues related to death and dying did not develop until after the publication of Elisabeth Kubler-Ross's watershed book *On Death and Dying* (1969). Families got along in their grief as best they could, and it was culturally normative for people not to discuss feelings about a death in the family.

In addition, my parents come from kin who did not talk about feelings; thus, they were not inclined to talk openly about what had happened. Mother and Father were in the impossible bind of still having to function in the parental role while also grieving the traumatic death of a baby. So life went on as if nothing had happened. My parents took Billy and me to Boston the day after Jimmy died so that we could ride the swan boat.[6] Well intended to amuse and distract us, the swan-boat ride left me confused that we would go on such an excursion but not talk about what had happened to Jimmy.

The privacy and silence of the grief experience within the family further challenged me to wonder whether he mattered to us. It contributed to my distorted, unconscious belief that I had to carry the grief for the whole family, since it seemed that Jesus and I were the only ones to whom he mattered.

Once we were at our family's home again we attended Jimmy's funeral in the cemetery chapel. This service functioned to "close the book" on Jimmy's life and death.[7] The trauma I experienced at the death of my brother, whom I loved and for whom I felt responsible, and the trauma of my grandmother's cruel accusation, could not have been spoken of in my family and the societal culture at that time. The silence and secrecy built on the guilt, shame, and sorrow enhanced the tragedy.

S. P. Bank and M. D. Kahn cite the work of Krell and Rabkin:

> Parents and child come to share a powerful bond through the spoken or unspoken feeling that, if any one of them had somehow acted differently, the child might still be alive. The guilt maintained by these unrealistic beliefs remains intact and intense, with each individual locked in a struggle with his own conscience and unable to share such painful feelings.[8]

In such families as mine,

> Bereavement must remain a private matter; one must stifle or choke back sadness, anger, or happy remembrances. Entombed within this conspiracy of silence, the family tries to regain its balance, and life goes on "normally," in the pretense that the death has never occurred.... The remaining child interprets the parents' unwillingness to talk about the dead sibling as an unspeakably angry accusation that somehow he or she is at fault.... The parent keeps silent because, "It would upset our remaining child to talk about it," and a child keeps silent because, "It would upset my parents to talk about it." Constricted in circles of mutual protection and self-protection, the sibling never fully faces the loss.[9]

As a five-year-old, I was developmentally disposed to make up reasons for why my brother died, and this built on my grandmother's accusation. Bank and Kahn continue: "Younger children are more likely to misunderstand or distort a death than are older children and adolescents; below the age of ten, magical attributions and fantasies about the dead sibling can go unchecked as can corresponding ideas about the responsibility of the survivor-sibling."[10]

Amplifying the family trauma and in parallel to my having been accused, my parents were accused by adults in the neighborhood and church community of abusing and killing the baby. I recall that a couple of months after Jimmy died Mother told me that this was one reason she stopped going to church. The fact that I remember Mother telling me this despite my having repressed my grandmother's accusation was a saving grace for me, although it must have been deeply traumatic for my parents. When I began in my late twenties consciously to mourn my brother's death, my mother's words helped me to see my own pain in a larger context. But as a child, affected by the death and by Mother's words, I began to wonder if the church is a safe place after all. Stunned and overwhelmed with grief, each of us who survived Jimmy's death was off in her or his own corner, coping as well as possible.

Jimmy's death was an experience of dislocation. It happened during the summer, far away from home and far from my church friends, neighbors, and schoolmates. I felt isolated by my shame and guilt. I felt that something must be wrong with me for needing to talk about my brother's death. The incongruity of the swan-boat trip caused me to question my sense of things. With my parents overwhelmed with grief, my grandmother to be avoided, and spiritual questions arising that challenged my trust in God, the safety and surety of family and church felt compromised.

The Search for Meaning: From Confusion to Discovering the Mystery of Love

As a teen and young adult I was confused about guilt and responsibility. I believed I was responsible for Jimmy's death and I lived unconsciously from that belief for many years as I tried to atone for my guilt. I engaged in codependent, "taking care of" relationships in my personal and early professional life, in order to make up for not having taken good enough care of my brother. This unconscious belief fueled my journey to become a priest and therapist, but I needed significant personal therapy to break the stranglehold of codependency. Because my family was unable to talk openly about my brother's death, I needed a lot of input from my early pastoral care and pastoral counseling supervisors as an antidote to the lack of confidence I had in my perceptions, timing, and style related to when and how to talk about sensitive issues. Abrupt terminations by clients in my early years of practice were occasions of what T. A. Rando calls "subsequent temporary upsurges of grief" or STUG experiences. "These are brief periods of acute grief for the loss of the loved one, which are catalyzed by a precipitant that underscores the absence of the deceased and/or resurrects memories of the death, the loved one, or feelings about the loss."[11]

It was God's providential care that enabled me to survive the trauma of Jimmy's death, my grandmother's accusation, and the splintering of my family's closeness. I attended church with Father. I watched him sit and pray in the pew, leaning forward toward the next pew with his hands over his eyes. Seeing my father look to God in brokenheartedness and earnest hope was an important factor in my spiritual growth, coping, and healing. I began as a five-year-old to search for meaning in life and in death.

The grace of the hymn "Jesus Loves Me" in my life cannot be underestimated. That hymn held me and worked on me unconsciously and consciously. Unconsciously, it enabled me to belong to Jesus and to dwell with him. The hymn's lyric "The Bible tells me so" claimed scriptural authority as an anchor that I did not learn about in church school but that said to me, "this is really true; this is something trustworthy." Consciously, and at a developmentally appropriate level for a child between the ages of five and eight, I experienced the disconnect between how could it be that a God who loves me would not allow a beloved child like Jimmy to live. It did not make sense to me that God would allow a precious child to be born and then allow him to die. This was before I knew anything about the Crucifixion of Jesus. The hymn says "Little ones to Him belong." I wondered if little Jimmy belonged to Jesus more than I did. I also wondered if perhaps Jimmy did *not* belong to

Jesus as much as I did, or else why would he have died? Why was his life so short? I was angry that God took away "my baby." What could be the meaning of a precious life that lasted only two months?[12] Many years later I realized that through Jimmy's death I became a spiritual seeker and praying person.

Mother also told me that some neighbors said that Jimmy would spend eternity in hell or in limbo because he died without having been baptized. It was hurtful for me to hear this, and I am sure this explicit condemnation was very painful for my parents. The idea that Jimmy was not in heaven further challenged my spiritual formation to date.[13] I could not and would not accept this belief because it was in direct opposition to what I had already learned, that "little ones to Him belong."[14]

I have come to understand that *belonging* and having a sense of belonging is not about membership but about *mattering*. Thus I may join a church, but that membership does not necessarily mean that my internal experience is one of mattering. "Little ones to Him belong" told me as a child that children matter to God, I matter to God, and that my brother's life was and is important to God whether or not he was baptized. Those words were a holding environment of trust and safety to me.

In Jesus' farewell discourse in the Gospel of John, Jesus gives his followers hope that there is a real relationship, a real presence despite physical absence or distance. The relationship Jesus' followers have with him will endure beyond his death. Jesus' followers will always belong to him. He says "on that day you will know that I am in the Father, and you in me, and I in you" (John 14:20). There is mutual indwelling, mutual object constancy. These words have been of profound comfort and guidance for me as I live into the truth that Jimmy matters to God and to me, and that I matter to God and to Jimmy. The relationship has not ended even though my brother died. We belong to one another and to God.

Recommendations for Ministering to Child-Siblings after the Death of a Child

J. W. Fowler states that,

> There are marker events that blast the landscape of our lives and shred the veil of our temples beyond all recognition. These devastating events, against which none of us finally has protection or guarantees, can be prepared for—in limited ways—only by shaping a life grounded in faith and a community of faith that can form and support us in spiritual communication with a Ground of Being beyond our finite bonds of love and our webs of woven meanings.[15]

The importance of the ways parents, pastoral caregivers, and the community of faith respond and do not respond to children who are mourning the death of a child in the family cannot be underestimated. Their responses will affect the child-sibling throughout her or his life.

We know that Christian education is essential in the formation of discipleship of Jesus Christ within the lives of young children. Pastoral care from clergy, church school teachers, and youth leaders is essential in helping children to cope with loss and other significant and difficult events in their lives and to find meaning in their suffering. This is a way in which the community of faith may enact the truth of God's love and that each life is precious in the heart of God.

All church leaders who minister to children should be notified when a death has occurred in a child's family. A plan for ministry to the child or children in the family should be developed as an essential part of the comprehensive pastoral care ministry to the family in its grief. A pastoral minister and/or a trusted Christian educator of young children can meet with a family in their home to help them talk about and reflect on the loss they have suffered. Young children can be encouraged to talk about their questions and draw their feelings. Church schoolteachers can use the story of the death of Mary and Martha's brother Lazarus (John 11) to teach children about grief in families and Jesus' compassion for Martha and Mary. Children who are in the bereaved child's class can learn how to express sympathy and care for their classmate, just as "many of the Jews had come to Martha and Mary to console them about their brother" (John 11:19). Jesus' treatment of both Martha and Mary showed how much they mattered to him. He engaged in what I call "the sacrament of tears" ("Jesus wept" [John 11:35]), an external manifestation of the love he held for Lazarus, Mary, and Martha.

Pastoral caregivers should be attentive to what the child says and does not say, and what the family says and does not say. These caregivers are in a position to ascertain over time if a child is experiencing an inhibited or disturbed mourning process and to help make an appropriate referral for the family and child to a pastoral counselor or bereavement counseling agency.

Allowing children to continue to ask their questions, and responding to them with receptivity and tenderness, is a way the community of faith can be a community of care. Many questions that children have are ones that reflect the great mystery of life and death. Many of these questions are ones to which we do not know the answers. It is important that pastoral caregivers not respond to children's questions with platitudes but with honest, developmentally appropriate answers, including "I don't know." Platitudes such as "God took your brother home" usually make the caregiver less uncomfortable but can have the effect of silencing the child.

The death of a child within a family is an occasion for teaching about the meaning of the Eucharist or Lord's Supper. In that sacrament we enact the truth that suffering is real and that God's love and power are at work in the midst of brokenness and sorrow to bring some kind of new life and joy out of that death. Pastoral caregivers can, over time, help children to be attentive to the tiny grace notes of God's presence that will be present in the midst of their suffering. From those grace notes woven within the sorrow they will over time begin to discover and experience God beckoning them to new life and joy.

Even though a child may not be able to believe or feel God's love in the early stages of grief the community of faith can serve as a faith-holding environment for him or her. Through its words and deeds of presence, loving-kindness, attentiveness, responsiveness, prayer, and teaching a congregation proclaims the most important truth that "[nothing] will be able to separate us from the love of God in Christ Jesus our Lord" (Rom 8:39b). This scripture text reflects the truth of God's enduring relationship with each person no matter what happens, no matter if the person is alive or dead. "So then, whether we live or whether we die, we are the Lord's" (Rom 14:8).

Notes

1. S. P. Bank and M. D. Kahn (*The Sibling Bond* [New York: Basic, 1982]) describe this role as *one-way loyalty*: being *my brother's keeper* (125–34). "'The parental child,' who is generally a girl, assumes primary responsibility for brothers and sisters in childhood and often into adulthood" (125). The term *my brother's keeper* has its origins in the Hebrew Bible (Gen 4:1–16). In that story about the two sons of Adam and Eve, Cain has killed his brother Abel, who was favored by the Lord. "Then the Lord said to Cain, 'where is Abel your brother?' He said, 'I do not know; am I my brother's keeper?'" (Gen 4:9). Cain asks "Am I my brother's keeper?" to deflect blame and avoid accountability for having killed his brother. Bank and Kahn use the phrase to denote a sibling who takes on the responsibility for the raising of a sibling or siblings. My use of the term in the title of this chapter reflects a full range of feelings I have about my relationship with my brother and his death: guilt, confusion, sorrow, anger, defensiveness, and gratitude.

2. Jesus loves me! This I know,
For the Bible tells me so.
Little ones to him belong;
They are weak, but he is strong.
(Refrain) Yes, Jesus loves me! Yes, Jesus loves me!
Yes, Jesus loves me! The Bible tells me so.
(Words by Anna B. Warner, 1859; Music by William B. Bradbury, 1862.)

3. Thomas G. Keens, MD, of Childrens Hospital Los Angeles, writes that "a number of epidemiologic studies have now been performed which look into the possible relationship of SIDS and DTP immunizations. The majority of studies, and the better studies, do not show a relationship. SIDS is most common between 2–4 months of age. Immunizations are routinely given at 2 and 4 months of age. Thus, by chance alone, one in eight SIDS babies will have died within a week of their baby shot. However, the larger studies do not show any greater frequency of SIDS near immunizations. The NIH collaborative study actually showed fewer SIDS victims had baby shots than controls.

"A number of years ago, our group took a different approach. We recorded the breathing pattern and heart rate of babies overnight the night before and the night after their DTP immunizations. We had three groups of infants: controls, SIDS siblings, and apnea of infancy (ALTE). There was no difference in the recording the night after vs. the night before the baby shot. In fact, there was a slight trend for breathing to be more regular after the baby shot. These two pieces of information indicate that SIDS and/or apnea are not due to DTP immunizations" (SIDS Network Web site, http://sids-network.org/experts/immunize/htm; accessed January 22, 2008).

4. "SIDS is the sudden death of an infant, under one year of age, which remains unexplained after a thorough case investigation, including performance of a complete autopsy, examination of the death scene, and review of the clinical history.

"In a typical situation parents check on their supposedly sleeping infant to find him or her dead. This is...a tragedy which leaves them with a sadness and a feeling of vulnerability that lasts throughout their lives. Since medicine cannot tell them why their baby died, they blame themselves and often other innocent people. Their lives and those around them are changed forever" (American SIDS Institute Web site, www.sids.org/definition/htm; accessed January 22, 2008).

5. J. Bowlby (*Loss: Sadness and Depression* [New York: Basic, 1980], 123) states that "when a baby dies suddenly and inexplicably at home, as in 'crib-death,' a distraught mother may impulsively accuse an older child of being responsible."

6. Bowlby (*Loss*, 153) describes my parents' overt response to Jimmy's death well. He states that "adults who show prolonged absence of conscious grieving are commonly self-sufficient people, proud of their independence and self-control, scornful of sentiment; tears they regard as weakness. After the loss they take pride in carrying on as though

nothing had happened, are busy and efficient, and may appear to be coping splendidly."

7. The whole family did not at that time and has not to this date discussed the impact of Jimmy's death on the family.

8. Bank and Kahn, *Sibling Bond*, 275.

9. Ibid.

10. Ibid., 281.

11. T. A. Rando, *Treatment of Complicated Mourning* (Champaign, IL: Research Press, 1993), 64.

12. Rando (*Treatment of Complicated Mourning*, 612) states that "when a pregnancy or infant is lost, parents are reminded that they can have other children and told they are lucky they did not have more time to become attached. Often, the fact that emotional bonding occurs well in advance of birth is totally overlooked." I believe that my emotional bonding with Jimmy began in midpregnancy, when my mother was beginning to "show." I began to learn about pregnancy and birth in a developmentally appropriate way. I was excited about the baby coming and about being a big sister. "However, others outside the family may not have had the opportunity to develop a bond with the child or to have experienced [him] as an individual. They mistakenly believe that the loss is minimal because the life was so brief....Usually the loss is negated and the family's mourning becomes disenfranchised" (Ibid., 613, referencing Kenneth J. Doka ed., 1989, *Disenfranchised Grief: Recognizing Hidden Sorrow.* Lexington, MA: Lexington Press).

13. In fact, this belief that a child who dies without having been baptized will not go to heaven is still alive. During the course of preparing this chapter I worked with a teen church school class, playing "Stump the Priest," in which the teens asked their spiritual and religious questions of me. One teen asked if it is true that babies who die without having been baptized go to hell.

14. I have come to see the sacraments of the church, including Baptism, not as rites that make something happen that has not happened before, but as ways the community of faith gathers to celebrate and lift up for blessing the truth that this person is a precious child of God, that this person "belongs to God."

15. J. W. Fowler, *Faith Development and Pastoral Care* (Philadelphia: Fortress, 1987), 106.

References

Bank, S. P., and M. D. Kahn, MD. *The Sibling Bond*. New York: Basic, 1982.

Bowlby, J. *Loss: Sadness and Depression*. New York: Basic, 1980.

Davies, B. "Sibling Grief throughout Childhood." *The Forum* 32, no. 1 (January/February/March 2006): 4. Association for Death Education and Counseling. Http://www.adec.org/publications/forum/Forum_Jan_06.pdf. Accessed January 14, 2008.

Fowler, J. W. *Faith Development and Pastoral Care*. Philadelphia: Fortress, 1987.

Herman, J. L. *Trauma and Recovery*. New York: Basic, 1992.

Moriarty, I. "Mourning the Death of an Infant: The Siblings' Story." *Journal of Pastoral Care* 32, no. 1 (March 1978): 22–33.

Rando, T. A. *Treatment of Complicated Mourning*. Champaign, IL: Research Press, 1993.

White, P. G. "Factors that Influence Sibling Grief." The Sibling Connection. Http://www.counselingstlouis.net/factors.html. Accessed January 22, 2008.

Woolsey, S. "The Grief of Children." KidSource. Http://www.kidsource.com/sids/grief.html. Accessed January 20, 2008.

18

"Here I Am, Standing Right Beside You"

Spiritual Accompaniment and Care of Alzheimer's-Impaired Parents

Janet K. Ruffing

A few months before my dad was diagnosed with metastatic colon cancer and when his Alzheimer's was already well advanced, I was with my parents and Dad's caregiver, Natalia Crook, at Eucharist in our parish Easter Sunday morning. During the communion procession, we sang Tom Booth's song, "Here I Am," which I was hearing for the first time. I dissolved into tears and into God, recognizing, deeply, how Jesus had been standing right beside me, beside us as a family in the entire circle of caregivers, who became part of our journey as we cared for my dad and subsequently for Mom.

At that time, Natalia Crook had been caring for Dad twelve hours a day for about two months, accompanying Dad minute-by-minute through his day and standing right beside him, bringing order to his day by guiding him through every moment and, as a result, calming his anxiety and bringing some peace to the household. She, too, was deeply moved when I was, and sensed what I was feeling as well. Intuitively, I also wondered if this was to be our last Easter with Dad, which it proved to be. For us, the meaning of the verses of the hymn seemed to have a powerful spiritual effect.

> Here I am, standing right beside you. Here I am;
> Do not be afraid. Here I am, waiting like a lover.
> I am here; here I am. I am here.
>
> Do not fear when the tempter calls you. Do not fear even
> though you fall.
> Do not fear, I have conquered evil. Do not fear, never
> be afraid.
>
> I am here in the face of every child. I am here in every
> warm embrace.
> I am here with tenderness and mercy. Here I am; I am here.
>
> I am here in the midst of every trial. I am here in the face
> of despair.
> I am here when pardoning your brother. Here I am;
> I am here.

In the compressed moment of communion with the Risen Christ, the parish community, and my parents and caregivers, Christ was everywhere and "standing right beside me." I knew I could trust that he had been and would be with me for the whole journey. And I trusted that he was present "with tenderness and mercy." It seemed to me that Dad's experience of Natalia was of her standing right beside him during his waking hours, in a very loving way. Theologically, in the terms of the song's image, Natalia had become a Jesus-presence, standing right beside Dad. When in our shared faith we talked about it on the way home, I discovered that she too recognized herself in this role.

As a family, we had always been faithful Sunday Catholics, participating in Eucharist with the parish community. By Easter Sunday 1999, my parents had been worshipping in the same parish church since 1960. Relatively recently, the church had been renovated, placing the altar in front of the original sanctuary on a raised platform, and the pews, removed from the nave, had been placed on either side of the altar. Four pews thus faced one another with the altar between them, and the first row on one side provided seating for the altar servers and on the other, for the handicapped and infirm. The weakest in the community were thus seated only a few feet away from the altar with a completely unimpeded view of the presider. Eucharistic ministers brought communion first to the handicapped and then to the rest of the community. Others who came in the front side doors filled in the rest of the seating. Often, they were the families of the lay ministers for the service. In this way, the ill and handicapped were cared for and included within the worshipping community. For many, such as my parents, they had never been as close to the sacred action before.

For my church-attending parents, the eucharistic ritual was utterly familiar, and, despite being ravaged in other ways by their dementias, they continued to respond to the entire ritual. It seemed to me that for both parents, liturgical music communicated as much as, if not more than, the reading of Scripture and the homily. The sung music, with its theology embedded in its words, touched their hearts and the intact parts of their minds, and they were always totally present and visibly connected to the service. Somehow for them, the kiss of peace reinforced the affection among us, and the holding of hands at the recitation of the Lord's Prayer joined us to the larger community as well as to one another. These embodied ritual actions may be for such patients a significant access to God and to prayer throughout their illnesses. For me and for our Filipino Catholic caregivers, it was as well a consolation.

Natalia and her husband, Leo, continued to take Mom and Dad to church every Sunday, as long as it was possible. In addition, the local parish had a team of lay ministers who brought communion to the homebound, and when Dad was brought home from the hospital after his cancer surgery, we arranged for one of them to make a weekly pastoral visit to my parents, including a communion service. As the adult daughter and the one responsible for overseeing my parents' care, I discovered over and over again that I had to make the request from the parish when I was in town and make church attendance an activity I expected the caregivers to provide. It helped that our caregivers were members of the same parish.

By September, I had taken a leave from the university in order to be with my parents in California more consistently. When I arrived home, Natalia told me that sometimes my dad would call her "Janet," and on one such occasion, she reported that Dad had said, "Janet, I don't know how much longer I can keep on going." This was my first experience of Dad's "nearing death awareness," despite his severe dementia. By the time I returned from retreat ten days later, Dad was in the hospital and had been diagnosed with metastatic colon cancer that had already reached his liver. They gave us a prognosis of three to six months.

Dad's dementia made his hospital stay something of a nightmare for him. He had to be restrained and was black and blue from pulling against the restraints and resisting care because of his confusion and fear. Mom, by this time, was already showing signs of moderate cognitive impairment and was functioning far below her normal level, given the impact of Dad's diagnosis on her. At this point, I spent mornings with my Dad in the hospital and interacted with the medical staff, and Natalia helped my Mom at home. She then brought Mom to the hospital in the afternoon and stayed with Dad, so he was not left alone so much in the hospital.

Before Dad's surgery, we arranged for a priest from the parish to administer the Sacrament of the Sick. I requested the priest whose grandmother had Alzheimer's and who, I knew, would be comfortable with Dad's dementia and with us as a family, since I had already made a connection with him from Sunday worship. I had indicated in the scheduling that both Mom and I would be present and that I planned a simple service. Instead of the pastorally sensitive priest I had requested, another priest, who was obviously challenged relationally, arrived with the chrism of the sick but without communion. He said, "I didn't know if your Dad was rational enough to receive communion." I said, "He is, but you knew Mother and I would be here, and this is part of the sacrament." The priest proceeded to say the prayers in a mechanical way. Just before he began the anointing with oil, I stopped him and said, "We need to listen to and sing a song, so Dad will know he has been anointed." I had brought a tape recorder with me and we played and sang Marty Haugen's song, "Healer of Our Every Ill" (1987). The music and the words powerfully expressed a hopeful sense of healing, comfort, and faith that extends beyond pain, fear, and sorrow. It captured the mix of feelings I guessed Dad might be having, but it also expressed those that Mom and I were experiencing and supported our efforts to move toward Resurrection-faith and a trust in God, despite Dad's diagnosis.

> Healer of our every ill, light of each tomorrow,
> Give us peace beyond our fear, and hope beyond
> our sorrow.
>
> You, who know our fears and sadness, Grace us with your
> peace and gladness,
> Spirit of all comfort: fill our hearts.
>
> In the pain and joy beholding, how your grace is
> still unfolding,
> Give us all your vision: God of love.
>
> Give us strength to love each other, every sister,
> every brother,
> Spirit of all kindness: be our guide.
>
> You who know each thought and feeling,
> Teach us all your way of healing
> Spirit of compassion: fill each heart.

Dad became peaceful in response to the song, and Mom and I were consoled and strengthened during this time of prayer and ritual together. The priest completed the anointing and left without making any relational connection with Mom or me.

Such an inadequate approach to the sacramental life in a church that claims to be sacramental at its core is too often the case. However, as a nonordained person who has been educated and trained in ritual, I found I could supply what was missing from the ministrations of the ordained by enhancing a minimalistic approach to sacramental life by including all of the senses, especially music. I knew the rituals themselves and I knew that, according to numerous neuroscientific reports, music with and without words can stimulate different parts of the brain more than words alone can do. In Alzheimer's-impaired persons, such music with meaningful texts can evoke heartfelt responses that help the impaired person connect again to deep parts of themselves and can help orchestrate a less-confused response to their situation (Sacks 1985, 36–38; Jourdain 1997; Lite 2008, 53–57).

In addition to music, I found that touch was often the most powerful and calming care I could offer Dad spiritually. I did not consider my dad to be a particularly religious person. He agreed to become a Catholic because Mom would not marry him unless he did. Only when he began instructions in the Catholic faith before their marriage did he discover that he had already been baptized a Catholic. Mom was deeply religious in her whole way of being. Dad expressed his spirituality in his love for Mom and for us and in the thousand details of householding and providing for his family. He was concrete and sensate in his expression of care and affection. Often, all I needed to do was to hold his hand; many words were not needed.

The hospital staff quickly discovered that if I was touching Dad or talking to him he remained calm and would offer no resistance to any necessary procedure. As a result, the staff allowed me to accompany him everywhere in the hospital. In the surgery waiting room, with the surgeon and orderlies standing with us, I gently laid my hands on Dad and prayed out loud for him, for the surgeon, and said to my Dad, "Now, you come back to us." He nodded and came through the surgery pretty well.

Throughout his recovery from the surgery in the hospital and later in the nursing home, despite his severe dementia, he would have a few minutes when I was with him when he was completely lucid. At one point, he said, "I have cancer." I said, "Yes, you do, and I am sorry you have to go through this. And we will help you as much as we can." Another time while still in the hospital, he said, "I miss your mother." I explained that Mom had a cold and she could not come to the hospital, but I called her on the phone and got her to talk to him.

Another poignant moment in the hospital occurred when I walked into Dad's room. He had a wild look in his eyes and was hooked up to some kind of inhalation machine. He was agitated and breathing very shallowly. He calmed only slightly when he saw me and, as I sorted out for myself what was supposed to happen with the machine, I placed his hand on my belly and invited him to breathe with me, making it a game. He finally got the hang of it, and when the Chinese inhalation therapist arrived, there we were peacefully doing deep abdominal breathing in perfect unison with each other.

Dad had a short stay in a nursing home to get a little stronger and to regain enough strength so that he could walk a little and we could bring him home to die. We had to intervene several times in the standard procedures of the nursing home, because Dad needed to spend more time in bed than the "rules" allowed. He tended to be more confused in the dining room, and I discovered that the TV was always on, always loud, and set to channels that appealed to the twenty- and thirty-year-olds who were on the staff. The music and images were agitating and disturbing to Dad. At one point, Dad asked, "What did I do to get stuck in here?" He was interpreting his experience there as punishment. I tried to reassure him by explaining that he was sick and that we would bring him home, as soon as we could. Within a few days, Natalia and Leo agreed to work together as team, and we were able to bring Dad home from the nursing home and initiate hospice. Dad arrived home the weekend before Thanksgiving.

The hospice team was wonderful. Once they were in place, I could receive more support emotionally and spiritually. And I could call on various members of the hospice team to work with Mom, my brother, and the caregivers. The hospice chaplain was a woman Episcopalian priest with a mixed Protestant background. I asked her to pray with Dad and to use some of his favorite hymns that he liked from revival meetings my grandmother took him to in the mining town where he grew up. On another occasion, I asked the social worker to help the caregivers and my mom to recognize and to respond to increasing instances of Dad's "nearing death awareness" (Kornfield 1998, 205–11; Callahan and Kelley 1992).

About three weeks before Dad died, we took him out in the yard in his wheelchair to show him the newly installed wrought-iron gate. He said something like "I feel lousy." And one of the caregivers told him everything was wonderful. Dad replied, "If this is wonderful, then you are the one who is crazy." When we put Dad back in bed after lunch, I noticed that his liver was quite enlarged. I was gently touching his side, and he asked me what I was doing. I explained, "Your liver is right here, and it has gotten very large all of a sudden. This is where the cancer is." Natalia said to me, "You can't talk to him like that." I replied to her, "He knows there is something wrong with his body. It isn't helpful to pretend everything is okay, when he knows it isn't."

The social worker was very helpful in addressing the difference in our cultural attitudes about speaking about the dying process. For instance, when he met Emily, the hospice social worker, Dad told her, "My name is George Ruffing" and then added something about "angels." He reported to me a series of hallucinations or fantasies that suggested death was nearing, because "people are coming for me," he said. Then he said, "I don't want to go with them. I am going to retire in two weeks. I'm tired of all this." He died ten days later. He reported seeing his dead brother, Rudy, bringing him black boxes. Three days before his death he said, "This is going to kill me! I'm in a mess." "I'm upside down, what have I done?"

Emily took several examples that I gave her of things Dad had said indicating he knew he was dying. She interpreted these statements as nearing death awareness. This explanation and conversation reduced the tension among us, and the caregivers learned not to contradict Dad's accurate awareness of what was happening to him, even if it was expressed in his unique symbolic language.

On Christmas Eve, Mom, Natalia, and I had a very tender and moving experience with Dad. He was very animated and wanted to know "Have I paid you enough?" Dad had been an accountant early in his career, and I understood that he wanted to know that he had treated us well and been fair. Each one of us around the bed described to Dad how loving he had been, how well he had treated each one of us, that he had always been fair. Dad's face lit up and he would question us, "Are you telling me the truth?" When we assured him we were truthful, he would reply, "Well, that makes a guy feel good." This process went on for maybe an hour. At one point, I said to my Dad, "we don't know anything that you have done to us that needs healing, but if there is something on your mind or in your heart that we don't know about and that you are sorry about, just tell God in your heart you are sorry, and it will be all right." Shortly after that, Dad became quiet and Natalia did not expect him to live through the night. Christmas Day, I went to Eucharist alone and brought communion home. I talked briefly with the pastor after Mass, and I told him how close to death Dad was. He was very kind, and he came to the house Christmas Day and anointed my dad again, while I was out running along the Santa Ana River, where I worked out my feelings.

In my opinion, the dying process is such that no official pastoral care person can necessarily be present when the dying person needs spiritual accompaniment. It is often family members who are present and, if they understand the complications of dementia, they may perceive that such patients' symbolic world offers important cues to what is happening as death approaches. My dad was actually engaging in a review of his life, and he needed our help and reassurance. My leading an appropriate response to Dad's question enabled everyone who was there to participate. And Dad received an infusion of love in response.

At other quiet times during that last ten days or so of Dad's life, I would sit and hold his hand. I was usually silent but would pray interiorly or just rest in God. Dad would become agitated if I left him, even for a brief time. I could feel him pulling on my spiritual energy. It was as if our souls were communicating with each other without words. And he knew I was not afraid of what was happening to him. At another time, Dad wanted to know what would happen when he died. I told him I really didn't know but suggested that he ask his sister, Sarah, who was a very spiritual person to help him and that he would meet her on the other side. I also said something like, whatever else happened, he could trust that God was love and that we didn't know much else about it. I told him that "God is nothing but love and the love will remain—that love begets more love." That seemed to calm him. Periodically through these last days, I would sing to him the "Suscipe" of Venerable Catherine McAuley, which has been adapted for a hymn (Nieratka 1979). The words of this song/prayer emphasize a loving God in such language as "You are a God of Love and Tenderness" and "it's you (God) who must teach me to trust in your providence" with the plea "Take from my heart all painful anxiety." Singing this song of entrusting surrender helped me and my dad. I think that it helped him hold on to God's lovingness, and he was soothed by hearing my voice singing it.

Dad lingered for another week and died on January 3. He was apparently waiting for my brother to arrive, and he and his wife came sometime during Christmas week. Even though my brother is not a particularly religious person, he was able to join us around my dad as we prayed aloud some of the prayers for the dying, and family members would choose a psalm from my community office book (1998) or would say a decade of the rosary. One of the things I discovered at my father's deathbed was that the prayers in the Catholic Prayer Books (1962) for the dying introduce many references to sin and judgment, which were not helpful in Dad's case, because he had already reviewed his life and by this time was quite incapable of sin. The prayers for the dying from the *Book of Common Prayer* (1979) were much more helpful and positive, offering reassurance and comfort.

I don't know how much this praying aloud helped Dad. None of the family had ever been present for a death, so we were not practiced in recognizing how the process was progressing. Dad was actually in pain and having trouble breathing when we first thought he might be actually dying. We needed the hospice nurse to give us a lesson on how much morphine to administer to relieve his difficulty breathing, and that made Dad's last couple of days less labored. His death was a simple gentle exhalation and we were all ready for his death and present for it.

Hospice was again very helpful. Verne, the hospice chaplain, came, even though a clergy friend had been present at the deathbed. Verne stayed with Mom as Natalia, my brother's wife, and I cleaned and anointed Dad's body with lotion before the undertaker arrived. Verne stayed with Mom and other family members until Dad's body was removed from the house and we had completed all the other necessary tasks under the supervision of the hospice nurse.

Mother's Story

My mom had been diagnosed with mild cognitive impairment a couple of months before my dad died. She had a previous history of stroke and was suffering small strokes. She had many complicating medical problems including a heart condition, diabetes, and breast cancer. Her postmortem brain autopsy also revealed Alzheimer's disease, but this was not entirely clear before she died. Like my dad, her basic personality remained intact, although she was cognitively impaired in terms of memory, executive function, and abstract thinking. She lost some of her social functioning at this time, and it became difficult for her to make any new friends or socialize very well. She developed Parkinson's-like symptoms the last two years of her life, which responded for a while to the Parkinson's medications. With Alzheimer's disease, there is no predicting when or which particular brain function will be attacked by the plaque. This makes every Alzheimer's journey unique to the person.

Mother was a survivor of multiple medical emergencies and adapted remarkably well and worked hard to recover from each major health challenge. She managed to survive my dad for nearly four years, although none of us, including Mom, expected Dad to be the first to die. Natalia continued now to care for Mom, since it was clear she could no longer drive nor manage her own household.

Pastoral care for Mom differed somewhat from that of my dad, because their personalities were so different. Mom continued to worship in her parish community after Dad died, with the assistance of her caregivers. However, the parish was completely nonresponsive when, more than a year after Dad's death, Natalia's replacement, Cora Ferrar, requested someone to bring communion to Mom when she was recovering from hip surgery.

Not quite a year after Dad's death, Mom broke her hip. Mom had undergone many surgeries and, since it was the last week of my school term, I thought that she could go through this surgery without me, simply accompanied by the caregivers. However, the doctors had to delay the surgery for nearly a week to wait for her blood thinners to dissipate. As a result, I was with her before the surgery. Mom was agitated in a way I had never seen her before a surgery. She seemed frightened and anxious. The afternoon before the surgery, Natalia, another religious sister named Judith, Roy, an Episcopalian priest friend, and I were with her. I asked Mom if she wanted us to pray with her, which we did. All of us laid hands on Mom and prayed both silently and with a few words. She alternately closed her eyes and looked at each of us. Her entire mood shifted, and she became totally peaceful and said how grateful she was to be surrounded and held by us all at the same time.

I continued to provide communion services every visit home, which was every three to four weeks. In these services, I always included her caregiver, and we developed a pattern of using the form of a Eucharist service with a lay presider. I always used at least three pieces of religious music: an opening song, a response to the first reading, and a communion meditation song. We read the Sunday Scripture selections, and I would often make a three-to-five sentence reflection on the word and invite Mom or Cora to speak, if they wished. We included the intercessions and then began the communion rite with the "Our Father" prayer. Cora was very sensitive and helpful, in that she helped Mom make the sign of the cross. We held hands at the "Our Father" and offered one another the kiss of peace and received communion and listened to a meditation song together. During the last year of Mom's life, I took a leave from school and, in addition to spending some time with Mom every day, we did these services at least weekly. Even when Mom could scarcely speak, I asked her on one occasion, "Is this consoling for you?" She immediately responded, "You know that it is." Despite her profound impairment in speech from the Parkinsonian symptoms, Mom always entered into her God-space, an embodied sense I have had of her since I was a small child sitting next to her in church Sunday after Sunday. I could feel her God-connection in my responsive body. I believed that by including all the senses in our communion services, I was tapping into her deeply embodied memories and, through the devotional music, helping her to organize her responses.

Despite Mom's loss of her day-to-day memory from a multi-infarct process, her caregivers, Cora and Nilda, surrounded Mom with such a loving and peaceful atmosphere that Mom showed no interest in dying. There was no wanting this to end. Her day-to-day experience was serene and reliable. She enjoyed attending some performance events, films, and regular programs on TV. Mom was obviously becoming weaker and experiencing swallowing problems. She was at high risk for aspiration pneumonia. I decided that we should anoint her late that fall, because I did not think I could rely on a timely response from the parish clergy. So when a priest friend was visiting, we celebrated Eucharist together and anointed Mom within that service. We used the prayer selections from the *Book of Common Prayer* (1979) that emphasized strengthening and healing instead of those focused on dying. Mom was quite clear in her responses that she was not interested in considering the possibility of dying quite yet.

Between that service and sometime in February, Mom was declining. She had nearly choked to death, due to her swallowing problems. When our priest friend was planning to visit us in the middle of February, I decided we would anoint Mom again, but this time in anticipation of her dying. A consultation with Dr. Bonnie Olsen, a neuropsychologist at the University of California at Irvine, explained to me that in a dementia such as Mom had the person's consciousness may not be organized enough to recognize that she is dying or that death is approaching. We again did a full eucharistic service in our home with Mom and Cora, and I explained to Mom that this time we were going to anoint her in anticipation of her dying. I explained that she was weakening, that we did not know exactly when she might die, but she would most likely die in the next few months and I wanted her to have the comfort and strength of the sacrament. Mom's eyes got wide, and she seemed to take it in. The service was moving and tender, and we all cried, except Mom.

I cooked a splendid dinner that had to be pureed for Mom, and the evening had a celebratory quality to it. And typical for Mom, we watched a video together that evening. She had no interest in talking anymore about dying, because she was now ready for a party. This shift of mood can be challenging for family members. With dementia patients, the feelings often stay intact, but once the moment is over, it's over. For family members, the shift in feelings is often very abrupt, so it is something of a discipline to stay attuned to the moods of the patients who are being cared for so as not to impose a more sustained mood on them.

Throughout this entire period of attending to my parents during their physical and mental decline, I kept the radio on the classical music station and also brought home CDs of classical music. Mom had introduced us to classical music, when I was only about eight years old. I knew she loved this music and was uplifted and transported by it. I was also aware of the effects of classical music on the brain. So I tried to fill the house with beautiful sounds, which I hoped would also offer some consciousness-shaping form for my parents' ravaged brains. Dad would just say "turn that off," if the rhythms and tones were not right for him. Mother never indicated that she did not want the music playing.

Mother's death process differed from Dad's in many ways. She did not have the diagnostic clarity of Dad's colon cancer diagnosis and the clear progression of that disease ending his life long before the Alzheimer's process did by itself. Mother, on the other hand, had multiple, long-term disease processes. She had heart problems going back to childhood, a multi-infarct brain process, Parkinsonian symptoms, diabetes, asthma, repetitive urinary tract infections, and the effects of treatment for breast cancer two years before Dad died. She was both fragile and fiercely willful about living. We were only sure of her Alzheimer's diagnosis from the postmortem autopsy.

Her dementia protected her in interesting ways. She and Dad had been married sixty-two and a half years when Dad died. She was already suffering some mild cognitive impairment, and so she suffered bereavement for only twelve to eighteen months before her dementia restored Dad's presence to her. She would take in the fact of his death on our occasional visits to his grave, but she would be even more shocked to see her name printed on the marker awaiting her death date. At home, it often seemed to her that Dad was still present, as I also felt him to be. I finally interpreted to her that this presence was like her having the feeling that Dad was so close to her and caring about her that she did not perceive a difference between his physical presence and his spiritual presence. She nodded in agreement.

In the same way, when her short-term memory became even more impaired, her depression lifted and she appeared to be quite content. Our caregivers were very good to her and with her. They created a reliable structure of care for meeting her minute-by-minute needs, and they were very loving. As I imagined her reality, I realized that she experienced very little distress and was pretty happy and content in her own home, surrounded by love. She had no reason for wanting to leave the planet.

Finally, however, her heart began to fail in congestive heart failure. When I placed her on palliative care, because she was too weak to take out of the house anymore, I only then discovered she had been in CHF for a while. I had been convinced previously that she had so many life-threatening illnesses that she would likely choose to die when she felt she no longer wanted to live. During these four months of her life, I was living full time in California on a research leave and seeing her every day. The family came to see her before Easter and then I told her Easter Sunday that I would be away for two weekends in a row for speaking engagements. After that, I intended to return to New York. When I left for the first event, she actively began the dying process. Although she had no pain, she had a perpetually surprised look on her face. Her neurologist told me on Easter Monday that she might die in anywhere between ten days and two weeks. She died two days after I returned from Miami.

I stayed continually at the house with her then, and would get up and sit with her if I heard her breathing change and recognized that she was awake. Her eyes were wide open and her breathing was a labored panting. On the morning of her death, after the caregiver awakened and cleaned her, I again played classical violin music and got in bed with her and held her, to both comfort her and to support keeping her head up so she could breathe more easily. Because we could not tell how soon death would come, we called her primary caregiver, who had not yet arrived. I believe Mom clearly knew she was dying, and the whole house was thick with peace. When the visiting nurse came, she said she wished she had filmed this death, so that she could show others what a home death could be like. Mom was surrounded by me and two caregivers. There was nothing but love and peace in the whole house. Music was softly playing in the background, and Mother's breathing pattern so resembled the way a woman in labor breathes that I intuitively felt that I was Mom's midwife as she was being birthed into another life.

I hope these abbreviated narratives of this double Alzheimer's journey may be helpful to other adult children who wish to provide quality spiritual accompaniment for their parents as well as appropriate physical care. To do so, adult children need to know about and share their parents' spirituality. If there happens to be a memory impairment, as in the case of my parents, I believe that keeping one's parents present in their worshipping community and participating as fully as possible is more important than any embarrassment about their physical appearance or behavior. The richness of a fully enacted ritual has the capacity for tapping into the soul of patients and their deeply embodied ritual memory and supporting their God-connection. Only family members really recognize the unique symbolic meanings of the hallucinations and fantasies that emerge into speech. Although Emily, my dad's hospice social worker, recognized the symbols of death—for instance the "black boxes"—she had no way of knowing that Rudy was my Dad's first sibling to die. Family members, thus, have the background knowledge of their parents' life stories to interpret their symbols and to draw on other experiences that would support them in their dying process.

Within this essay, I have described some of the ways I prayed with my parents. I tried to illustrate that this activity of "praying with" has to be tailored to the style of spirituality and personal history of the person who is dying. Adult children need to follow the cues of attentiveness or disinterest of parents and must not impose their own piety on their parents or deny their parents spiritual comfort by not adapting to them. I also learned that I could not count on the local parish community to meet my parents' needs; although I still sought all the help I could get, because it is important to maintain the connection with the larger parish community.

Finally, it is important for adult children to get as much help as they can from the hospice team, which provides both a social worker and a chaplain. Although chaplains may not come from the same denomination or faith tradition, they are frequently more skilled in ministering to the dying than the average clergyperson. The responsibility of caring for Alzheimer's-impaired parents is daunting on every level. I received considerable support from the hospice social worker and nurses, who helped educate and comfort family members who were less present to the process because of distance or other reasons. The neuropsychologist, who was part of a multidisciplinary team assessing elders at the University of California at Irvine, was consistently the most helpful in providing me with the neurological information needed for giving direction to our caregivers and in offering emotional support to me over a period of five years. This included in Mom's case especially how her brain was or was not functioning. So above all, adult children accompanying their parents need to rely on help from many sources, including both professionals and other spiritually oriented adult children who have journeyed with dementia-impaired parents.

References

The Book of Common Prayer and Administration of the Sacraments and Other Rites and Ceremonies of the Church, together with the Psalter or Psalms of David according to the Use of the Episcopal Church. 1979. New York: Church Publishing.

Booth, T. 1996. "Here I Am." Portland, OR: Oregon Catholic Press.

Callahan, M., and P. Kelley. 1992. *Final Gifts: Perspectives on Death from Christianity and Depth Psychology*. New York: Poseidon Press.

Haugen, M. 1987. "Healer of Our Every Ill." *Gather*. Chicago: GIA Publications.

Jourdain, R. 1997. *Music, the Brain, and Ecstasy: How Music Captures Our Imagination*. New York: William Morrow.

Kornfield, M. 1998. *Cultivating Wholeness: A Guide to Care and Counseling in Faith Communities*. New York: Continuum.

Lefebvre, Gaspar, and the monks of St. Andrew's Abbey, eds. 1962. *Saint Andrew Daily Missal with Vespers for Sunday and Feasts*. Bruges: St. Andrew's Abbey.

Lite, J. 2008. "Sonic Health Boost." *Prevention* (January): 53–57.

Nieratka, Dolores, RSM. 1979. "Suscipe." Sisters of Mercy, Detroit, MI.

Sacks, Oliver. 1985. *The Man Who Mistook His Wife for a Hat and Other Clinical Tales*. New York: Summit Books.

Sisters of Mercy. 1998. *Morning and Evening Prayer of the Sisters of Mercy*. Silver Spring, MD: Institute of the Sisters of Mercy of the Americas.

Weil, A. 1997. *Sound Body, Sound Mind: Music for Healing with Andrew Weil*. New York: Upaya (2 compact disks).

19

Losing Sight of Loss

Emilie Trautmann

"Health Hell" began for my husband, Jay, and me on a stunningly clear late spring day. Jay is an artist, and to supplement his income from the sale of paintings, he did development work for an artists' community. I am a freelance writer, and, at the time, both of us were working for the community. When Jay returned to our New York City apartment on that spring afternoon, I was sitting at a small table in our living room, trying to concentrate on the research in front of me despite the beauty of the sky cushioning a waning sun. I said hello to him and then launched into an explanation of the approach I was taking to the task before me. Undeterred by Jay's lack of response and somewhat blank look, I chattered away. Jay often engaged in what he called "space traveling." As far as I could tell, his space travels took his mind and spirit to unexplored realms that often appeared, in one form or another, in his paintings.

Growing tired of conducting a monologue, I demanded his opinion on the plan I had just outlined. He answered, "I had the sonogram today. They said I have a very enlarged liver and spleen." I wanted to know exactly what that meant. Immediately. I wanted to know who said what. All the details. But there were no details. A technician had delivered the news to Jay and had told him to call his doctor.

"So did you call Dr. Colbert?" I asked. Jay said no. I strongly suggested that he make the call instantly, which he proceeded to do. Dr. Colbert said that he wanted Jay to have a CT scan. "What does he think the problem is?" I asked. The answer was that there was no answer yet.

While patience is usually one of my strong suits, I have never been good at accepting the proposition that no answer exists. So that afternoon, I began to create an answer. On an artist's grant a few years earlier, Jay had been to the Balkan area that used to be Yugoslavia. He had stayed on farms and eaten all sorts of things with questionable origins and served in circumstances that, to say the least, lacked basic hygiene. Hepatitis or a slow-moving parasite of some sort, I decided, was the reason for Jay's enlarged liver and spleen. Dr. Colbert would, of course, take care of everything. For Jay's part, the primary concern remained his long-standing digestive problem. This problem was his reason for visiting Dr. Colbert in the first place, as well as Dr. Colbert's reason for ordering the sonogram.

Jay scheduled and underwent a CT scan the following week. His mother, who had been a nurse and a hospital's director of nursing, agreed with me that he probably had picked up a nasty bug in Yugoslavia or maybe in the Communist countries of Eastern Europe, where he had also traveled on an artist's grant. Alternatively, she suggested, he could have picked up something in New York City. She lived a few hours south of us and considered the city to be fundamentally uninhabitable because of the pervasive grime. Neither she nor her son nor I seemed terribly anxious during the week between the sonogram and CT scan. I added to my prayers a request that Jay's bug, along with the digestive problem, would be cured expeditiously.

The next step after the CT scan was to visit Dr. Colbert and find out what the problem was and what the solution to the problem was. I decided to accompany Jay on this visit, and he was happy to have me tag along. Jay had started a file on his ailment, and he had doodled all over the front and back covers of the file folder. I figured that if he went into artist mode in Dr. Colbert's office, or worse, began to space travel, I would never get a clear idea of his medical condition or the necessary treatment.

By the time we saw Dr. Colbert, the weather had turned quite warm. I remember that I didn't need a jacket that day. Jay and I joked in the waiting room about possible implications of his doodles on the file folder. I asked if the drills and pipes and saws he had drawn indicated that he was getting ready to build me a home in the country. He wondered if surgeons ever had an urge to use simple woodworking tools rather than sophisticated medical instruments. We decided to stop at a favorite delicatessen on our way home from Dr. Colbert's office and sauntered into his examining room holding hands. Dr. Colbert greeted us somberly and said that the CT scan had shown lesions in bones throughout Jay's body. "Are you saying the lesions are connected to each other and to the enlarged liver and spleen?" I asked. "Yes, probably," he answered and then showed us a list of oncologists whom he knew and highly recommended. He also wanted to examine Jay, so I said that I would wait for him in the waiting room.

As soon as I sat down in the waiting room, I felt the walls closing in on me. I panicked. A nurse in the office was suddenly helping me into a small private room. At some point I had started crying but was only aware of the tears when I heard the voices of Dr. Colbert and Jay in a hallway a few yards away. The nurse handed me a box of tissues, and I quickly wiped my eyes and blew my nose. Then I stood up very straight, left the room, and calmly asked Dr. Colbert what the next step was. He said to choose an oncologist. Jay mused over the list for a few moments and announced that he liked the name Starr. "I have good associations with stars," Jay said cheerfully. We forgot to stop at the deli on our way home to call Dr. Starr.

Dealing with "Health Hell"

Jay has a characteristic that I find endlessly intriguing and that I have never encountered in anyone else. He has absolutely no fear of his own death. He always said that he considers death to be an adventure, and he is quite certain that it will be a wonderful adventure. This belief probably had roots in his spirituality, which I respect but consider to be unrelentingly idiosyncratic and incomprehensible. He went to Mass on most Sundays because I did and because he especially enjoyed space traveling in church. Sometimes he tried to figure out how he could get from a particular pew to the highest point in the ceiling of the church using only a rope of a certain length. Sister Anne, the nun who appeared to keep most operations going at the church to which we belonged, always seemed to treasure Jay's unusual spiritual wanderings.

I never doubted the veracity of Jay's claim that he didn't fear death, but if I had harbored any doubts, they would have been laid to rest as "Health Hell" unfolded for us. He was concerned for a while about leaving me with huge medical bills after his death, and he was concerned that certain people receive designated drawings and paintings after his death, but he showed no fear of experiencing death or its aftermath.

From the early days of Health Hell, I took a different approach to the fear of death. I buried the possibility of Jay's death deep within my heart and made sure that it stayed buried. My new operating principle was that we would find out what kind of malignancy he had, we would find a treatment, and normal life would resume. I felt prepared to argue eternally with anyone who challenged my position, but no one took up the challenge. For the first couple of weeks after receiving Dr. Colbert's news about the CT scan, however, I experienced odd little fissures in my granite stance. I jogged pretty much every morning, grateful for the time to be alone with my thoughts, or with no thoughts at all, at daybreak. As I jogged during those weeks, thinking of nothing in particular but the weather or the East River or the skyline, I would burst into tears without warning and have to stand still in order to breathe. In a minute or so, the tears would stop, and I would continue my jog. In less than a month, the teary episodes came to an end. My slate of relentless optimism was wiped clean, and I didn't cry again for years.

The oncology unit of the hospital where Dr. Starr worked was overcrowded and visually appalling. The waiting room had been seconded for examination rooms, which were still in short supply. We waited for our initial appointment with Dr. Starr in a hallway crowded with battered plastic chairs of several colors and vintages. Jay brought a large black portfolio to the appointment because he planned to show some drawings to another artist after seeing the doctor. I bought a silly beanbag lizard on my way to meet him at the hospital, thinking it might cheer him up.

After over an hour of waiting, we were summoned to see Dr. Starr. Jay left the portfolio, with the lizard perched on top, in the hallway. Dr. Starr, upon first meeting, appeared soft-spoken and intensely serious. He looked overworked and a bit underfed. Jay seemed satisfied that he had chosen the right oncologist, so I decided that I was going to be satisfied too—at least for the time being. Dr. Starr was talking about some tests that needed to be done when screams and yelling and major commotion broke out in the hallway-*cum*-waiting room. The doctor went right on talking, giving the distinct impression that time was too precious to accommodate interruptions such as mayhem ten or twenty yards away. To my great relief, the environment eventually calmed down. When we returned to the hallway waiting area, we learned that a couple of women had seen the beanbag lizard and thought it was some sort of voodoo curse. They had gone berserk and had to be taken from the area by security guards. Jay was thoroughly enchanted by the incident and spent the evening calling friends to recount the story. I was vaguely aware that I had crossed a threshold into a bizarre new existence.

Happily, the oncology unit of the hospital moved a month or so later to brand new, wonderfully patient-friendly quarters in what had been an enormous warehouse a few blocks from the hospital. Dr. Starr had a lofty title in the new cancer care center. By this time, I had settled into the pattern of attending every appointment Jay had with Dr. Starr. I stayed with him during all the examinations and asked a lot questions. I took notes, keyboarded my notes at night, filed a copy, and sent a copy to Jay's mother. Being a freelancer, I had some flexibility in when and where I worked. I informed all of my employers that Jay was undergoing a series of medical tests but that I foresaw no significant conflict between attending to his needs and carrying out my assigned work. As time to myself became more limited, I eliminated nonessential bits of my daily routine. I jogged for shorter distances and gave up daily jottings in my journal. Anyway, the journal was beginning to sound like the worst whining of the country and western genre. The effects of spending hours at the cancer care center in the middle of my work day did not appeal to me as subjects of close analysis.

At this early stage of our encounter with Health Hell, I made another error. Dr. Starr was ordering tests to identify Jay's particular type of malignancy, and I was searching the Internet for information about the doctor's early hypotheses. The prognoses I found on various Web sites were devastating: a person might live two years with one type of malignancy, maybe three or four years with another type. I was terrorizing myself with a lot of contradictory information that I didn't fully understand, so I asked a friend with a degree in medical history about online sites that might be useful to me. She informed me that according to a study by a major teaching hospital, the vast majority of medical information available to the general public on the Internet is either out of date or patently wrong. A person like me without medical training, she continued, could easily misinterpret even accurate information. She successfully cured me of amateur online medical researching.

Jay was experiencing no discomfort from whatever his still-undiagnosed medical condition was at this time during year 1 of Health Hell. With ease, he had perfected the art of space traveling during medical tests. He looked perfectly normal. If life wasn't normal now, I often thought, it would be normal soon. Reinforcing my belief, Jay made plans for his annual month of painting outside the city. He was using a painting technique that he had invented and that involved undiluted dry pigments. Some of these pigments were pure, highly toxic metals. I recalled with increasing trepidation stories I had heard about several of Jay's artist buddies from the 1970s who had worked in plastics and died of leukemia and various other malignancies. Jay knew more than I did about the hazards of what he was doing. Along with a lot of other people, he also knew that he was producing some magnificent art with the pigments.

Jay cheerfully informed Dr. Starr one day that he would be using his favorite colors during his painting retreat that summer. Dr. Starr gave him a cold stare and advised him, without further comment, to use an asbestos mask. I made a conscious decision that day. Jay's identity was inextricably bound to his art, and I wasn't going to place any barriers between him and his art. If he insisted on using cadmium yellow straight from the jar, and if he agreed to use an asbestos mask, I wouldn't raise objections. After an excruciatingly painful bone marrow biopsy, which he later said sorely tried his capacity for space travel, Jay left New York for a month in the cabin he had rented in Massachusetts.

The gallery that had scheduled an exhibition of his work in the fall had cooperated with a donor to produce an exhibition catalogue. Jay insisted that I write some of the catalogue text. Having neither the expertise nor the inclination to write about his art, not to mention having copy deadlines of my own bearing down like rampaging elephants, I capitulated and agreed to the task only because of his precarious health. When the catalogue arrived from the printer, Jay was enormously pleased and thanked me profusely. A couple of days later he mentioned, quite matter-of-factly, that the catalogue was especially important to him because it might be the last testament to his work. I responded by asking if he wanted to rent the Massachusetts cabin again the following summer. Once again, I assured both of us that we would prevail over whatever was attacking his health. I believed what I said, and I probably was very convincing.

Late in the fall it appeared that Jay might have a malignancy that could be treated with a bone marrow transplant, although neither Dr. Starr nor the colleagues with whom he had been consulting at other hospitals had pinned down exactly what Jay's condition was. Jay had a daughter, his only child, from his first marriage. She flew from San Francisco to New York to be tested as a possible bone marrow donor. It turned out that Jay's sister, his only sibling, was a better match. She lived about an hour's drive from New York and was planning to visit the Holy Land with a church group in early winter. There was a lot of violence in Israel/Palestine that year, and I was aghast that she would even think of putting herself at such risk when Jay might need her to donate bone marrow.

A friend, fortunately, convinced me not to confront Jay's sister over her impending trip. A part of me understands that she was right not to deny herself an eagerly anticipated adventure because of her brother's illness. But another part of me still accuses her of self-indulgence that could have had tragic consequences. At least, the latter part says, she could have made the trip sometime after the transplant issue was settled. It turned out that Jay did not have the kind of malignancy hypothesized by several doctors toward the end of year 1. Since a bone marrow transplant was now moot, I dropped my plans to repaint our entire apartment, to clear all unessential items from surfaces, and to create as sterile an environment as was humanly possible in order to increase his chances of surviving transplantation.

Reckoning on some sort of economy in the universe of transplants, I had signed up as a bone marrow donor and deposited the requisite blood samples with the national bone marrow bank. If I could help save the life of an unknown bone marrow recipient, according to my logic, Jay's life also might be saved. But there was no logic in the equation. I was, in fact, making a deal with God. As a child, I made many deals of this kind: If I do X, God will do Y. I suppose I was so frightened, beneath the solidly cheerful demeanor I presented to both myself and everyone else, that I had regressed to deals with the trickster God of my childhood.

When Jay's sister returned unscathed from Israel/Palestine, she was clearly relieved to hear that Dr. Starr was proceeding with chemotherapy rather than a transplant. There was still no diagnosis, although a consultant from the National Institutes of Health had joined the team working on Jay's case.

The first chemotherapy Jay underwent involved a spanking-new substance that required an injection lasting four to five hours and that would be administered weekly in the cancer care center. I knew my way around the center quite well by then. I was on a first-name basis with everyone from the center's receptionist to members of the chemotherapy treatment staff. I truly liked almost all of them. Motivated by a dogged intention to smooth the way for Jay whenever and wherever possible, I was unremittingly friendly even to the few people at the center whom I found disagreeable. Most of all, I depended on Dr. Starr's exquisitely competent nurse practitioner. I consulted with her about Jay's diet, an exercise regime, and anything else I could think of that might strengthen him for the treatment ordeal he was facing.

Dr. Starr described the substance used in the chemotherapy for us and said there was a good chance Jay would lose his hair. Jay said no, he didn't think he would lose his hair. The nurse practitioner gave us a tutorial on other effects of the chemotherapy, including loss of appetite. Jay said no, he didn't think he would lose his appetite. I prepared myself for dealing with his hair loss, which I considered rather minor, and his loss of appetite, which I considered more serious. He never wore hats, and I was pretty sure he would prefer to walk around bald rather than wear a baseball hat. I thought a lot about how all this would affect his self-esteem. From a nurse at the center, I learned about foods that would be especially nutritious, and I hunted down recipes using these foods in ways that sounded pretty good. During the first chemo session, which began in the early evening, Jay asked me to bring him a hamburger and french fries. I brought sandwiches and pastries to subsequent sessions. To my delight and to the amazement of many on the cancer center staff, he devoured whatever he was given. He also didn't lose any hair.

My work schedule and social schedule now depended on Jay's chemotherapy appointments. I always met him in the cancer center's treatment area, remained with him as he underwent hours of chemotherapy, and went home with him. The treatment area was comfortable, with a sensitive and confidence-inspiring staff, a nice collection of plants, and all the juice you could drink. Jay was relaxed during his treatments. We talked about art, politics, and people. At times he happily space traveled. If he fell asleep, I read. Chemotherapy soon became just another part of our weekly activities.

After a couple of months of this regimen, it became apparent that the chemotherapy was not improving Jay's condition. Dr. Starr assured us that there were many options, and my outlook remained utterly optimistic. Spring had come around again, and Jay was looking forward to his summer month of painting. More medical tests ensued. Data from another bone marrow biopsy were sent to the National Institutes of Health, but no one could identify Jay's disease. Jay made plans to paint at the home of a couple from Upstate New York who spent their summers farther north.

I usually stayed in New York City during Jay's month of painting, taking one or two long weekends to visit him and enjoy whatever serene and sylvan setting he had chosen. When I visited him that summer, after being away from him for a couple of weeks, I detected something unsettling about his face and complexion. An artist lived across the street from the couple's house, and he asked me if Jay was ill. I conjured up a chipper voice to say that he was undergoing some tests, and the doctors weren't quite sure what might be ailing him. It had become crucial to me that Jay and I remain outside cancer's vortex of fear and dread. I thought that if I touched the edge of this vortex, both of us might be lost forever. More to the point, Dr. Starr had assured us that his quiver of treatments was far from exhausted.

Year 2 of Health Hell

An acquaintance who directed a private equity firm, and who had an interest in art and a propensity for experimentation, offered Jay a job one day at the firm's midtown Manhattan office. As year 2 of Health Hell progressed, Jay had a new job that fascinated him and that offered us some financial security. My enthusiasm for the job was rooted in the very good health insurance that went along with it.

After protracted consultations with colleagues at a couple of other hospitals, Dr. Starr decided on a second type of chemotherapy. This one did not require the long hours of treatment necessary for the first type, but the frequency of treatment increased. Jay's new employers were amenable to his unconventional working hours, and I once again explained to my employers that although I would be accompanying Jay to all chemotherapy sessions, I could maintain my present work load. I figured that I would just sleep less. And visit with friends less. And be more efficient about everything I did. In other words, I would work harder and receive less support.

Another problem arose as the second chemotherapy began. I had an excellent working relationship with Dr. Starr's nurse practitioner. I trusted her judgment and depended on her timely answers to my questions. She explained medical tests and side effects to me, enabling me to feel at least somewhat prepared as I accompanied Jay on invasive and painful procedures. When she told me that she had decided to leave New York in order to care for her ailing sister, I lost my bearings for about a day. For the first time in quite a while, I wondered if I could continue gliding through life dominated by Jay's illness and visits to the cancer center. "You don't have a choice, so just keep on keepin' on," I firmly told myself. In combination with some intensive prayer, the admonition worked.

In a couple of weeks, Dr. Starr's new nurse practitioner and I were becoming friends. She was as wonderful, in very different ways, as her predecessor had been. I adjusted my never-ending search for information to accommodate her working style, and I respected her opinions and suggestions without reservations. One day, as Jay was undergoing chemotherapy, she and I started talking about the oncology culture. She said that the people in the cancer center loved their work and were generally very supportive of one another. "There's so much we can do for people," she explained as she looked over the treatment area and all the peaceful patients ensconced in their recliners. I asked if she ever felt discouraged. She admitted that she sometimes felt sad but insisted that she never felt discouraged. She looked like a satisfied woman, which boosted my spirits considerably.

A little while later she confided that she and her colleagues shared oncology jokes. "Like what?" I asked. She tried to dissuade me from pressing the inquiry, but I persisted. "Okay," she finally said and proceeded to tell me the latest joke making the rounds at the cancer center. Question: Why do they nail the coffin shut after someone dies of cancer? Answer: So the doctor can't get in for one more course of chemo. I laughed, keenly aware that I was now sharing space with the cancer and chemo insiders who didn't get discouraged. I laughed because I recognized the imperative that members of this special group take advantage of every opportunity to release tension in the company of supportive friends. And I laughed because I believed that everything was going to turn out all right and that Jay was not going to end up in a coffin nailed shut to keep out Dr. Starr.

The second type of chemotherapy seemed to be missing the mark, so Dr. Starr called a halt to it. Jay's spirits were still good as spring was emerging toward the end of year 2. By that time, he and I had a hard time imagining life without Dr. Starr. We had assigned him the role of third nuclear family member. No one but a family member, after all, would pursue Jay's health issues with the persistence that he demonstrated. When Dr. Starr decided that he wanted another series of tests before subjecting Jay to further treatment, Jay acquiesced without any argument whatsoever.

The tests were so extensive that they required Jay's admission to the hospital. The first few days progressed without problems. I spent each day with him at the hospital, accompanying him to tests or waiting in his hospital room if technicians barred me from the testing area. At night I worked, sometimes until sunup, to keep up with my writing assignments. With the arrival of the weekend, however, the hospital systems underwent a meltdown. Jay became increasingly frustrated as he waited for procedures and tests that never took place. I was unsuccessful at running interference between him and some of the more intransigent hospital staff members. His pent up anxiety seemed to be exploding, and it broke my heart to see him so helpless before a mindless bureaucracy disguised as a healthcare entity.

On Sunday, I slipped out of the hospital for Mass. Sister Anne asked, as I left the church, where Jay was. In my weary and weakened state, I broke down and told her about the past two years of Health Hell. I suddenly felt ridiculous for not having told her sooner. "I kept thinking it would all be over in a couple of weeks or months," I told her, "or that things wouldn't become this serious." As she listened closely, I realized that another unhelpful tenet had appeared from my past. When I was growing up, people did not go out of their way to mention an illness to a priest or a nun unless it was life threatening. By talking to Sister Anne, I was ratcheting up the possibility of an outcome I refused to consider.

When I arrived at Jay's hospital room on Monday morning, Sister Anne was already there. She had opened a window on springtime with a bouquet of yellow tulips. Her calming aura had restored Jay's good humor, and that restoration brought back my equilibrium.

Year 3

The tests that Jay underwent indicated a lot of things, but not the cause of his condition. As spring came and went, he began to lose his robust appearance. Friends started asking, with concerned expressions, about his health. My newly developed stock answer was: Jay has some very weird health issues that are baffling doctors in three New York City hospital systems. Dr. Starr, always respectful of Jay's vocation, did not try to dissuade him from going Upstate again during the summer of year 3. I chose to interpret the doctor's laissez-faire position as an indication of his confidence that Jay's health would hold up under a physically rigorous painting regimen.

When I visited him Upstate toward the end of the month, it was clear to me that his illness was getting worse. The artist neighbor invited me for a walk in the woods and bluntly said that Jay looked like a very sick man. "The doctors are working on it," I assured him. I was probably trying to assure myself as well. When I returned to New York City, I began a new prayer routine. I was very focused and very specific in my requests for Jay's return to health—that outcome the sole intention of my prayers. And just to cover the bases, as my grandmother wisely advised throughout my childhood, I wished on the first star whenever I spotted one over the city.

Soon after Jay returned from his month Upstate, Dr. Starr sent him to a surgeon to begin making arrangements for the removal of his spleen. His abdomen was swelling with fluid, and he was finding it difficult to sleep at night. Within a couple of weeks, he could no longer lie down and spent nights sitting in a chair. People in the neighborhood who had always been friendly suddenly looked frightened when we passed them on the sidewalk. The men working in a local delicatessen showed discomfort when we spoke to them. I hid my anger and stayed close to Jay at all times, somehow convinced that I could protect him from people's hurtful reactions to his appearance.

I also questioned Dr. Starr about the plan to remove Jay's spleen, since no one was sure about what was causing his condition or even about the nature of the condition itself. Without patronizing me or showing an iota of impatience, Dr. Starr explained that the trouble might be originating in the spleen and that Jay's spleen was in very compromised shape. When I demanded to know why he couldn't just do a biopsy, he gave me a quick lesson on the anatomy of the spleen. My illusions of being on top of medical decisions concerning Jay were dissipating before my eyes. I felt useless.

Jay was losing his grip too. He was in terrible discomfort and hardly slept at night. The surgeon, during one of our final visits to his office, said that Jay needed another CT scan before surgery. Jay refused, declaring that he couldn't possibly go through another scan. Dr. Matthews, the surgeon, calmly responded, "I'm not in the habit of losing my patients, and I don't intend to lose you. Am I making myself clear?" When we later compared our reactions to this comment, Jay and I found that we had the same thought: Everything's going to be fine because Dr. Matthews doesn't lose patients. Jay acquiesced to the CT scan and was admitted to the hospital for surgery a couple of mornings later. As Jay lay on a bed in a terribly cold room shortly before going into surgery, I made him promise that he would endure the surgery and come back to me.

I had kept in touch with his mother and sister throughout each medical ordeal, providing them with details of all the twists and turns in our long trek. His mother decided to come to New York the day before his surgery and to stay for an unspecified length of time with one of her friends who lived about twenty blocks from our apartment. The arrangement was fine with me, in principle, until about the fifth hour of what was supposed to be a three-hour operation to remove Jay's spleen. Having been a nurse, his mother began sketching various scenarios that could account for the extended surgery. None of them were good. By the sixth hour, I desperately wanted to escape from her rendition of fatal and near-fatal possibilities, but I was afraid that I would miss Dr. Matthews's promised report on the surgery if I left the waiting room. After seven hours the surgeon came through the waiting room doors and explained how difficult the operation had been. They had removed thirteen liters of fluid, and that was just the beginning. Additionally, it appeared that the surgery had yielded nothing conclusive about Jay's condition.

Jay's mother told me that it was time to face the fact that he might die. I said that I didn't think either of us should be engaging in such a conversation at that point. I was thinking, however, that if she ever said anything like that to me again, it would be her health that she should be worrying about.

Totally exhausted, Jay's mother went back to her friend's apartment. I was exhausted too but stayed at the hospital until he was settled in the intensive care unit. Jay's vital signs were not good, and he lay amid a mass of tubes and monitors and medical personnel. I couldn't get near his bed, so I watched all the activity from several yards away. Early in the morning, when everything except his blood pressure was stabilized, I decided to go home and sleep for a couple of hours. But after I arrived at home, I couldn't resist calling the intensive care unit every half hour to check on his condition.

The next morning, I found Jay awake and in foul humor. Fluid was again building up in his abdomen, and an intensive care nurse had dropped a malfunctioning monitor on his leg. It was the beginning of a grim week. Longtime friends and a bevy of relatives gathered in New York for what appeared to be a death watch. Only Sister Anne's appearance seemed to bring Jay peace, and I limited the others to ten-minute visits. Fatigue probably helped me to get through the week. Dr. Starr had the fluid buildup under control with a strong drug, but the drug was only a temporary measure. Jay told me that at one point during the surgery, he found himself settling into water that felt like velvet. Each time he blinked, he saw another one of his favorite color combinations in the velvet. The experience was so delightful that he didn't want to leave, he said, but suddenly he remembered his promise to come back to me. So he came back up from the velvet water.

All sorts of tissue slides had been made as a result of the operation, and Dr. Starr explained that the best way to get these slides to other doctors consulting on Jay's case was for me to transport them. I spent a couple of surreal afternoons messengering slides among three hospital systems in New York City.

A week after the operation, Jay was moved from intensive care into a run-of-the-mill hospital room. He began to feel better and to joke about his circumstances. The friends and relatives went home. Even his mother eventually went home. Finally, he was able to go home.

Because the operation had not resolved his health problem, we soon began a new regimen at the cancer care center. By this time, going into the final months of year 3, I was so focused on

Jay's health and comfort that I was turning down work assignments and adding a caveat to any plans I happened to make. "Of course if anything comes up with Jay's health," I would tell people, "I may have to cancel." For perhaps the first time in my adult life, I was absolutely certain of my priorities and unflagging in my efforts to arrange every part of my days and nights around these priorities. I felt almost giddy when I said to people, "No, I can't do this or that. I have to focus on Jay for the time being." There were no difficult choices to make, because there were no competing demands on my time. Jay's needs, as I perceived them, came first. Everything else was a very distant second.

My social concerns were gradually changing too. The receptionist at the main entrance to the cancer care center was having issues with his teenage daughters, and I usually chatted with him while Jay was having lab work done. Jay and I would then proceed to the financial section of the center to take care of insurance and co-pay matters. The people working there were extremely competent, and I was friendly with all of them. The next step of each appointment was to wait in a large and comfortable room outside the corridor leading to the examining rooms. A young man who worked in the waiting room was planning to take courses in forensic medicine if he could make it through his biology courses. We had long talks about the ups and downs of college curricula. A woman who also worked in the waiting room planned to join her boyfriend on the West Coast after she saved enough money to put a down payment on a car and an apartment. We commiserated about the size of our bank accounts. I had more contact with these people at the center than I had with friends and coworkers who had been dear to me for many years.

When called from the waiting room, Jay and I would follow a nurse into an examining room. After she recorded his vital signs, we would wait for Dr. Starr. I usually had a copy of *The New Yorker* magazine in tow, and we would look at the cartoons while we waited. By the time Dr. Starr arrived, we were usually laughing. During the examination, Dr. Starr talked with us about medical matters or art or a recent social or cultural development. It all seemed like a perfectly normal visit with an interesting and highly intelligent friend. Jay didn't seem to be getting any better or any worse. When he returned to his office job, he reinforced the appearance of normalcy.

The next chemotherapy, no. 3, started out alright. It consisted of an injection, which Jay was to give himself at home. He was intrigued with this process and injected the substance into his thigh without so much as a grimace. After a couple of weeks, however, he became very lethargic and then depressed. I checked with the nurse practitioner, who said that his symptoms were common side effects of this particular chemotherapy. One morning he said that he couldn't get out of bed. I brought him the telephone so he could let someone in his office know that he was sick, but he just shook his head and curled up in a fetal position. As I begged him to call the office, he curled up tighter. I found the situation so distressing that I called Dr. Starr's office and, for the first time, told his assistant that it was an emergency situation.

Dr. Starr fit us into his schedule that afternoon. I somehow got Jay dressed, pleading for his help throughout the process, and pulled him out of the apartment and into a cab. Dr. Starr took one look at him and halted chemotherapy no. 3. Life soon returned to normal—that is, what had come to feel normal. Soon it was spring again, and we were into year 4 of Health Hell.

Year 4

Year 4 brought chemotherapy no. 4. Jay complained of tingling in his fingers, which was an anticipated side effect of that chemotherapy, but he took the weekly needles and injection sessions at the cancer care center with equanimity. We established a routine for the chemotherapy, which entailed chatting or reading followed by a short nap and a snack that I packed for each appointment. I think that by that time, I considered the chemotherapy as much a part of my life as it was a part of his. We joked, not entirely in jest, that after the chemo sessions ended, we would miss hanging out in the comfortable chairs and chatting with our friends on the oncology staff.

Jay seemed in good enough shape by the summer to return Upstate for his annual month of painting. His condition remained undiagnosed, and in addition to the tingling in his fingers, he was experiencing numbness in his toes. When he returned to New York City in late August, Dr. Starr said that we would discuss new treatment possibilities.

Dr. Matthews, the surgeon, was an art collector. Jay decided to give him a painting as a gesture of friendship and gratitude before he left for his summer retreat. We visited Dr. Matthews's office with slides of several paintings and invited him to choose the one he wanted. The doctor was clearly delighted as he looked at the slides. Jay's work at the time was abstract and minimalist. All of a sudden, Dr. Matthews looked shocked. "My God," he said. "I just remembered what these paintings remind me of. It's the slides we made from your spleen." Jay had never seen the slides, of course, and he was thrilled at the idea of such synchronicity. The abnormal had become so normal to me that I hardly saw anything unusual in the doctor's observation.

Jay had a fine month of painting and returned to New York City in the fall full of optimism about his art in particular and life in general. The good feelings were soon pushed into the background, however, with the resumption of chemotherapy and increasing numbness in his feet. On September 11, 2001, he got out of bed and couldn't feel the floor beneath his feet—which meant that he couldn't walk. To this day, I remember 9/11 primarily as the first day that Jay couldn't walk. He settled back into bed, and I went out for a jog. On my way home, I stopped at a bakery to buy some pastry for him. In the bakery I heard that a plane had hit one of the Twin Towers.

By the time I got home, the second plane had hit. Jay was watching television when the towers fell. At that time I was trying to get through to the cancer care center in order to make an emergency appointment for him. The cancer center and the nearby hospital had been designated as primary facilities for receiving people wounded in the Twin Tower attacks. By the time I reached the nurse practitioner in the late afternoon on 9/11, everything in New York seemed so confused and terrible that we decided to talk the following day. Jay wasn't in pain, and like so many other New Yorkers, sat mesmerized in front of the television.

By the end of the week, he was able to hobble around the apartment with a cane I had found at a local pharmacy. The masses of wounded people expected by the cancer center and hospital never materialized, because most people in the Twin Towers either died or escaped from the scene. We were able to see Dr. Starr early in the week after 9/11, and he sent Jay for another battery of neurological tests.

After some seemingly routine tests, we were directed to a renowned physician whose office was in a hospital basement. The doctor was hunched over, shuffled, and spoke with what sounded to me like a Transylvanian accent. His nurse was about a size 0 and had one roving eye. The doctor ordered Jay to sit on a gurney and began tapping him with an electrified wand. I got a severe case of the giggles. Jay tried to staunch his laughter by coughing. The doctor and nurse probably thought we were pretty odd. When the test was finally over and we were safely in the rising elevator, Jay and I collapsed on each other laughing.

We got the good news a short time later that the nerve damage in his feet probably was not permanent, although it might be a long time before Jay could walk without a cane. His feet sort of flapped as they hit the ground, a phenomenon I had noticed in a few patients at the cancer care center. As his feet began recovering, however, he completely lost his voice. Chemotherapy no. 4 went the way of nos. 1, 2, and 3.

Jay's voice started to return after about a month, but the improvement in his feet was minimal. By Thanksgiving, he was getting discouraged. I spent a lot of time trying to cheer him up but wondered how much longer my optimism would hold up. Dr.

Starr had another treatment in mind for the new year, and I was beginning to search for signs that his stamina was flagging too. I detected no loss of drive, however, in the good doctor. The nurse practitioner, however, was becoming very pregnant, and I knew we were about to face another unsettling change in the dream team.

When I talked with Dr. Starr about Jay's flagging stamina, he immediately recommended a consultation with the oncological psychiatrist who worked at the cancer care center. Jay wasn't enthusiastic about the idea and never seemed to get around to making an appointment with Dr. Tripp. So I went ahead and made an appointment for both of us to see her. I cajoled and then threatened Jay, before finally dragging him into Dr. Tripp's office. Happily, it was love at first sight. She was an elegant woman with a hearty laugh and great sensitivity. She prescribed an antidepressant for Jay and continued to see us after each of his appointments with Dr. Starr. By the third or fourth appointment, I had seen only happiness in her face and asked how she remained so chipper. "I adore my job," she said. I must have looked skeptical, because she continued, "Most psychiatrists work with abnormal people or people with abnormalities. I work with very normal people who just happen to be in abnormal circumstances." Much as I appreciated her insights and laugh, I decided that Jay would benefit more from sessions alone with her. It never occurred to me that I might be in need of some counseling too.

The new year and new nurse practitioner came along with a new drug treatment. The drug was a pill with such a sordid history of side effects that I had to sign a statement pledging that I would neither consume nor even touch any of Jay's pills. The prescription had to be renewed monthly, with each renewal preceded by a telephone questionnaire for Jay. Pharmacies near our apartment were loath to carry the pills because of many obstacles to dispensing them. I often landed the task of picking up the pills at a downtown pharmacy.

The new nurse practitioner was a challenge too. Jay called her the Princess. Her saving grace was that she adored Dr. Starr and truly wanted his respect. It took a few months, but I finally figured out a way to work congenially with her. The nerves in Jay's feet healed, and his spirits picked up considerably.

Year 5

Year 5 began uneventfully. Jay continued taking the drug with the nasty background, which had been resurrected for treatment of certain malignancies and malignant-like conditions. The chief pathologist of a major teaching hospital at long last issued his report on Jay's lab tests and pancreas slides. He concluded that he couldn't identify the disease.

We visited the cancer care center regularly for Jay's lab tests, checkups by Dr. Starr, and sessions with Dr. Tripp. When the lab tests began showing improvements, Dr. Starr took it in stride. There was no definitive reason for the improvements. Maybe the pill treatment was helping. Maybe one of the four previous chemotherapies, or a combination of them, was kicking in. When summer rolled around, Jay went to the couple's house Upstate.

I visited him toward the end of the month. The artist neighbor remarked on how well he looked. Jay mentioned the same day that he wanted to start jogging and asked if he could tag along with me the following morning. I took a long look at him and realized that he had the appearance of a normal man with a bit of a pot belly and spots of paint on his topsiders. Yet the first comment I made was: "Do you have enough of those evil pills to last until you get back to the city?"

After looking at Jay's lab results that fall, Dr. Starr announced that a checkup every three weeks should be sufficient. Soon monthly checkups sufficed. The lab results continued to improve. During the winter, a major art gallery about three hours from New York City invited Jay to become its interim director. The financial firm where he worked was still suffering from a post-9/11 slump, and Jay was eager to move on to another job. Dr. Starr saw no reason why he couldn't take the gallery job, and I encouraged him to take it too. In my fantasies, I saw the gallery job becoming permanent and enabling me to move from the city to a house in a delightful town far removed from the Health Hell of the last five years.

I remember feeling profoundly weary as I helped Jay pack for his temporary move to the new job. He said he would take every opportunity to come back to the city, and I promised to visit him regularly. When he drove off, I expected to find his absence, and the accompanying peace and opportunity to catch up on work, rather enjoyable.

Instead, I found myself alone with someone I no longer knew. I had lost connections with my friends and my work. I had been supporting myself on the framework of my husband's mysterious illness for nearly five years, and when that framework disappeared, I could no longer find my identity. I reread a note that Jay's mother had written during year 4 of his illness. In it she said, "I will always be enormously appreciative of the care you gave Jay. You saved his life. If you do nothing more in your lifetime, it would be enough." The sentiment horrified me. I had prayed fervently for Jay's survival, while neglecting every other important aspect of my life. Including our marriage. An impossible quid pro quo arose: I expected Jay to take care of me now in the same way that I had taken care of him. Even if he weren't trying to get back on his feet, literally and figuratively, he is so different from me that he couldn't possibly undertake the caretaking I had done. Still, I expected him to save me. And, of course, I was disappointed. I was so disappointed that our marriage collapsed.

Today, several years later, Jay is still healthy. I have re-entered my own life, which is now an unmarried life. I pray regularly for Jay's continued good health, but that's only one of many items on my list. At a recent party, a woman I know complained to me about her daughter-in-law's unconscionable behavior. The woman's son is very ill with cancer, and the daughter-in-law continues to go to yoga classes and to eat out with her friends. "I'll tell you my story," I told the woman, "and maybe you'll look at your daughter-in-law in a different light."

20

Pancakes in Mumbai

Roberta Troilo

As I begin writing this, it is Sunday night in Mumbai, India, at the beginning of October, and it is very hot and extremely humid. It's a long way from New York, where I have lived and worked for most of my adult life. I'm a bit surprised that I am in Mumbai, but I'm here pretty much because of the story I'm about to tell. When I ordered pancakes for breakfast this morning, I was reminded that I had committed to write about this time in my life. You see, I haven't had pancakes for over four years, not since Cono used to make them for me, not since before he got sick. Cono died three and a half years ago, one year after he was diagnosed with stage 4 lung cancer. But I'm getting a bit ahead of myself.

Cono and I met when we were somewhat "on" in life; I was forty-eight, Cono fifty-nine. I had a nice community of friends and was not seeking a relationship. Our meeting was a "fix up," and our first date, which went on for twelve hours, started on Sunday, November 1 (All Saints' Day) with Mass. I always loved telling the extended story of how we met and was thrilled whenever I was asked to tell it. Actually, I still love talking about it or even just thinking about it, and I can still hear Cono saying, "Please Roberta, you're not going to tell that story again, are you?" But as I would begin to tell it, a twinkle would come into his eyes, and I knew he loved hearing it as much as I loved telling it. It was a very special time.

Neither of us came into the relationship without baggage. Cono was going through a divorce, and his professional life, a business forty years in the making, had just gone up in smoke…literally; the building blew up and burned to the foundation it had been standing on. And for me, well, I was having a hard time trying to figure out where a career path was going to take me. I had always completely identified with my work life and had had a very focused and successful career until I messed up, leaving me in a job hunt with absolutely no direction in the search.

Our infamous first date of twelve hours was really quite *nice*. As previously mentioned, it began with the Solemn High Mass at St. Ignatius Loyola, where the music is always spectacular, then followed with a Broadway matinee in which one of Cono's clients was the star, and ended with an early Sunday evening dinner, where we sat and talked for hours as though we had known each other for years. Cono and I didn't exactly fall in love that day, but we were immediately and extremely comfortable with each other. As I think about it, I'm not so sure that we ever actually fell in love in the storybook kind of way; but, at some point along the way, we found ourselves loving each other completely and became totally committed to each other. I guess history would refer to us as having been "in love."

When we said good night that evening, I hoped that I would hear from him again and looked forward to seeing more of him. Since I was from the school where women did not call men, I waited for the call to come but, thankfully, did not have to wait very long. And after *that* call, we spoke for extended periods of time every day, and our "dating" fell into a regular routine, although nothing about Cono could ever be considered "regular." We did things we both loved doing and went places where we both loved going; it was incredible how much we had in common. Cono was convinced we had most likely stumbled into each other at some point in our past lives, but our lifestyles back then had been so different that our meeting during that period in our lives would never have happened. Cono used to say that he wished we had met forty years ago, but I wonder if our love would have been as deep or as committed as it was in the twelve short years we had together.

What's in a Name?

During one of our first phone calls, I asked him, "What kind of a name is Cono?" To which he replied, "What do you mean what kind of name is it? It's my name. Haven't you ever heard of St. Cono? Ask your mother." And so I did. I also called the Archdiocese of New York, who said there was no such saint; perhaps they didn't know about Google at that time in the Archdiocese. Come to think of it, did Google exist in 1992? Whether it did or did not, my mother was very well acquainted with St. Cono, and was also convinced that *my* Cono was most likely a distant relative.

Apparently my grandmother had a cousin named Cono, who was a chef and had landed in Brooklyn upon coming to the United States. Cono's father was a chef, and Cono himself was an incredible cook, so there was the connection! Along with that, St. Cono was born in Teggiano, Italy, where Cono's father was born and close to Naples where cousin Cono was born. Google *Cono* and you'll find that "Generations of Teggianese boys were named Cono, and the name spread as Teggianesi, fleeing the poverty of southern Italy's Mezzogiorno region, settled in Argentina, Brazil, Uruguay and, of course, in Brooklyn." (Charles Gasparino, "The Cono's of Brooklyn...Many Brooklyn Italians Favor Cono as a Name for Their Sons," *The Wall Street Journal*, November 10, 1998). How I wish that I had seen that article at the time it was written and shown it to Cono. It would have made him very happy, and he would have sent it to everyone he knew and handed it to each of his clients with a great deal of pride.

Cono's clients came to know every achievement in my life, no matter how small or insignificant. I was back on my feet again with a very good position in a well-known and highly respected company; Cono told his clients. I was recognized for an accomplishment at work; Cono told his clients. We went somewhere that required formal attire; Cono told his clients what I wore and how I looked and that nobody could "pull herself together" the way I did. Work took me fairly often to Europe and Asia; Cono told his clients, and from me he wanted a detailed account of each day of each trip. He often said that, as soon as he retired, he would come with me on some of those trips and what a great time we would have doing them together. Yes, we would have, could have, should have....

As I said, Cono was an incredible cook, one who never used a recipe; everything was in his head. He loved cooking, and he loved cooking for me. When he saw that I really enjoyed something like soft shell crabs or his linguini with baby clams or those wonderful pancakes, he would make them. Usually, he would make them at a time when I least expected them, and he so loved the idea of the surprise. And if I wasn't feeling well, there was always a bowl of his delicious bone marrow soup made special just for me to make me feel better. And you know what? It really did make me feel better. Maybe it was the love that went into making it that did the trick?

This must sound like a bit of idolization; and perhaps in some way it was, but it was definitely not one sided. I loved talking about Cono; I loved caring for him, and he loved being cared for. Cono never ceased to amaze me; he had an endless knowledge of history, politics, art, theatre, movies, literature, and music of every kind, although his greatest love was opera. He'd hear a baritone, a tenor, or a soprano and immediately know the voice; he'd hear a snippet of an opera and immediately name both the piece and the composer. Since I was such a novice in classical music, I was always rather impressed with his ability to do that. After I had already been introduced to a piece, if we heard it on the radio and I didn't recognize the opera or the voice, I'd receive a bit of a reprimand like, "Shame on you, Roberta, for not knowing that."

Cono truly appreciated all kinds of music, so I asked him to listen to a particular piece of popular music—Rod Stewart's "Have I Told You Lately That I Love You?"—and to pay particular attention to the lyrics. I thought the lyricist must have been tuned into my heart, but I didn't tell Cono that. The crooner begins by asking his love how often and how recently he had expressed his love for her, and whether she was aware of how important a figure she was in his life since their first meeting. I knew I had yet to express those bold words of love and commitment to Cono, particularly since in the words that follow, the crooner sings of his exploding heart that was so filled with a happiness he had never experienced before, and that since meeting her, all he needed to do was just think of her and all of his sadness...all of his troubles...would vanish. But, even though I had yet to express those thoughts to Cono, I thought surely one day I would. I never for a minute thought it might be too late. I often wonder why it had been so hard for me to say, "I love you." Cono told me often how much he loved me, and I would answer, "Me too." But it wasn't the same, and Cono told me so.

Have I Told You Lately That I Love You?

I think Cono must have felt the same way I did about the words to that song, although he may have just been playing to the sentimental side of me. There were numerous occasions when I'd come back to the apartment at the end of my workday, and the message on my answering machine was simply Stewart crooning the words to what had become, cornily enough, "our song." Much to Cono's dismay, the staff played popular music nonstop, but whenever "our song" came on, Cono simply dialed my number and put the receiver against the speaker. It always brought both tears and a smile, and I knew that I loved him. Why didn't I tell him?

I used to tell Cono, as well as everyone I knew, that he was absolutely the smartest person I had ever met, bar none. Cono's formal education was through high school, so his incredible and vast array of knowledge was self-mastered, and that awed me all the more. He was also extremely creative with incredible vision and an incredible eye for color, decorating, designing, landscaping, gardening, cooking, and on and on and on. And yet, his mechanical skills were endless; anything electrical that needed fixing, he did it himself. He did all the plumbing work himself, all types of carpentry work himself; and if a car needed repair of any kind, he did it himself. I once asked him if there was anything he couldn't fix, and he simply said, "No, Roberta, there is nothing I can't fix." Later, when he began to lose feeling in his fingers because of the chemo, it was hard for him to accept that that fact was no longer so, and he would remind me that "there once was a time...."

Right from the get-go, Cono had told me that he had no interest in ever getting married again and that, if I wasn't okay with that, we shouldn't continue seeing each other. Being forty-eight years old and never having been married, I was more okay with not getting married than I was with not seeing Cono anymore. So basically after that, the subject never really came up again, and we just continued being with each other and loving each other, totally and unconditionally.

As a result of not having a wedding anniversary to celebrate, each year we celebrated the date that we met as our own special anniversary, and each year on our anniversary there were always surprises. November 1, 2000, fell on a Saturday that year. I had been out and about doing things all day, and Cono arrived at the apartment before I got back. When I opened the door, there was just a dim light shining, and Cono had his back to the door. When he turned around, I saw that he was holding a small bag, and all of a sudden out jumped the cutest little puppy I had ever seen. Talk about surprises!

I had never had a pet of any kind, but I knew that Cono had pretty much always had dogs in his life. He had been introducing me to different types of breeds, and I found myself asking questions about them and starting to be much more aware of dogs than I had ever been. I had never heard of a cockapoo, but Cono had once had one who he truly loved; unfortunately DJ was stolen from him. Makes me sad to think someone could do that. And so it was a cockapoo that Cono brought into our lives. When he came to us from his mother and the breeder, he was twelve weeks old and pitch black except for a little white spot in the middle of his tiny little chest. Cono said I could name him, but it was Cono who in the end gave our new little one his name, and so he came to be known as Jetta.

Jetta did something to us that it is difficult for me to try to explain, but in a very short time, I started to refer to him as our little "Holy Spirit" and by no means in a sacrilegious manner whatsoever. It was just that somehow or other Jetta brought Cono and me closer together. And I know this probably sounds a little silly to some, but he was almost like having a child. He did, after all, require a great deal of care and demanded a great deal of attention, which I willingly and happily gave him. Cono used to say to people, "My dog, Roberta's son."

But Cono loved Jetta just as much as I did, and Jetta really was Cono's dog, as it was Cono who took care of him. During the week, Cono and Jetta lived in the country house, and Jetta typically accompanied Cono to work. Cono was the one who fed him, walked him, groomed him, took him to the vet, trained him, disciplined him; Jetta was Cono's dog. I think Cono would have liked to have taught Jetta to sing, but Cono seemed to be happy enough with Jetta making howling noises as Cono whistled along with an opera. They were good bachelor buddies, who lived on their own during the week, as I went about living my own City life kind of thing.

But when Friday night came, and I took the train up to spend the weekend with them, we became the happy threesome. I'd come walking down the platform and see Jetta hanging out the car window with his tail wagging a mile a minute, and my heart leaped. When I finally arrived at the car and opened the door, he'd jump out and then back in over and over again; then over the front seat onto the back seat and then back up to the front seat and, finally landing on Cono's lap, he'd wait patiently, tail wagging, panting until I'd settle in. Then finally the time had come for him to jump into my lap and he'd lick my face a few times to make sure it was me and to let me know how happy he was to see me. Then he'd finally settle down, having reached his nirvana, as he was now tucked into my arms. And so began our typical weekend, the three of us attached at the hip. Although Cono and I went off to do our own thing on Saturdays, we were inseparable on Sundays. As such, Sunday now is a very difficult day for me and the time when I feel the loneliest.

I pause now in writing, as remembering that period in our lives is giving me too much cause to think about and to remember how happy we were in just being together. And that is bringing tremendous grief and sorrow to me right now. I miss Cono so very much, and while I am sad in that, I do know how blessed we were to have had the love we shared for each other. We were God's gift to each other.

Most likely this is going to sound peculiar to anyone who has never shared the love of a pet with someone, but I honestly believe that our relationship grew stronger through Jetta, strong enough for Cono to ask me to consider marriage. Cono knew that I would only marry in the Catholic Church, and so he began the process of annulling his first marriage. This is neither the time nor the place to talk about why the church granted the annulment. I can only say how painful a process it was for Cono to relive all the details of that period of his life, as we went through the documentation that the church required. We worked on this every Sunday for at least two hours for over a year.

Coincidently, Cono received the papers from the Archdiocese granting the annulment on the day we closed on our new apartment, bought jointly in anticipation of our upcoming marriage. We drank champagne that evening celebrating our love and our blessings. Since I was the organizer, I took control of all the wedding preparations and Cono's creativity and mechanical skills took over the renovation in preparing the apartment for our move-in date. Never could there have been a more aptly suited pair; we were ecstatically happy.

Married Life and the Unexpected

We were married on May 18, 2002, with a perfect wedding ceremony celebrating our marriage at a Nuptial Mass at St. Ignatius, witnessed by our families and close friends and followed by a spectacular New York City party. We both loved everything about that day and about each other. We moved into the new apartment the following week, and as clear as day I remember saying to Cono, "I am so happy, it hurts." Hurting from happiness is a good hurt, but little did I know about bad hurting.

As we approached our first anniversary, Cono had had a chronic cough for over three months, and I finally convinced him to visit our doctor to have it checked. The chest x-ray showed a spot on his lung. The next step was a CT scan; the step after that was a visit with a pulmonary specialist. We had no idea of the severity of the situation until we were sent to an oncologist, who immediately went into a long dialogue on the process they would want to follow and the type of chemotherapy they would want to do. Even then, we didn't know how serious the situation truly was.

It was at a point when the doctor started talking about anticipated outcomes that I stopped him and told him we were a bit confused with what he was talking about. He then realized that we had not been advised that Cono had inoperable lung cancer that was most likely "terminal," although the doctor never used that word. Instead, he told us that, while we didn't need to go home and get affairs in order that day, we needed to start the process, as they had no idea how long we would have from that time on. Cono and I were dumbfounded. Hit by a ton of bricks smack in the face, we simply reached for each other's hand and held on, as the doctor told us what to expect and what his life expectancy might be.

Once alone in the car, we sat and cried, but we said we would get through this because of our love for each other and that we wanted to celebrate our second, third, fourth, and so on wedding anniversaries. On the night of our first anniversary, we had dinner in a small, unassuming neighborhood restaurant in the City and vowed that we would fight this. But we were both scared and sad, because we had no idea how strong our hope could be. It was a far cry from the way we had planned to celebrate our first anniversary.

One of our neighbors told me the next day that she had seen us walking home and that her heart had ached for us. She said it was apparent how much we loved each other and that it was obvious this had happened to both of us. She was so right. As part of our "celebration," Cono had brought me calla lilies, our favorite flower. I had carried them in my arms as I walked down the aisle on our wedding day, and, two years later, they sprayed Cono's coffin as he was taken down that very same aisle. But there was something so amazing about those anniversary calla lilies that Cono had put on our dining room table. After a week, they were still as fresh as the day Cono had put them there. When I remarked about this to Cono, he said that he would then certainly continue to use the florist where he had bought them. Had this been an in-person conversation rather than over the phone, I wouldn't have been so gullible. Two weeks later, I took a closer look to find they were artificial. Sounds crazy, I know, but they really were that real and so perfect. I honestly believe it was Cono's way of telling me that he, and everything we loved, would always be with us. Those calla lilies are still on the dining room table. Like our love, they will never be taken away.

Shortly after the diagnosis, when Cono began his chemo treatments, I realized that I could not go into the office anymore or live apart from Cono, so we took up full-time residence at the house in the country, only occasionally going into the City apartment. Cono continued to work, and I made arrangements with my office to work from home. We tried to go on with business as usual, until Cono was put into intensive care with pneumonia. Because of the severity of his condition, I asked the priest to administer the Sacrament of the Healing. After a long ordeal, Cono came through that period and came home.

His time in the hospital was difficult for me. I was scared that he wouldn't pull through this, and scared as I drove home each night on that dark and curvy road. Also, I had committed to a work assignment that was taking up a great deal of time, and I'd sit in his room working online rather than focusing on him. The assignment was also mandating that I travel to Europe for a week. I did not want to go, but Cono insisted, and my sister came to stay with him. In hindsight, I wonder why I continued working and why I was putting that kind of pressure on myself. Cono refused to listen to me about quitting my job. Perhaps, after all, he was right.

I have related the history of our meeting, our growing relationship, and the depth of our love for each other, because it was how we were able to manage the year of cancer before Cono died. I can't take you through that year, because it is much too difficult to relive in words. Unfortunately, during that time, some rifts in relationships with Cono's family occurred, which have never been healed and which I do regret. I grew bitter and resentful with some things that were said and done. From my experience, I would caution others against falling into that devil's trap. When someone you love is suffering so much, it is probably best to let everything outside your love simply not exist, so as not to offend. I wasn't wise enough to do that.

It was a hard year for both Cono and me. Neither of us was prepared to go through what was required of us, and sometimes it tested our love. My biggest regret during that time was arguing with him about two weeks before he died. I am ashamed of that and much too ashamed to say what the argument was about. But in that shame also came my reaching out to Cono to ask for forgiveness. His response was that he loved me so much and knew what I was going through. He knew the argument was a senseless one but that I had to act it out nonetheless. Again, I can only say how blessed I was to have had his love.

Cono never gave up hope of remission, and sometimes we pretended the cancer didn't exist and tried to get on with our life together. We typically celebrated New Year's Eve at the New York

Philharmonic, as we had done on our first New Year's Eve celebration. We always went black tie, and it was always a very special night for us. So on December 31, 2003, the year of the diagnosis the previous May, Cono wanted to return to the Philharmonic. He said that the best way to do so was to continue our black-tie tradition and surround ourselves with family and friends. In spite of his now being on continuous oxygen, Cono decided that, after the concert, we would all return to our apartment and have one of his very special dinners. That decision made, we headed down to Chinatown, where he bought lobsters and clams and calamari and cooked the entire day on December 31, 2003, before showering and donning his tuxedo. He then waited patiently for me to appear.

I had gone all out for that evening and wore a gown that Cono had not seen before. He was awed when I finally presented myself. And I was happy to give him this small gift. I held back my tears as I put his onyx cufflinks into his shirt cuffs, one of our small dress-up traditions. I think I knew that this would be our last New Year's Eve celebration. Like Sundays, it is now a very hard time for me and fills me with a great deal of both loneliness and happiness. Had I not met Cono, would I ever have experienced such a special evening? Who can say? I'm just happy that I had those special evenings with this very special man.

The following March, Cono came home from work one day and said that was it—he would not be able to continue working anymore. We had opera tickets for that night, and for the first time ever, just we, not anyone else, used them. The next day, Cono began to call each of his clients to tell them he would no longer be able to take care of them. He cried, they cried, and as I sat at my desk trying to focus on work, I cried listening to the one-sided conversations. I knew it was tearing him apart. And that became the beginning of the end. I saw Cono begin to lose some hope of his going into remission. He was tired all the time and couldn't eat. He began to lose his strength. We both kept fighting the reality of what was happening; so much so that in late June, when I was asked to travel for work, Cono insisted I go. I insisted I couldn't.

He became terribly agitated by my not wanting to go, and I realized it was probably best for the two of us to get some time and space between us. We spent that week apart.

Cono spent the week with his son, a week that he would most likely not have had if I had not traveled. In the end, it became my gift to the two of them. They spent the week ignoring the cancer and went out on the boat and fished and cooked together. Of course, Jetta was right there by their side. Each time I called, I heard a special happiness in Cono's voice, and I knew that he had once again been right in sending me away.

I became somewhat revitalized during that week by not having Cono's cancer in my face 24/7. It was the week of the Fourth of July. I returned the following week and thought we would start anew in our fight to overcome this ugly disease. But I was so wrong. I watched Cono get progressively worse, and on July 19, my mother's birthday, Cono had a chemo appointment. He could barely make it down the path to the car, and I wanted to call an ambulance, but he said no. When we arrived at the cancer center, the oncologist took one look at him and sent him for a CAT scan. We learned that the cancer had spread to Cono's liver and that there no longer would be any need for chemo. The oncologist tried to tell us in a gentle manner, but what can be gentle about having death look you in the face? He sent Cono home to die, saying that it was only a matter of days at that point. And with that, Cono gave up his battle. He made me promise that, after he died, I would go on with my life. I said I would, but I wasn't sure how or even why I would want to. That was a Monday.

Cono's last will and testament still was not signed, and so we scrambled to get that accomplished. That got us through Monday and Tuesday. He could barely sign his name, because he was losing all of his functional skills. When the estate lawyer left, I walked her to the front door, and as we stood on the porch to say goodbye, her eyes welled up with tears. Cono had changed so much since she had first met him. And she, like everyone who met him, had been taken by his inimitable charm. Her tears were only a natural result of having met this man.

It was all happening so quickly, but for whatever reason, I was thinking weeks instead of days and wanted to make him as comfortable as possible. Unfortunately, we had a bad experience with the hospice that was assigned to us, and so while Cono was fighting for his life, I was fighting with everyone around me. Little did I know that all that I was insisting on was going to be for naught. They brought in a massive oxygen tank, a hospital bed, rubber sheets, and those undignified diapers. I was trying hard to remain in control.

Cono's son moved into the house to keep watch with me. Ignoring the hospital bed in the adjoining room, I took Cono to bed on Tuesday night and held him in my arms until he fell asleep. During the night he lost control of his faculties and, as I struggled to change the sheets and clean him up, I knew I would have to succumb to putting Cono in the hospital bed. I called my brother and asked him if he could come. That day he arrived to help. It was Wednesday. I thank God for Cono's son and my brother for never leaving our side.

On Thursday, my brother took me to the cemetery to buy a burial plot. I had no choice. I knew that I could not put it off any longer. I was terrified of leaving Cono because death was now at our door. But thankfully nothing happened while I was gone. It was important for me to find a plot that was right for Cono, and so I did. It was on the hillside under a tree, with an Italian name on the tombstone next to his. I smiled and quietly said to my brother that I hoped Cono wouldn't mind the Irishman, who would be lying on the other side of him.

Friday morning, I knelt by Cono's bedside. I don't think I prayed, although maybe it was a form of prayer. Cono couldn't see anymore, but he still had his hearing, and so I put my arms around him and whispered in his ear the words that I should have said out loud at an earlier time. I knew all the words from our song verbatim, so, singing quietly, I asked him if I had told him how deeply I had loved him and would continue to love him, and that he would continue to be the most important person in my life. Through my tears I told him that since meeting him, I had only to think of him or see him, and a smile would creep across my face. I told him that he had always made me happy and never once, since knowing him, had I been sad—until now. I then heard myself say, "I love you, Cono." He smiled; it wasn't too late after all.

I thought about how we had danced to "our song" on our wedding day, and I knew Cono was thinking the same. I saw him smile as I whispered the words. Shortly after, Cono died, while still in my arms. God had indeed been good to us.

Our parish pastor arrived, and we all sat by Cono's side and prayed for the repose of his soul. Then Cono's body was taken away. The first thing I did was clear the house of everything that reminded me of his sickness. I asked the men to fold up the bed and put it out on the porch and the same with the oxygen tank and everything else that the hospice had brought in. I threw away anything that reminded me that Cono had been sick and flushed all his medicines down the toilet.

Dealing with Death, Mourning, and Grief

I went through the mechanics of planning and arranging the funeral. The music had to be a great tribute to him, and it was. Cono was buried the following Thursday. It was Jetta's birthday. He turned four that day and was now my full responsibility. I was scared to face what was ahead for both of us. I felt the great loss of love and security. In some way, it was the same loss I felt when my father died. The two men I loved most in my life were with me for such a short period of time, Cono for twelve years and my father for nine years.

I had no idea how to mourn, or even what it meant. But I knew that I had to stay in the house, because I couldn't face the apartment by myself. I threw myself into work and worked long hours at home—stopping only to take care of and play with Jetta.

And then, I began the process of getting rid of things. Cono had put the house on the market before he died, and, within the year of his death, there was a buyer. I was grateful for that because the legal end of the sale kept me even more occupied. Unfortunately, no one in the family could use the furniture from the house, so I hired someone to hold a tag sale. I was making lots of decisions at that time, and that was one of my worst. But I was operating in fear and simply didn't know what else to do.

After the closing, I packed up whatever was left in the house and drove away. That brought that era to a close, or so I thought. I was driven to keep busy and to preoccupy my thoughts, so I decided to sell our apartment and buy something else—another decision made too soon after Cono's death. But the selling and the buying gave me the excuse for activity I was looking for, as did the eventual moving into the new apartment.

By mid-September 2005, a little more than a year after Cono had died, I had sold the house, the furniture, and the apartment that Cono and I had bought together, and had found and bought a new one and was completely moved in. And now I had nothing mechanical left to do, so the unbearable loneliness set in and took over. I kept Jetta by my side day and night, and he was happy to oblige. It was only in Jetta that I was finding any kind of happiness and solace, and he was there for me to cry with.

I sought psychological help and went on some mild antidepressants, but that didn't help. I wasn't looking for help from my family, and I felt I had no friends. I didn't return phone calls from the couples Cono and I had shared activities with, because I didn't want to know them without Cono by my side. I went to Sunday Mass at St. Ignatius and would cry so hard that it hurt, particularly when praying the Our Father. Cono and I had always held hands during the prayer. I had been away from St. Ignatius for two years, and there were so many new faces I didn't know. The ones I did know, I hid from. I didn't reach out to anyone, and no one reached out to me—until I met Sr. Kathryn.

During the time of my absence from St. Ignatius, Sr. Kathryn had joined the staff as a pastoral associate. There was something about her presence and her essence of peace that drew me to her, and I found myself speaking freely to her—mostly complaining about how abandoned I felt by the priests at St. Ignatius and the people there, who I thought were my friends.

I met Sr. Kathryn when I signed up to take a course she was teaching regarding discernment. At the conclusion of the course, I knew that I would want to be part of whatever Kathryn would be doing at St. Ignatius. And so when I saw that she was co-leading a women's retreat, I decided to go. There were three other women on that retreat whose husbands had recently died. Was God's hand guiding me in my decision to go that weekend? It became the catalyst in the formation of a new bereavement ministry at St. Ignatius under the direction of Sr. Kathryn.

Then there was an item one Sunday in the church bulletin regarding care for the sick at Goldwater Hospital, a hospital for the chronically ill run by the City of New York. I wasn't sure that I was ready for this, but I decided to go to the first meeting anyway. I learned that the hospital was on Roosevelt Island—a real drag to get there—and that in order to volunteer, you needed to go through a physical that the hospital mandated and that only they could administer, as well as a battery of shots also done only at their site. To this day, I do not know what drew me to this and why I became committed.

This ministry then became a part of Partners in Healing, which was another course being introduced at St. Ignatius and spearheaded by Sr. Kathryn. "And there," as the saying goes, "by the grace of God go I." I was beginning to keep the promise I had made to Cono to go on with my life.

That promise is what brought me to Mumbai and got me eating pancakes again. When I was asked to take on this three-month work assignment, the only thing I could hear was Cono's voice telling me that I needed to do this. I needed to experience all that I could in life and be open to everything new and different. The assignment has gone from three months to six, with two trips back home to see Jetta, my family, and those friends I didn't think I had. It has also opened up other work opportunities for me. Having proved the quality of my work here, I have been asked to take on a new experience; one that will take me to Japan, this time though for intermittent trips rather than prolonged periods of time. Jetta is being well cared for by Cono's son. They have a very strong mutual adoration between them, and so I am okay with the travel.

God has filled my life with many blessings. I am thankful for all of them and most of all for Cono, who opened my heart, my mind, my eyes, and my ears to love, to understand, to see, and to hear the beauty of God's gifts to all of us. The fear and the loneliness are still part of my life, and that is alright for now. Perhaps someday they will disappear. But if not, I know that I will never really be alone, not with God and Cono and Jetta by my side—and, oh yes, with the family I didn't reach out to and the friends I didn't think I had.

Contributors to This Volume

John J. Cecero, SJ, PhD, is associate professor in the Department of Psychology at Fordham University. He is rector of the Jesuit community and director for the Center for Spirituality and Mental Health at Fordham. His primary teaching and research interests are in personality assessment and the role of spirituality in mental health. He published *Praying through Lifetraps: A Psycho-Spiritual Approach to Freedom* (2002).

Rev. Pamela Cooper-White, PhD, is the Ben G. and Nancye Clapp Gautier Professor of Pastoral Theology, Care and Counseling, Columbia Theological Seminary, Decatur, Georgia, and recipient of the American Association of Pastoral Counselor's 2005 national award for Distinguished Achievement in Research and Writing. She holds PhDs from Harvard and the Institute for Clinical Social Work, Chicago, and is the author of *Many Voices: Pastoral Psychotherapy and Theology in Relational Perspective* (2006); *Shared Wisdom: Use of Self in Pastoral Care and Counseling* (2004); and *The Cry of Tamar: Violence against Women and Church Response* (1995). An Episcopal priest and pastoral psychotherapist, Dr. Cooper-White is certified as a clinical fellow in the American Association of Pastoral Counselors and currently serves as publication editor of the *Journal of Pastoral Theology*.

Robert J. Giugliano, PhD, is a licensed psychologist, spiritual director, and adjunct faculty member in the Graduate School of Religion and Religious Education at Fordham University. He currently has a private practice in psychotherapy and spiritual direction, runs a spirituality group for mentally ill adults at South Beach Psychiatric Center, and is on the preaching team at Mount Manresa Jesuit Retreat House.

Rev. George Handzo, MA, MDiv, is ordained in the Lutheran Church in America, is vice president of pastoral care leadership and practice at Health Care Chaplaincy and leads HCC's consulting service. Rev. Handzo is author of numerous articles and chapters in *Health Care Chaplaincy in Oncology*, co-authored with Dr. Laurel Burton. He is a board certified chaplain in the Association of Professional Chaplains and is past president of that organization.

Janna C. Heyman, PhD, is associate professor at the Fordham University Graduate School of Social Service and associate director at the Ravazzin Center on Aging. She received both her PhD and MSW from Fordham University and teaches social work research, social policy, and program evaluation. Dr. Heyman has published numerous articles on end-of-life planning, spirituality, and social-work education. She has also received grants to develop end-of-life planning interventions for older adults and their families.

Rev. Margaret Kornfeld, DMin, is an American Baptist minister, diplomate and past president of the American Association of Pastoral Counselors, and author of *Cultivating Wholeness: A Guide to Care and Counseling in Faith Communities*. Rev. Kornfeld presently resides near Berkeley, California, where she continues to counsel, consult, and lead workshops and retreats on community wholeness.

Marylin Kravatz, PhD, is an assistant professor and the executive director of online graduate programs in religious education at Felician College, Lodi, New Jersey. In addition to her administrative and academic responsibilities on the graduate level, Dr. Kravatz continues to teach a course on healing, spirituality, and morality for health care undergraduate students. She also works as a presenter for the purpose of catechist training and formation in various Catholic dioceses.

Neil J. McGettigan, OSA, DMin, professor of theology at Villanova University, adds editing to his more than forty years of teaching in various institutions along the East Coast. The consonance of theology with other areas of academic study impacted by acceptance of the process of evolution in creation is of special interest in his presentation of Christian doctrine. Experience in the study and teaching of English literature is a valuable asset in his efforts at writing and editing.

Rev. Paul A. Metzler, DMin, is director of community and program services for the visiting nurse services of New York Hospice Care. He is an Episcopal priest and psychotherapist, a fellow at AAPC, and a New York State licensed marriage and family therapist. He serves as a book review editor for the *Forum*, the publication of the Association for Death Education and Counseling.

Beverly A. Musgrave, PhD, is presently a professor of mental health and pastoral counseling in the Graduate School of Religion and Religious Education at Fordham University. She has taught in Ireland, India, and Canada. Dr. Musgrave is a pastoral psychotherapist with a private practice in New York City and is certified as a clinical Fellow in the American Association of Pastoral Counselors; she is also a New York State licensed mental health counselor and a trained spiritual director.

Mary Ragan, PhD, LCSW, is senior clinician at the Psychotherapy and Spirituality Institute in New York City. She teaches at Columbia University School of Social Work. Dr. Ragan has clinical experience with trauma from working with first responders and family members from 9/11 as well as with survivors of Hurricanes Katrina and Rita.

Eleanor M. Ramos, MS, is executive director of the New Citizens Committee on Aging, an advocacy organization for aging issues. Prior to this position, she spent twenty-five years at Catholic Charities of the Archdiocese of New York, overseeing services to seniors and developing a model parish volunteer program.

Sarah Rieth, DMin, is a pastoral psychotherapist and consultant who has an independent practice in Charlotte, North Carolina. Her dissertation and published articles focus on healing needs of survivors of abuse and recovery from Internet pornography.

An Episcopal priest, she is a diplomate in the American Association of Pastoral Counselors.

Janet K. Ruffing, RSM, PhD, is professor in the practice of spirituality and ministerial leadership at Yale Divinity School in New Haven, Connecticut. Dr. Ruffing is currently offering a new extended workshop for spiritual directors entitled "Love Mysticism and Spiritual Directions" and continues to publish in the areas of religious life, mysticism, and ministry, and is working on a complete revision of *Uncovering Stories of Faith*.

Kieran Scott, DEd, is associate professor in the Graduate School of Religion and Religious Education at Fordham University. Dr. Scott's expertise is in foundations of religious education, curriculum theory, adult education, and ecclesiology. He has published in religious journals and educational periodicals. Recent published works include *Perspectives on Marriage* with Michael Warren and *Human Sexuality in the Catholic Tradition* with Harold D. Horell.

Yvette M. Sealy, PhD, MPH, is an assistant professor at Fordham University Graduate School of Social Service. Dr. Sealy received her PhD from Fordham and her MPH from Mt. Sinai School of Medicine. Dr. Sealy is currently working with the New York City Department of Health and Mental Hygiene to design detailing kits that address public health issues on obesity, intimate partner violence, and breast feeding.

John J. Shea, OSA, PhD, teaches religious development and pastoral counseling at Boston College. He has taught in Australia, Rwanda, India, Ireland, Malaysia, and Canada. In 2005, he published *Finding God Again: Spirituality for Adults*.

Emilie Trautmann, MDiv, is a freelance writer living in New York City; her background is in international human rights. Her published works include *Coming Home*, a collection of interviews with long-term prisoners; *In Your Hands*, a community human rights action guide; and many country and issue reports published by Amnesty International.

Roberta L. Troilo is senior manager of Global Client Relations PRI, PricewaterhouseCoopers. She recently spent six months in Mumbai, India, leading a work project. With the overwhelming heat and humidity, the overcrowded streets, the never-ending begging of mothers and babies, when asked if she would return to India, her reply is always "in a heartbeat."

Paulist Press is committed to preserving ancient forests and natural resources. We elected to print this title on 30% post consumer recycled paper, processed chlorine free. As a result, for this printing, we have saved:

9 Trees (40' tall and 6-8" diameter)
3 Million BTUs of Total Energy
822 Pounds of Greenhouse Gases
3,959 Gallons of Wastewater
240 Pounds of Solid Waste

Paulist Press made this paper choice because our printer, Thomson-Shore, Inc., is a member of Green Press Initiative, a nonprofit program dedicated to supporting authors, publishers, and suppliers in their efforts to reduce their use of fiber obtained from endangered forests.

For more information, visit www.greenpressinitiative.org

Environmental impact estimates were made using the Environmental Defense Paper Calculator. For more information visit: www.papercalculator.org.